WHY WAR?

CHRISTOPHER COKER

WHY WAR?

HURST & COMPANY, LONDON

First published in the United Kingdom in 2021 by
C. Hurst & Co. (Publishers) Ltd.,
41 Great Russell Street, London, WC1B 3PL
© Christopher Coker, 2021
All rights reserved.
Printed and bound in Great Britain by Bell & Bain Ltd, Glasgow

The right of Christopher Coker to be identified as the author
of this publication is asserted by him in accordance with the
Copyright, Designs and Patents Act, 1988.

A Cataloguing-in-Publication data record for this book
is available from the British Library.

ISBN: 9781787383890

This book is printed using paper from registered sustainable
and managed sources.

www.hurstpublishers.com

CONTENTS

CONTENTS

INTRODUCTION

'It is quite in keeping with man's curious intellectual history that the simplest and most important questions are those we ask least often' (Norman Angell quoted in Gray, 1999).

Whatever else you may say about Tolstoy's *War and Peace*, it is a long book. My paperback version weighs in at 1,300 pages. It is one of the longest novels ever penned. It is one of those novels that I dare say you probably think you should have read but probably haven't. But then, the classics are those books which you always claim you are re-reading, even if they are likely to remain unread.

The point is that books that are embedded in our personal life are rich in association, and re-reading them often re-triggers the emotions they first provoked. Even so, we often prefer to watch a movie version; it is less effort than ploughing through a novel. 'No, but I have seen the film' is a familiar refrain. It saves a lot of time, although the Soviet version of Tolstoy's novel, which was made in 1967 to coincide with the fiftieth anniversary of the Russian Revolution, is seven hours long. Even then it scarcely did justice to the original campaign in which 800,000 soldiers lost their lives. Think of the Battle of Borodino where the Russian army finally made a stand (to put this into perspective, the death rate was equivalent to a Boeing 747 crashing with no survivors every five minutes over a period of eight hours; McLynn, 1997: 519). What we remember about it most of all is the disaster that overtook the French army as it haemorrhaged away, both on the long march to Moscow (from cholera) and the even more famous march back (from the cold). On the long retreat home, the French wounded were left to freeze to death in their sleep. Some 200 bodies, covered by snow and then forgotten, were only discovered in 2002, perfectly preserved, locked together in foetal positions just as they had died. Forensics showed that their average age was 21 (Nolan, 2017: 243).

Whether you prefer to read the book or watch one of the many screen versions of the story, the 1812 campaign leads back to one name, Leo Tolstoy. His tale captures the startling intensity of emotional extremes—fear and hatred are among the strongest motivating forces in war, but so too, ironically, is love—a love that excludes no expression of longing, whether love of friends or love of country. And his enthusiasm for his characters is infectious. The death of the hero Prince Andrei is one of the most poignant scenes in literature, as too is the scene of his friend Pierre fleeing from the battlefield of Borodino seeking 'ordinary conditions of life' and discovering that they are nowhere to be found (Tolstoy, 1982: 996). The real hero of the book, by the way, doesn't appear on the page. She lived off it. It was his wife Sophia who wrote out the entire text eight times in between bearing the couple's thirteen children.

At the heart of *War and Peace* is the same question that I pose in this book: why war?

> What does it all mean? Why did it happen? What made these people burn down houses and kill their own kind? What were the causes of these events? What force made people act that way? These are the involuntary, simple-hearted, most legitimate questions that mankind poses for itself (Tolstoy, 1982: 137).

INTRODUCTION

Tolstoy's novel wrestles with the most difficult and troubling questions—why are people motivated to act so murderously and with such selfish or thoughtless cruelty; why are young men drawn to war in the first place; and why, even when they have first-hand experience of the reality, are so many drawn back to it again and again? But then, you don't have to read a novel, however well-regarded, to ask the questions that Tolstoy asked—they have probably popped into your head many times when you have watched the news of violent conflicts on television.

Since Tolstoy's day there have been many answers to the questions he asked. In his day it was commonplace to trace war back, like every other ill that humanity suffered, to a single impulsive act: Eve's disobedience in the Garden of Eden in going scrumping for apples. We have been infected with original sin ever since (Mark Twain cynically remarked that it would have been better for all of us if she had eaten the serpent, and not the apple—a matter best left perhaps to theologians). If you were a Christian, you could argue—and many did—that it was the product of the gift that God had given us: free will. We are permitted to make choices. Dostoevsky, a contemporary of Tolstoy's, didn't believe a word of it. In every one of us, he wrote, a beast lies hidden, 'a beast of lawlessness let off the chains.' Other writers have preferred to avoid such value judgments and to wax political. One is Charles Tilly, who claims that war makes the state and the state makes war. At times we have given up trying to find a single explanation: R G Hawtrey tells us that the 'principal cause of war is war itself', which explains everything by explaining nothing very much.

Tilly's explanation has the virtue of being short and pithy, and it is undoubtedly correct. In Tolstoy's novel it is the state that makes war—it is the French who invade to satisfy the political ambitions of one man, Napoleon, and Russia's resistance is enthused with patriotism, the defence of the motherland. War came first, and the state followed a very long time later—war dates back hundreds of thousands of years as we shall see; the state has only existed for about seven thousand. In this work, I shall not ask why states make war—there are endless books on the subject, on the causes of the Hundred Years War or the world wars of the last century. The scope of this work is much broader—why do human beings ply this trade, why are they prepared to kill so many of their fellows, and why, more mysteriously, are they prepared to put their lives on the line and sacrifice themselves for others. These are all species-related questions.

In the course of writing this book, I lost count of the number of 'why' questions that can be asked, but they all touch upon aspects of human behaviour. Why do we still kill each other; why is war still predominantly a male activity; why does it survive across time and culture; and why do soldiers surrender their lives for so little personal gain? It is tempting, is it not, to cut to the chase and ask: why can't we sober up and see the absurdity of mass murder? Isn't war pathological? To call war pathological, however, really tells us very little. If you really think this is the case, then you will fail to grasp what war is all about; the subject will slip away from you into elusive darkness. The use of the term in this case is really a confession of failure to solve the mystery of war. It is merely a restatement of the mystery. The real question is, where to draw the line between those behaviours that are so obviously adaptive that no-one doubts their evolutionary origins, or the benefits they confer, or are deemed to, and those which are not so obvious, including war.

Anger is an example of the former, religion is another. According to the psychologist Robert Plutchik, anger blunts feelings of personal insecurity and prevents feelings of helplessness from reaching levels of conscious awareness. And if directed at an 'outsider', it solidifies the group, making one feel more secure (Asma, 2018: 181–2). Religion also reinforces group solidarity. It establishes social norms as well as penalties for those who break them; it promotes group selflessness (it encourages us to put group interests ahead of our own). Religion has been invoked over the centuries to justify every conceivable human activity from imperialism to slavery. And most states have gone to war claiming to have God on their side. The comforting belief in God's approval or displeasure is a central aspect of human nature that spans time and culture (Johnson, 2016). It also affords a great alibi of course. I recall these lines from a poem by Ilya Kaminsky: 'At the trial of God, we will ask: why did you allow all this? / And the answer will be an echo: why did YOU allow all this?' (Gabbert, 2020: 245).

Unfortunately, when it comes to war itself, its adaptive value is not so obvious and needs to be puzzled out. If we concentrate, as we are encouraged to do by scientists, on the survival value of a behaviour, war is particularly problematic, is it not? Most mammals will die to defend their kin, and some will also go so far as to kill in their defence, but often we are prepared to put our own lives on the line for such 'imagined communities' as the nation-state; we will even hazard our lives for an abstract idea such as 'the brotherhood of man'. Surprisingly, however, such behaviour does indeed seem to have adaptive value. It has allowed us to surpass every other species on the planet by building civilisations from the bottom up and establishing even more all-embracing political communities. The great eighteenth-century philosopher Immanuel Kant conceded that we are violent by nature—that we are driven by passions and hatreds that are difficult to contain; nonetheless, he believed that war had a hidden 'cosmopolitan purpose'. The phrase he coined to describe this process does not trip lightly off the tongue—it is 'asocial sociability'. We have programmed into us a desire for honour, power and status. Without these asocial qualities, which are in no way admirable in themselves, we would never have developed. Those different drives have fuelled war over the ages as we have gone to war to win a reputation or win it back, or to increase our power and status, but war in turn has helped widen our circle of acquaintance through conquest and empire building and made us less distrustful of others. As we have come to know more about each other, so we have grown more peaceful. Kant died convinced that cooperation would eventually supersede competition as the driving force of history (Wright, 2001: 238).

It's a great story to tell, is it not, and it fits in well with Tilly's formula. Respect and honour are common to all of us, and are central to the way states still behave—they still fight for honour, in order to maintain or restore it, although these days the word they tend to prefer is 'credibility'. And in the past, states went in for empire building on a grand scale—even today they still have their own agendas; they still go to war to maximise their power. But then again, Kant's thesis is only really compelling if you believe in teleology: that history has a narrative drive that is leading to a pre-scripted end. You also must accept metaphysics, in this case, that there's a hidden plan behind events scripted either by God, or by more material forces that historians will one day discover. And that, today, is a bit of a stretch; we live in a post-metaphysical age. We prefer scientific explanations if they are there to be found.

Nevertheless, as it happens there is a perfectly convincing scientific explanation that may bear out Kant's hypothesis. Conquest really can extend the size of the in-group by promoting inter-marriage, and that has a genetic impact too—it produces a selective advantage. Mingling the gene pool tends to improve both physical strength and mental development. This can be seen at work in the global movement of population in the twentieth century, which includes refugees from conflict. It has contributed to the Flynn effect, a world-wide rise in measured intelligence by as much as three IQ points (Kinsbourne, 2012: 194–5).

So, I think that it is possible to conclude that war is not pathological. There is a perfectly rational reason for why we engage in what often appears to be such apparently irrational behaviour. This book tries to explain, with reference to some of the latest scientific discoveries, why we as a species fight wars and have done so for a large part of our history, long before states were even conceived. Humans are inescapably violent. Violence is a feature of our evolution as is our propensity to spin stories that celebrate it and theories about its place in our lives and those of our ancestors. But, if all this is true, where to begin? Presumably, you are interested in war since you are reading this book, but are you very interested in seagulls? To be honest, they are not the most beautiful of birds, and unless you are an ornithologist you are unlikely to find them very interesting. But think again. Seabirds enjoy a rich and complex social life. And although the gulls, which now invade our cities looking for food, may not be much loved, they fascinated a Dutch scientist of whom you are unlikely to have heard. And it is his work that I believe offers us the best way to answer the question: why war?

The Man Who Watched Seagulls

When he was a boy, Niko Tinbergen used to leave his home in The Hague for the Dutch coast where he spent hours observing gull behaviour. Later, while studying them as a teacher of zoology at Leiden University, he discovered that they were marvellously adapted to their environment. He loved studying them for that reason, though he never surrendered entirely to their charm. He was the first to confess that, missing any incubation instinct in himself, he couldn't understand the satisfaction which presumably a female bird feels when just sitting on an egg all day (Tinbergen, 1961: 134). And after observing them for years, he came to the conclusion that their intelligence was distinctly limited. They knew, for example, that if you dropped a shell from a height it would break open, but they never learned that to do this you needed to drop it, not on water, but on a rock, or firm sand. And while they could distinguish the faces of other gulls in the colony, they couldn't always distinguish between their own eggs and those of their neighbours. In his book, *The Herring Gull's World*, there is an especially instructive photograph of a gull, eyes closed, and wings folded, contentedly sitting on an empty nest while its eggs (which had been helpfully removed by an ethologist) nest in the cold, only a foot away.

And it wasn't only the intelligence of the adults that could be questioned. The youngsters could easily be fooled, too. When presented with a red knitting needle that was a simulacrum of an adult mother's beak, herring gull chicks would peck at it excitedly simply because it was redder and longer than the norm. Size, it appears, matters in the world of gulls as much as it does in our own. Not that we should congratulate ourselves for being especially superior. We too are influenced, are we not, by super-stimuli like fast-foods (even though they are less nutritional than others) and photo-shopped models (who though attractive are often less intelligent than other people).

None of these limitations, however, had ever threatened gull's survival. And survival is what ultimately counts. After all, for most of their history gulls never had to contend with ethologists removing eggs from their nests to test their reactions. They have thrived for a reason: they are well adapted to their environment. All of Tinbergen's later work was concerned with asking why animals behave as they do and how that behaviour enhances their chances of survival. 'The Tinbergen Method', as it came to be known, involved the long and careful observation of birds' habits and the constant search for an explanation that would explain them.

What intrigued Tinbergen most about seagulls was their aggressive behaviour. Why, he asked, were some gulls, like gannets, more aggressive than others when hunting for food? Like many other animals, gulls often turned their violence against each other. When two gulls met on a boundary of their territory, they would begin to pull out lumps of grass with their beaks. At first, he surmised, they were doing what many animals do: marking out their territory. Later, he recognised that they were acting on stimuli from the immediate environment. In the case of grass pulling, they were divided by the desire to fight and the desire to flee. Their thwarted urges were displaced into a new activity; what they were doing to the grass is what they wanted to do to their opponents, if only they dared to put up a fight.

Aggression is hard-wired into many species. Surprisingly, it was only noticed in gulls in the early 1950s in the work of one of Tinbergen's students, Esper Cullen. When Tinbergen visited her in the Farne islands in the summer of 1952, he was excited to discover that one member of the genus—kittiwakes—were the most aggressive of all in the competition for nest sites. The reason was that they had made an evolutionary exchange from shore-nesting and a coastal life to one spent nesting on cliffs, which often jutted out into the open seas. Rather than make the effort to collect it, some preferred to steal material from a neighbouring nest (Nicolson, 2017: 86–88).

But what struck Tinbergen most was the apparent senselessness of much of their aggression. In his laboratory in Leiden he noticed how sticklebacks would hurl themselves against the glass walls of their tanks whenever they saw a red mail van pass in the street outside. Red, in their minds eye, was the colour of a rival male. Their response was of course senseless. It was no longer functional. In the language of evolution, it had badly 'misfired'. And when our own behaviour misfires too, we get economic depression, social violence, and even worse, the prospect of nuclear war. As he grew older, he became even more convinced than ever that our belief in our own rationality was much exaggerated. Unlike most other animals, we don't go in very often for ritualistic aggression. Rituals are intended to minimise damage. When alpha males among the great primates fight for dominance, the loser is rarely killed; in submitting to the other he acknowledges that he has lost the fight, at least for now. We tend to fight for real. Tinbergen was in general pessimistic about human nature for that reason. He had been a hostage in a POW camp in the Second World War. At that point, his confidence in humanity had been brutally shattered. He continued to look on in horror as the Cold War deepened and the threat of nuclear war continued to grow. The universal is often born of the particular; in his own life story he saw the depressing story of humanity, of passions unleashed and hopes disappointed, and dreams rendered still-born by our own perverse behaviour.

Tinbergen recognised, sure enough, that we are different as a species. But the fact that our behaviour and that of other species is so different did not discourage him from applying the same methodology in his study of animal behaviour to our own. Human behaviour is not that different from that of other animals. It is a compromise between the instincts we are born with and those we later acquire, when our aggressive instincts are turned into aggressive desires.

Tinbergen was a scientist of note, and his research won him a world-class reputation. He was awarded the Nobel Prize in 1973 together with two other ethologists, Konrad Lorenz, who made his public reputation as the author of a bestselling book *On Aggression*, and the now largely forgotten Karl von Frisch. Lorenz spent most of his life promoting his own work with shameless application; Frisch, who proved that bees can see colours, played the electric bass and didn't say very much. Of the trio, Tinbergen was the real thinker. Their work was not entirely new, of course. Darwin had clearly and convincingly begun the evolutionary study of behaviour and linked it to the principle of natural selection. But in a famous paper dedicated to Lorenz (from whom he later distanced himself when his Nazi past came to light), Tinbergen raised four questions about animal behaviour, both human and non-human alike:

1. What are its origins?
2. What are the mechanisms which allow it to flourish?
3. What is its ontogeny—its historical evolution over time?
4. What is its function: its adaptive significance which facilitates its reproductive success?

What Tinbergen basically came up with was a scientific scaffolding upon which to build explanations for why animals behave as they do—a scaffolding that could be used not only in zoology, but other disciplines including the social sciences. He crafted an investigative strategy that made the fewest possible unsubstantiated assumptions that could be tested with real data. He was the first to acknowledge that it was a self-consciously derivative project that created no new knowledge of its own. But in drawing upon the knowledge provided by other fields of enquiry he believed that it could illuminate animal behaviour more vividly than any other.

But is Tinbergen's work illuminating enough? It is a question that we have continued to ask. As it happens, the methodology that he provided us with has survived remarkably well despite the passage of time (Bateson and Laland, 2013: 1). Young, and not so young Turks may find fault with it, but the questions he encouraged us to ask are still the ones we are asking fifty years after he won the Nobel Prize. That is not to say that its details have not had to be occasionally updated. Tinbergen himself largely limited his study of ontogeny to genes. Since his death, major research has been undertaken in understanding the impact of parental genomic imprinting and other epigenetic factors on gene expression. Likewise, the question of function. For

Tinbergen, this was entirely about survival, but biologists have spent a lot of time recently looking at the concept of 'adaptive significance': its contribution to fitness, including exclusive fitness. They have discovered that some characteristics can change function over time (for example, feathers that evolved for temperature regulation were eventually adapted for flight).

Tinbergen's model has continued to invite criticism on three other counts.

Some critics tend to dismiss the ethology approach to human behaviour as methodologically flawed. As a species, we have no single habitat unlike gulls. Hence can we really identify a species-typical conduct related to a specific territory? Doesn't it matter that we find ourselves living in wetlands, jungles, and polar-regions, with each environment different from the other? And isn't human behaviour not only influenced by biology but also teaching? Isn't it socially and culturally conditioned from an early age? 'Man is a product of evolution', writes one scientist, 'but he is not merely a puppet jerked by genetical (sic) or phylogenetic strings' (Barnett, 1979: 106–25).

But the objection that animal behaviour is different from ours is no longer as easy to sustain as it once was. One of the major advances in knowledge in recent years has been the realisation that animals share many of the same emotions that govern our lives; they also have a rich cognitive life. Darwin, as usual, got there first. In *The Expression of the Emotions in Man and Animals* (1872), he came up with the heretical idea that emotional complexity is not exclusive to one species. If the idea never really caught on, this was largely because the evidence that was available at the time was entirely anecdotal. It is now backed up by hard science. Today we know that animals have perspectives and purposes of their own, as subjects with lives that matter to them and should matter to us. As we continue to learn more about them, so we can see what has previously been invisible to us—that their lives are rich in emotional expression.

INTRODUCTION

Almost a hundred years after Darwin's book came the publication of Donald Griffin's *The Question of Animal Awareness* (1976) which seeded a new field: cognitive ethology—i.e., the marriage of cognitive science and ethology, a study which allows scientists for the first time to ask questions about the mental state of animals. We now recognise what has been hiding in plain sight: we now ascribe to them mental representations, intentionality and the processing of information. Animals, we have discovered late in the day, also have a rich cultural life. Birds, for example, sing different songs when defending their territory against a neighbour or a stranger. A recent study of wolves finds they have twenty-one different types of howling, and different breeds, red and timber, have identifiable calls (or dialects) (Radinger, 2019). And take the behaviour of whales who sing songs—some only five minutes long, others that last half an hour. Some, though living thousands of miles apart, even sing identical songs. The only explanation for this would appear to be cultural transmission. As one group hears a new variation, another takes it up, just as we often unconsciously find ourselves humming a popular tune (Brooks, 2015: 34–5). A 2017 study led by evolutionary biologist Susanne E Schultz into the social skills of ninety different types of cetacean—whales, dolphins and porpoises—found that they even have 'names' for each other. One day, perhaps, we may discover that they also have names for us (Moody, 2017).

All of this has led some primatologists to suggest that we are not especially special, we are just natural selection's way of turning a quadrupedal ape into a big-brained biped. But let's not get carried away. The great apes, in the words of one scientist, may be 'inching closer to humanity' as the distance between us continues to narrow (Bering, 2011: 24). Even so, we have progressed mightily since we split off from the same genealogical tree. 'Have you studied quantum physics?' asks Ant Man in *Avengers: End Game*. 'Only to make conversation', replies Scarlet Johansson's Black

Widow rather archly. The fact that very few of us understand quantum physics is not the point. As Michael Brooks reminds us, we have never seen a chimp struggle over the philosophy of quantum physics, and we never will. But then, we are the only species that insists on giving existence at least the illusion of meaning and trying to find out how nature works and what our place is in the cosmos. Chimps don't even realise that there is anything to worry about; they cannot imagine a world other than the one in which they live (Brooks, 2015: 257). We, by contrast, spend much of our time worrying whether we will survive global warming, or another global pandemic like the Black Death. And although we may never win our battle to understand the reality around us, at least we struggle to do so, and it is language, of course, which allows us to continue that struggle.

To the old claim that ethologists had nothing to tell us about human behaviour, there is another argument that Tinbergen's approach was highly reductionist in explaining behaviour (the whole) in terms of its distinctive parts. Isn't this, writes Rupert Sheldrake, to understand a computer by analysing its component parts, such as copper and silicon. Yes, we will know what it is made of, but in the process of reduction, the programmed activity of the computer vanishes, and no amount of mathematical modelling of the interactions between its atomic constituents will reveal the computer's programs or the purposes they fulfil (Sheldrake, 2012: 4). We now know what our forefathers didn't: that it is quite impossible to shrink anything down to its essence.

True up to a point, but as Steven Pinker argues in *The Blank Slate* (2002), there is a huge distinction to be drawn between bad reductionism and good. Bad reductionism consists of trying to explain a phenomenon in terms of its simplest constituents. It is not difficult to explain why it is wrong.

As the philosopher Hilary Putnam has pointed out, even the simple fact that a square peg won't fit into a round hole cannot be explained in terms of molecules and atoms, but only at a higher level of analysis involving rigidity (regardless of what makes the peg rigid) in geometry. And if anyone really thought that sociology or literature or history could be replaced by biology, why stop there? Biology could in turn be ground up into chemistry, and chemistry into physics, leaving one struggling to explain the causes of World War I in terms of electrons and quarks. Even if World War I consisted of nothing but a very, very large number of quarks and a very, very complicated pattern of motion, no insight is gained by describing it that way (Pinker, 2002: 69–70).

Good reductionism, on the other hand, consists not of replacing one field of knowledge with another, but of connecting them, and that is what Pinker claims Tinbergen did in establishing the connections between biology and culture. As Edward O Wilson argues, 'the cutting edge of science is reductionism, the breaking apart of nature and its natural constituents ... It is the search strategy employed to find points of entry into otherwise impenetrable complex systems. Complexity is what is of most interest to scientists, not simplicity. Reductionism is the way to understand it' (Wilson, 1998: 58–9). The great advantage of reductive explanations is that they tend to leave the phenomena just as they were, only better understood.

The last argument against the Tinbergen method is that it's an egregious example of scientism. It suggests that once you have discovered the scientific explanation of a phenomenon, there is nothing more to say. He never made that claim himself and with good reason. Science is not the sole authority; if it were, we would find ourselves living in a one-dimensional world. Take the case of love, one of the primal emotions that has more adaptive value than most in the struggle to procreate. No real insight, for example, is gained by reducing it entirely to pheromones. As the author Julian Barnes rightly maintains, there is surely something intellectually impoverishing in claiming that love boils down to pheromones.

This bounding of the heart, this clarity of vision, this everything, this moral certainty, this exaltation, are all caused by one partner and subconsciously nosed by another. We are just a grander version of that beetle bashing its head in a box at the sound of a tapped pencil. Do we believe this? Well, let's believe it for a moment because it makes love's triumph the greater. What is a violin made of? Bits of wood and bits of sheep's intestines. Does its construction demean and banalize music? On the contrary, it exults the music further (quoted in Byatt, 2000: 71–2).

Barnes is surely right: reducing love to its neural correlates and the brain states associated with it is indeed an egregious form of scientism. We would end up reducing the great romantic novels like *Wuthering Heights* and *Anna Karenina* to a kind of evolution-ary handbook in which human beings cease to be characters and instead become 'complex thermostats fabricated out of carbon chemistry' (Rosen, 2005: 297).

Science can explain much, but it is not the only, or even the last, word on the subject. It can help us find answers to most questions. In other cases, the human intellect may have boundar-ies; some of nature's greatest mysteries may lie beyond our com-prehension. If this is the case, science's ultimate achievement may be to reveal its own limits. But even when it comes to explaining why we behave as we do, science is best at posing questions in the right way.

By now, if you managed to stay the course you may well be asking yourself: what does all this have to do with war? Well, I would suggest that if applied correctly, it offers the best under-standing of why human beings are willing to kill each other, at some risk to themselves. The genius of Tinbergen's model is that it invites us to ask four different questions that, in the case of war, take us into the realms of art and literature, and history and history making, as well as into our psychological predisposition as a species to seek glory, to emulate the actions of our heroes (both fictional and real), and to follow our religious impulses or 'religious appetites' as the philosopher William James liked to call them.

Consider by contrast, the behaviour of ants who have been on the planet longer than we have and may well survive us. Thomas Hobbes, writes Alan Ryan, claimed that ants are naturally political, whereas human beings are not. Ants automatically build colonies, many of them hundreds of miles in extent. Our ancestors by contrast had to 'negotiate' a contract with the state to keep themselves from being murdered in their beds by their closest neighbours. The mythical social contract is the powerful myth that is still at the heart of Western democratic theory (Ryan, 2014: 93).

But let's not get carried away. Ants are an impressive species, to be sure. They have practiced agriculture for 50 million years and kept livestock twice as long; they grow fungi and keep aphids. It is also true that ant colonies fight each other all the time. Some ants also possess a highly developed military organisation. They march in columns 12–15 inches wide and 100 feet long, and they can march for days without having to set up camp at night or forage for food. When they attack other colonies, they either force them to leave or they wipe them out. They often engage in 'myrmicide', to coin a term. But though warrior ants do most of the fighting, we must remember that they are individual cells that act collectively without any central direction. In an ant colony, there is no leadership, no counsel of advisers and no strategic planning. There is also no political ambition. The queen, who was once thought of as a kind of commander, is merely a glorified larvae factory who possesses no more than 250 neuronal cells compared with the approximately 100 billion each of us has (Johnson, 2001: 30). And there is another critical difference that needs to be noted: individually, because ants are offspring of a single queen, they share three-quarters of their genes with each other. Sacrificing themselves makes perfect genetic sense. As a collective organism, each member exists purely to pass on its genes; it would never occur to an ant to die for a cause, like making the ant world 'safe for autocracy'.

Tinbergen was an ethologist, and he was interested in the life of insects too. His model applies to every species on the planet including the seventy or more that have been observed to go in for intra-specific violence—the killing of their own kind. But only we engage in war, and only in the case of humans is war so central to our own being: this is where his model really helps understanding.

1. *Biology.* How far do you have to go back to discover the origins of war? Not that far back, you may be relieved to know, no further back in fact than our encounter with *Homo erectus,* the longest living human species which was very like us both in body build and shape. The species went extinct and we didn't because its members only had basic weapons, like the hand axe; we had spears and slings which meant we didn't have to come in so close for the kill. War gave us the edge, and we have kept it ever since. Along the evolutionary highway lie the wrecks of numerous unsuccessful species—*Homo erectus* may have been one harried to its death by us. Which is not to deny that we probably lived in peace with another species—the Neanderthal. Unlike Schrödinger's cat', which poses the quantum paradox of being alive and dead at the same time, war and peace are not contradictory truths. They are merely different sides of the same coin.

2. *Culture.* Thomas Hobbes' description of the state of nature is famous; it is also telling, for he paints the picture of a life without 'arts or letters' or society (Hobbes, 1972: 26). What strikes one most is how plain and barren such a life really would be; there would be nothing to appease the soul. And yet, stories allow the eruption of colour and significance into

war. Imagine it without its tales of heroes and heroic last stands, of nations fighting for their freedom or for the privilege of oppressing others. Imagine war without its Tolstoy's. Literature, in fact, does a lot of the heavy lifting in fusing war with life.

3. *Ontogeny*. Consider the cattle grazing as you pass by, Nietzsche exhorted his readers in his first major essay: 'The Uses and Disadvantages of History for Life'. 'They do not know what is meant by yesterday or today' (Nietzsche, 1983: 81). Animals have only biology; we have a history. We make it thanks to changes in our historical situation, such as new technologies that have enabled us to pass from one age to another, from the Stone Age to the digital. Our understanding of our own humanity is also tied to our understanding of the future, of what one day we may yet 'become'. And from the outset war has been one of the most effective ways of improving our 'future fitness'.

4. *Functions*. War continues to meet social and psychological needs. It exploits our zest for glory and our willingness to sacrifice ourselves for others, for family or friends. It also feeds upon our fear of others and taps into our ill-defined anxieties about the future. 'Anxiety is the dizziness of freedom'—the phrase is Kierkegaard's. In other words, it is a product of free will, which we all think we enjoy, perhaps mistakenly. The claim that war is dangerous is true, but any account that is more equivocal about the human forces shaping it is likely to be better for it. Nothing is to be gained from refusing to confront our own humanity.

So, let us return to Tolstoy's questions. Let's agree with him that war is brutal and often mindless; that people kill each other with abandon, often for no real reason; that we still fall prey to the cover stories of people like Napoleon. Let's say he was also fortunate to be spared having to witness the total wars of the twentieth century, which saw his own country suffer the ravages of the greatest struggle in human history. Let's concede all that and more. But let's also ask how it is possible for humans to endure so much pain and make so many sacrifices; how it is possible for war to inspire a work such as *War and Peace*, which was broadcast on the radio in the darkest days of the Great Patriotic War (1941–5). There are a lot of questions that Tolstoy didn't ask that still need answering.

They are all to be found in our humanity. War is what makes us human. It's not the only factor, of course, and it not even the primary one, but in its absence, we would not be the people we are. As the only species to have invented language, we have been able to coin a term—humanity—to describe not only a particular species of big ape but the best attributes that we can consider it to embody. How we behave is deemed by many of us to define what makes us human.

Ad Hominem

My own interest in war began when I was very young. I was born in the early 1950s when war was an activity waged by and for men. Women did not begin to join the armed forces until twenty years later. If many boys of my generation were interested in war it was because we knew that for most of history there had been no escaping it. Boys anyway are more wired for physical aggression than girls; they like to play at being soldiers from an early age, and still do. At the age of fifteen, I volunteered for the school cadet force. Cadet forces were set up at the end of the nineteenth century to prepare a generation of male adolescents for the possibility of a European war. The basic training that I received would have secured me an officer's commission had I ever been called up. A commission would have been quite useless of course in the event of a nuclear war, but I was given the choice of joining either the cadet force or social service, and for me the former had much greater appeal. My parents and grandparents had fought in two world wars and I had spent years listening to their stories.

But if young men and now women—a real sea change—still join up, they are often influenced by what Tinbergen would have called the 'cultural mechanisms' that tap into their sense of self. For me, reading history was an incident-packed plunge into the distant past. I particularly liked the story of the Trojan War and its heroes, and I warmed to the biographies of great generals like Alexander and Julius Caesar. It was all so straightforward in those days—history appeared to be given shape by heroic deeds, usually, in Britain's case, on the frontier far away from home, against villainous and exotic enemies, with small units, always outnumbered but (usually) coming though for queen and country. Of course, I was reading the redacted version of history. Even then I suspected that there was probably another story waiting to be told, a darker version of events which I would encounter later in life.

I was also, in my adolescence, an avid player of war games. I collected hundreds of toy soldiers (the Napoleonic era was my favourite). The rules for these war games were first set by H G Wells in a little monograph, *Little Wars* (1913). Or to give it its full title: *Little Wars: a Game for boys from 12 years of age to 150 and for that matter ....the intelligent sort of girl who likes boys' games and books.* It is not a title that would pass muster today. War games allowed children the freedom to live in the past while they still could. Wells himself was nostalgic for the Napoleonic era of set-piece battles whose outcome was usually decided in a day. His nostalgia was amplified by his fear of what war was about to become. Fearing for the future, he found solace in the certainties of the past. He lived long enough to live through the London Blitz and to see the atomic bomb dropped on Japan.

Wells wrote his book *Little Wars* so that young boys and intelligent girls would get it out of their system while they were still young. A far more realistic note was struck by his contemporary, H H Munro (aka, Saki) who went on to end his life at the Battle of the Somme (1916). In a short story called 'The Toys of Peace', Munro set out to satirise the campaign that had been launched by the National Peace Council to promote 'peace toys' in place of toy soldiers. On Easter Sunday, two little boys are given a set of toys including a model of a municipal dustbin, a lead figure of J S Mill, the political economist, and a facsimile of the Manchester branch of the Young Woman's Christian Association. Their parents throw in some model ballot boxes for good measure. Alas, not all goes to plan. Asked to play at a General Election, they opt to play a war game instead. They convert the municipal dustbin into a fort, transform the civilian figures into soldiers, and lay siege to the Young Woman's Christian Association in the hope of abducting the girls. The experiment is judged to have been a crashing failure.

When I was not playing war games, I was often to be found at the cinema. Movies are yet another cultural mechanism that have fuelled our universal fascination with war. The films of my youth included such great yarns as *Zulu* (1964), which told the story of the defence of Rorke's Drift (1879) where a small band of British soldiers won the highest number of Victoria Crosses ever awarded for a single day's action. Even at the time it came out, the film was criticised for glorifying the British Empire, though the Zulus themselves were happy enough to take part as extras. They still remembered the British as brave soldiers. And outside Britain, the film was celebrated for what it was: a great adventure yarn. When it was shown in Kingston, Jamaica, the audience happily cheered every time a British Redcoat was killed.

And then we come to history or ontogeny in Tinbergen's model. Throughout the ages, war has pulsed in and out of focus, and it has never been out of focus for long. I went up to university to study history, but the question I have asked myself: why war, is not like the question 'why the Big Bang' which led to the greatest discovery in the history of science—the knowledge that there was a day without a yesterday. War was not born of one cosmic or even Earth-sized event. There was no single moment like the scene in Stanley Kubrick's movie *2001: A Space Odyssey* when a monolith from space 'programs' an ape man to use an animal bone as a weapon for the first time. You may recall one of the movie's most famous scenes when the ape man throws a bone high into the air in celebration of his first 'kill' and Kubrick cuts to a satellite orbiting the Earth. In the book that Arthur C Clarke wrote to accompany the film, it is not a satellite, but an orbiting space bomb aimed at the Earth below. The connection is clear if crude; human progress is measured by the lethality of the weapons we produce. But Kubrick's point is that war is indeed bound up with our own evolution. It evolved slowly, and it is continuing to do so. Indeed, I suspect that we will never see the end of it until it has finally exhausted its evolutionary possibilities.

As for the functions of war, I suppose my career illustrates some of those too. War ignited my imagination because it tapped into something in my nature. I have spent most of my professional life studying wars and revolutions and civil insurrections, and the rise and fall of the world's Great Powers (as Martin Wright once wrote, Great Powers don't die in their beds). The study of my subject, International Relations, began in 1919 with the analysis of the causes of war. I have spent a lot of time, in other words, in the shadows, but then I have never expected much of human nature, which is one reason why, unlike some of my colleagues, I am not particularly surprised by the way things are now turning out. But then, anyone of my generation who survived the Cuban missile crisis and the nuclear war we just missed in 1983 is probably less exposed to the ambient anxieties of the early twenty-first century. If I had to sum up in one sentence why war has been of such interest to me, I would cite a passage from Charles Dickens' valedictory address to the reader of *The Pickwick Papers*, his first major work: 'There are dark shadows on the Earth, but its lights are stronger in the contrast. (But) some men are like bats or owls and have better eyes for the darkness than for the light' (Dickens, 2003: 518). Dickens' novel of course has that most unlikely of literary endings—a happy one.

In short, I wasn't brainwashed or socialised, misled or suborned by war's cover story. No one forced me to play war games or to join the school cadet force. And certainly, my interest in war novels and movies was entirely undetermined by others (my parents had no interest in either). Most of my friends made other choices in life. The choices that are not made, and the paths that are not taken, are as important as those that are. Even military history, which seized my imagination early on, was the Cinderella subject at the time of my schooling, and to some extent still is (in the US only three universities now offer PhDs in military history). I think, therefore, we can say that war was in my 'blood'; it sought me out. That's just the way it was.

Why War?

There is a specific reason I have written this book. In the Western world, we don't prepare our children for war. We tell them to dream. We offer them visions of a globalised world where ethnic identity and national chauvinism have lost out to the logic of the market. We preach the politics of cosmopolitanism, cultural diversity and digital oneness. We have long claimed in Europe to have discovered a version of Immanuel Kant's 'perpetual peace'. Many years ago, the Czech author Milan Kundera reassured his readers that the Germans and French were now 'anthropologically' incapable of going to war against each other.

INTRODUCTION

Note, not economically or politically or even culturally but anthropologically. In other words, war was no longer encoded in their cultural DNA.

Browse the bookshelves and you will find many authors spinning a similar tale. One is Steven Pinker, the author of *The Better Angels of Our Nature* and *Enlightenment Now*, another John Mueller, the author of *Retreat from Doomsday* and then there is John Horgan, a former editor of *Scientific American* and author of a book called *The End of War*, whose title leaves you in no doubt about its conclusion. The arguments vary but they share the same premise. War is deeply irrational, and one day we will wake up to that fact and discover what is in our best interests. This appeal to rationality makes all three writers heirs to a Western tradition of liberalism. Also carried over into their writings is a belief in progress, a thesis that remains central to the historical narrative the West has told itself for 300 years. They believe that despite the state of much of the world around them, they are living in enlightened times. It is a great delusion. Unfortunately, they have mistaken the baggage of their own cultural inheritance for human nature in the round.

In telling our children much the same story, what we don't prepare them for is loss—the loss of illusions. Cast your eye around the world: at Syria's broken cities, like Aleppo, a city once rich in history but whose medieval seminaries have been destroyed and its ancient citadel damaged beyond repair. Or look further west to the continuing fighting in Ukraine which has seen the displacement of several hundred thousand people. Or give a thought to the Global War on Terror, now almost 20 years old with no end in sight. Some American soldiers now serving in Afghanistan were first grade students on the day the World Trade Center was attacked. A depressing fault line in fact runs through the world dividing those regions that are at peace with themselves and those that are not. And if you wish to extend your horizons

further into the future, consider the possibility of another Great
Power war. My students, until recently were confident that there
wouldn't be another. Today, they are far less sanguine, and they
have every reason to be. The new buzzwords in the military field
are 'directed energy', 'hypersonic missiles', 'space', 'cyber' and
'quantum computing', and very soon artificially intelligent
machines will be waging war on our behalf, or possibly theirs.

Our children must expect to be disappointed. What their parents have forgotten is what their own parents knew: at any
moment peace can crack. War can erupt often when least
expected. It doesn't need profound causes. And when it does, it
shatters lives very quickly and denies us the fundamentals of
happiness even though, paradoxically, it seems to be so fundamental to our lives. We forget, however, how tenacious and
recurrent war can be. It can flare up when least expected as it did
in 1914 or sneak up unsuspected as it did in Syria ten years ago.
And when it does, it can derail the lives of an entire generation
and rob them of their hopes for the future. 'You may not be
interested in war', Trotsky famously remarked, 'but war is interested in you'. The sentiment, though hackneyed, is still as true
as the day he said it.

Nevertheless, let me flag up that I shall end this book on quite
a different note by asking how long war will continue to remain
'the human thing', which is the definition—the only one—that
history's first military historian Thucydides was willing to offer.
To call something a 'thing' you might consider evidence of a
writer's lexical deficiency, or poverty of imagination; I prefer to
take it as evidence in this case that Thucydides recognised the
innate complexity of the subject under discussion. The fact is
that any attempt to analyse war nearly always eludes us; any general theory is likely to always fall short. Thucydides himself
believed it was powered by fear, interest and honour—not a bad
explanation but one that falls short of being a unified theory.

That said, our recent scientific advances raise a question that would have astounded Thucydides: how long will we continue to remain in control? Or to put it more dramatically, how long will war still need us? Thanks to ethologists like Tinbergen, we have discovered that our own intelligence is not general purpose. It's not general at all. It is specific to one species. It's different from that of other animals, and it will be totally different from the machine intelligence we are about to create. Will artificial intelligence take war out of our hands? Already algorithms are making value-laden decisions on whether to grant people a bank loan or a job offer or to hand out a prison sentence. Their cognitive evolution has only just begun, and we have no idea where it will take them. One day, they too may pose the question: why war? And some already fear the answer they may come up with.

1

ORIGINS

Long before Darwin told us about our consanguinity with apes, we had begun to recognise something of ourselves in them. The playwright William Congreve could never look upon an ape without feeling deeply mortified because it reminded him of his own humanity. When in 1842 Queen Victoria first set eyes on Jenny, a female orangutan that had recently arrived at London Zoo, she is reported to have commented that she found the ape 'disagreeably human' (Fernandez-Armesto, 2004). Like Charles Darwin, who had visited the zoo a few years earlier, the monarch saw in Jenny our near kin. A bit of a stretch? Perhaps, not. According to *Science* magazine (2003), orangutans are 'almost human'—some of them use napkins when eating and kiss each other goodnight (Ibid: 56). If an orangutan looks in a mirror, it knows instinctively that what it sees is a reflected image of its own body. Rousseau even thought that they shared with us a capacity to improve or 'perfect themselves' (Rousseau, 1994: 105). Unfortunately, they haven't, which is why they are almost extinct. Their greatest challenge is that they probably won't survive us. We have hunted them almost to extinction. The question that Victoria might have asked herself was why humans and not orangutans ran the zoo.

One possible answer to that question is that we are the only species on the planet to wage war. War has allowed us to spread across the globe into habitats that have long been closed to us—for example, we only began seriously studying orangutans in the late 1960s when Richard Leahy visited the east Java Sea. They have never been able to study us. If they had, they would have recognised that we are a particularly violent and aggressive species and that we are never happier than when hunting each other.

When you think of war, you don't tend to think of that however. Probably you prefer to think of Homer's *Iliad* and its bloody duels between warriors who were evenly matched. I think we warm to the Trojan War heroes several thousand years after the poem was written because of their individuality. We know their names; they have not faded into the anonymity of history. There is also an equality between slayer and slain which you don't find in war today; Achilles called the Trojan Warrior Lycaon a 'friend' before dispatching him to the Underworld. We learn where the heroes hail from—their hometowns and their patronymic names, and their deaths are recorded in surgical detail. We are much more sparing with the details of war today, and we hardly ever get to hear who was responsible for taking the lives of the soldiers who are killed. Being blown up by an improvised explosive device in Afghanistan or Iraq is about as soulless a death as it gets.

What we don't tend to recall is the darker side of Homer's narrative. The heroes are compared at times to 'eaters of raw meat', a term applied exclusively to warriors in the epic. 'Raw flesh eater' is Hecuba's description of Achilles; when he meets Hector in the final and fateful encounter, he tells him that he would like to chop off his flesh and eat it raw (Griffin, 1983). The metaphors to be found in the *Iliad* are dark indeed; they are a throw-back perhaps to an earlier practice of our distant ancestors who would eat their enemies in the hope of possessing their strength and power. Indeed, the fact that the heroes of the poem spend so much time imagining their enemies being fed to wild beasts or left on the field of battle for the birds to devour may betray a deep instinctive desire that has to be internally repressed. Even Achilles is a much more conflicted character then we imagine him. True, he embraces Priam and releases Hector's body to his care, but he is capable of reverting back to type at a moment's notice. At one point, he is so angered by the old man's interminable lamentations that he threatens to murder him where he stands. Homer employs another animal metaphor to describe his reaction—he only restrains himself by bounding out of his hut 'like a lion' (*Iliad*, 24: 572). These days we don't tend to compare our animal natures to lions so much as killer apes though we do so with scant respect for their true nature. Achilles remains a killer to the end—an incomplete man our forefathers might have said, though they would have been wrong. We are all incomplete in our journey to become human. For us, humanity is a work in progress, and we need to understand war and why we conduct it if we are ever to complete the work. One port of entry is to grasp our animal nature, while at the same time trying to also understand what makes us different from the other great apes.

Why We Don't Live on the Planet of the Apes

When you think about war, there is a good likelihood that you may recall the great battles of history. If you are from England, there are several that stand out—Hastings (1066), which is the butt of that great satire *1066 and All That* (it is the one date English children used to remember, but many no longer do), and Waterloo (1815), which takes centre stage in one of the great Victorian novels, Thackeray's *Vanity Fair*. Battles zoom in and out of English history, but there is one that has lodged itself particularly firmly in the imagination, thanks to one of the most patriotic plays ever penned by a playwright. What would the battle of Agincourt (1405) be but for Shakespeare's rendition of it; it is the set piece of his heroic pageant, *Henry V*. In the movie version, which Laurence Olivier made in 1944 at the height of the Second World War, the play takes flight cinematically as we watch from on high an army invading France, a veritable triumph of the will in the face of overwhelming odds. This is war as we all know it from cinema, with its heroes from central casting, its dramatic clash of arms as two armies struggle to prevail and write themselves into the history books. As Shakespeare gets the king to declare, we live only through history; we will be remembered only if successes on the battlefield 'with full mouth / speak freely of our acts'.

At the very heart of the play is a scene, 'a touch of Harry in the night', as the King converses with his soldiers on the eve of the next day's battle about the justice of the cause for which they are fighting. If you remember your Shakespeare, you'll recall that even Harry has doubts about his own claim to the throne of France though they are not sufficiently strong to deflect him from his purpose. Strong enough, nevertheless, to give him a sleepless night. The commoners among whom he mingles in a rare democratic impulse are not entirely convinced either. Why are they fighting, so far from home? If the King's cause is not just, will they be dispatched to hell? War gives rise to questions, an endless series of them. But in the end, battle is joined the next day. What Shakespeare shows us is an army led by a king with a taste for glory. We see him at the head of a ragtag bunch of men, some impressed, some seeking adventure, most fighting for their own profit. None of them in real life imagining that an English playwright would immortalise them in blank verse.

Picture a quite different scene, an aboriginal battle that was filmed in 1961 in New Guinea in a mountainous region that history had yet to discover. The battle had no playwright to celebrate it, or historian to record it, but it can be seen on a remastered version of the original documentary *Dead Birds*. It was filmed by the Harvard Peabody expedition and offers a unique insight into what war must have looked like for thousands of years. Two villages announce beforehand that hostilities will soon commence. They line up on opposite sides shouting out grievances at one another, singling out for special attention one or two individuals for special abuse. They fire arrows and throw spears, mostly missing the target. Neither side is willing to fight hand-to-hand. There are none of those brutal but dramatic encounters between warriors that are so vividly described by Homer. In the *Iliad*, we read of the 148 different ways in which it is possible to kill another man. Even so, the battle clearly deserved the name. Both sides had debated whether to go to war. Some had urged caution; others couldn't wait to begin the attack. The battle, such as it was, also saw the repaying of old scores and the use of cultural 'threat displays', such as the hurling of obscenities. What we see is not a clash of arms so much as a battle of words, not all of them probably carefully chosen (France, 2011: 395).

From the vantage point of the film crew in the helicopter from which it was filmed, the battle, such as it was, bordered on farce. But it would be wrong to reach this conclusion. In New Guinea, until quite recently, some social groups became extinct every century because of war. And just because the conflicts had few features that we would recognise in most state-to-state warfare, including organisation, logistics and leadership, did not make it any less lethal—in fact, the absence of all these things make it more lethal still (LeBlanc, 2003: 151).

Picture another scene. This time, it is not of a battle but what looks like an extended campaign of intimidation and violence that was observed in Uganda's Kibale National Park by the

University of Michigan's John Mitani. For ten years, a band of chimps persistently penetrated enemy territory, killing any lone male they happened to stumble upon. Recent work on the social lives of chimpanzees shows that they base their aggression on rational rules of thumb such as their numerical strength and that of their enemies, and they engage in consequence management—they usually go in for low-risk attacks (Wilson and Wrangham, 2003). The struggle which Mitani witnessed was eerily human—every ten or fourteen days patrols of up to twenty males penetrated enemy territory moving quietly in single file and halting cautiously whenever they heard a noise. If they encountered a force larger than their own, they would break ranks and retreat. The war only ended when the other group eventually left, dispossessed of its land. Why the violence? For the usual reasons, including access to resources which every community needs for its survival. Collective violence drives group selection in chimpanzees as it does in human beings too (Wilson, 2019: 117–18). But even this savage display of violence differed from the battle witnessed in New Guinea. Chimps go on raiding parties, but they don't fight battles. We don't attack isolated individuals when we go on campaign: we attack groups, and that is just one of many differences between us and the other great apes.

The kind of sustained aggression which Mitani observed in Uganda is called 'coalition violence', a term employed by primatologists to distinguish it from human warfare (Rutherford, 2019: 74). We tend to set the bar high because war—unlike isolated attacks—requires a degree of planning, organisation and even strategic thinking or 'manual-mode reasoning' if you wish to use a technical term. It enabled us to make a great leap forward in becoming the dominant species on the planet. It enabled us to think ahead, and to come up with rudimentary strategies for everyday living. And the difference was critical. Like us, the great apes have continued to evolve; they have evolved violence to maximise the chances of their own survival, but they have not yet evolved war. That is why their violence needs to be understood in its own terms, not merely as a model for understanding our own behaviour (Rutherford, 2019: 74–5).

We have been classifying other species for a long time, subdividing them into categories that have differed over the centuries. We like to pigeon-hole, to put our subjects of study on the right library shelf so that we can find them easily. We do this by finding attributes or features that help us to demarcate their possibilities and limits. And we usually fail. The Greeks thought we were defined by our use of reason; others have preferred to see us as *Homo quaerens*—questioning man (from the Latin word *quaerere*, which not only gives us the word 'quest' but also more ominously 'conquest'). In fact, we now reject the idea that reason or language or the use of tools sets us apart from the rest of the animal kingdom. But if we are indeed the only species to wage war, perhaps we should designate ourselves by another term: *Homo rapiens*. Not only are we very good at killing our own kind. We are even better at hunting to extinction other species, which is why of course we have zoos; they ensure that some of the most endangered may survive a little longer, at least in captivity.

From Prey to Predator

Chimps hunt too, of course, but only some groups do, whilst violence is common to them all. We have only observed chimpanzees hunting since the 1960s, so it might well be the case that they have observed our behaviour and adapted, especially as we have encroached on their habitats. Nevertheless, it is worth noting that very few chimps go on hunting expeditions. Life does not revolve around the hunt. And as the primatologist Frans de Waal suggests, aggression in chimps is not motivated by hunger, but by fear and the two imperatives are generated by very different neural circuitry (Maschner and Reedy-Maschner, 2008: 59). If this is indeed the case, this would suggest that for both us and chimps organised violence evolved before organised hunting. But in our case, violence eventually became a general-purpose tool. And as we climbed to the top of the food chain, so we began to see other human beings in an especially predatory light. Our transformation from prey to predator left behind a genetic imprint—an instinct for the hunt. No longer fearing any other species, we became the 'hunter ape'—the ultimate predator (Burkert, 1983).

For Barbara Ehrenreich, the great transformation in the human story was the escape from prey to predation. Until about 70,000 years ago, we lived side-by-side with other animals apparently peacefully enough except for those animals who preyed upon us. We spent our time scavenging for things that other animals had left behind, just as today's slum children rummage for plastic bottles and phone parts on the rubbish tips of Mumbai and Nairobi. And then we began to kill in earnest. It started probably with 'mobbing', for which you don't need weapons. All you need is co-ordinated behaviour. Such behaviour in animals other than humans can appear spontaneously; the perception of danger often prompts moments of group solidarity— chimps often scream loudly when watching a killing. But with the invention of weapons, we far surpassed ourselves. We went on to systematically hunt to extinction the great animals: 50,000 years ago in Australia, we polished off tortoises as big as small cars, kangaroos that were carnivorous and flightless birds twice the size of an emu. The large mammals of the Americas disappeared almost 10,000 years ago, after the first humans turned up; the reason wasn't climate change but the human disposition to hunt them to extinction. We used to think that our distant ancestors had a much more rewarding phenomenological and emotional engagement with the flora and fauna around them. Think again. It is just a myth.

So what cultivated this frenzy of killing? Possibly, Ehrenreich speculates, folk memories of the past. Darwin was once surprised by the fear of large caged animals in London Zoo shown by his two-year-old son. He later hypothesised that 'the fears of children which are quite independent of experience are the inherited effect of real dangers ... during savage times' (Ehrenreich, 1997: 87). And those fears were amplified by cultural role play. If women were excluded from going on hunting expeditions fairly early on in our history, they took over the education of children, and so began the cultural transmission of predator-related anxieties from parent to child. The helplessness of children (another feature unique to our species) would have made them especially susceptible to stories about wild animals who once hunted their ancestors (Ibid, 94–5). Monsters are a stock in trade of many fairy stories and folk-tales. The great authority on fairy stories, Bruno Bettelheim, claimed that they allowed children to confront exaggerated versions of everyday realities. It is an important social skill for the real monsters have always been us, lurking in plain sight.

Once we saw off the sabre tooth tigers and other predators, we began hunting each other. In no time at all, the great campsite stories of hunts soon became stories of hunts against people. Go back 2,000 years and you will find Aristotle dividing hunting into sub-categories—game-hunting, people-hunting (slave raiding), plundering and the hunting of people and possessions together, a practice he chose to call 'war' (Rihll, 1993: 83). The Greeks were less squeamish than we are in describing what they thought war was all about. Unlike many of us, they had no difficulty 'getting with the programme'. There is an ancient Greek epigram of uncertain authorship: 'Hunting is a practice for war; and hunting teaches one to catch a thing concealed, to wait for those coming on to pursue the fleeing' (Rihll, 1993: 84).

So, nothing much has changed since then, has it? 'How do we organise the Defense Department for manhunts?' asked Donald

Rumsfeld at the beginning of the War on Terror, and drone warfare can be seen as man-hunting on a grand scale. The fundamental structure of this type of warfare, writes Grégoire Chamayou, is not that of two fighters squaring off against each other on a battlefield, but of a hunter advancing on his prey (Chamayou, 2015). And we have chosen at the same time to turn man-hunting into a science. It now has its own technocratic jargon that is derived in part from social network analysis and 'nexus-topography', a pseudo-science which enables us to map the social environments that bind individuals together, and thus to find—and take out—the critical nodes in a network (such as terrorist cells). In his book, Chamayou ranges widely over the theoretical modelling that the American military has undertaken since the 9/11 terrorist attacks, such as pattern-of-life analysis (using the evidence collected by cameras on unmanned aircraft to profile the behaviour of those under surveillance). The military has also drawn inspiration from the way in which sports broadcasters, using cameras from all angles, are able to index every sequence of play on a database and so seize upon the critical moments and stratagems in a game so that lessons can be learned and acted upon in future.

But the Ehrenreich thesis invites another thought which is more disturbing in its implications. One of the fears that now haunts us when contemplating our own future-fitness is the arrival of 'killer robots', which are vigorously opposed by organisations such as the United Nations and the International Committee of the Red Cross. Quite apart from the doomsday scenarios in which machines eventually turn on us with extreme prejudice, there would appear to be a compelling explanation for our aversion to being killed by a robot that is able to take that decision without referring back to a human operator. There is a particular reason, I suspect, why the *Terminator* franchise does so well at the box office. The 'right' to be killed only by a fellow human, even if he is unleashing a missile from thousands of miles away, may be the most basic of human rights that we claim for ourselves. If Ehrenreich is right, and the transformation from prey to predator is indeed the central story in the early human narrative, as Darwin was among the first to suspect, and if the transformation may have been more or less complete only as recently as 25,000 years ago, then no wonder we fear the prospect of being hunted by machines of our own making, especially if they turn out to be far more intelligent than us.

Talking Ourselves to Death

Organised hunting requires organised planning, such as working out a strategy to hunt down an animal group, determining who takes the lead and who stays in the van, and ultimately how the kill will be distributed. Other animals of course work in packs— wolves are among the most sophisticated of all; they can stalk a group of animals for days and communicate with each other over long distances. Animals have evolved many different ways of communicating with each other and working as a team. Whales sing (they can vocalise the pain of bereavement); dolphins gossip; chimps learn basic sign language; and some monkeys give different warning cries depending on the type of predator that is approaching—an eagle in the sky or a snake in a tree. They are all telling examples of what is known as 'convergent evolution' in which the same solution to a problem, such as communication with others, emerges independently. What we humans have is language, and that makes the critical difference.

Chimps may well have pre-linguistic expressive powers (they have been observed in the wild misleading each other for their own advantage), and they also have a rudimentary theory of the mind (the ability to read another chimp's intentions), but it is language with its own syntax and semantics that really does make all the difference. If you doubt this, think of this paradox. There is nothing more instantly communicative than silence. For if chimps use grunts and nods and even silences (like us, they often sulk), humans are silent in ways that only language paradoxically allows—the silence of assent or dissent; the silence of disgruntlement; the silence of disobedience or defiance; the silence of drawing someone out in a conversation further than might be wise. When two people deliberately fall back on silence they are often declining to add a single word to what has already been unsaid.

Think of the many other advantages that language confers. With it, we can communicate an intention or aim. It creates a web of co-operation by allowing us to make promises that we are expected to keep. It allows us to enter into covenants with each other which, unlike contracts, can be open-ended, provided that trust in a partner is unreserved. Thanks to language, we insist on arguing out the terms on which we live. Language affords us a way to evaluate reciprocity, to ask whether we are getting the best out of a contract and how far can we place our trust in the person with whom we are cooperating. Possibly even more important is our ability to talk to ourselves. The American philosopher Daniel Dennett suggests that we might have developed the skill so that we could explain our actions to other people; our minds are 'clearing houses' in which we can rehearse justifications for our actions and run through the reasons that might persuade other people to follow our advice. In other words, language is vital in persuading others to do our bidding such as coercing other people (Dennett, 2017).

Language is vitally important for another reason, still. Over time, humans have become utterly dependent on socially transmitted information. The young are taught social skills which help them to develop emotional and social intelligence; they are taught social etiquettes and moral codes, and language allows them to develop enhanced cognitive skills which lead in turn to enhanced performance (Laland, 2018: 36). There is even a hypothesis that language emerged to help teaching—to reduce its costs and increase its accuracy, and that learning through language in turn produced a diverse and dynamic cultural world which demanded talking about (Ibid: 38). And a world that is worth talking about is also one that invites us to identify and correct its injustices, if we can.

As Michael Tomasello observes, we know that apes and wolves have sympathy for those in distress. In a wolf pack, the alpha male often follows at the back, checking on the condition of other members who may be falling behind because they are ill or injured. We know that Neanderthals looked after their ill and disabled, often for years at a time. But only we have developed a sense of fairness and justice, and when we believe we are being treated unjustly we try to correct it (Tomasello, 2016). The Sapir–Whorf thesis, which is now discredited by linguistics but still loved by philosophers, suggests that language does not describe the real world so much as create it. Or at least our sense of it. We are what we talk. Whether true or not, language does allow us to change reality if we think there is something that urgently needs changing, and war is one way, if a crude one, to make the change. Throughout history, in other words, we have found it very easy to talk ourselves to death.

The Myth of the Noble Savage

So, are we violent by nature? Or have we been conditioned to act aggressively? Two giant thinkers disagreed on whether aggression or social harmony were the grounding of history. The first was Thomas Hobbes, the other was Jean-Jacques Rousseau. And we have been arguing the toss between them ever since they committed their thoughts to paper.

WHY WAR?

In 1973, a Mexican anthropologist, Santiago Genovés, set out to prove that Hobbes was right. His experiment called for eleven people to be set adrift on a raft across the Atlantic. He chose to pick his candidates, largely for their looks. If you look at the photographs of them taken at the time, they look as if they might have auditioned for one of today's TV reality shows or soft porn movies. What he set out to test was whether humans were like many of the great male primates who fight each other over access to ovulating females. To add to the tension on board, he ensured the raft would set sail just as the hurricane season began in the Caribbean. Genovés was a neo-Hobbesian who expected that when you put a group of men on a small boat with attractive women, they would be at each other's throats in no time at all. To put it more bluntly, he imagined that they would 'revert to type'.

Some men, of course, given just the right amount of pressure, and taken out of their usual comfort zone don't need much encouragement to act monstrously. But Genovés was astonished to find that instead of turning on each other the men tried their hardest to have sex with the women, though they felt deeply inhibited because they could only do so in the open, in front of their peers. In the end, although they didn't turn on each other, they did eventually turn on him. When his navigation skills were shown up—he almost steered the raft into an oncoming container ship—they removed him from his command. He grew quite depressed and sulked for the rest of the voyage. His academic career didn't go far after that.

So, what does this failed social science experiment have to tell us, apart from the fact that social scientists are often quite foolish? Can we conclude that humans are more like peace-loving bonobos, the flower children of the primate world, who prefer to eschew violence and spend most of their time screwing each other? Unfortunately, not. Hobbes was right to argue that we are driven by fear. He is still remembered for his depressing description of the state of nature into which our distant ancestors were born as being 'nasty, brutish, solitary and short'. We tend to ignore the 'solitary' because we are by inclination a sociable species if often capable of very anti-social behaviour indeed. That is why we are driven to purchase security through 'dense sociality' as anthropologists call it, such as membership of a family, or kinship group or tribe. All of which separate 'insiders' from 'outsiders'. The very same propensity to be communal and socially cohesive makes us aggressive to others. It also makes us excessively fearful of being attacked by people from other tribes.

Although gregarious by nature, Hobbes went through life being fearful. He remained convinced that we will always be what our genetic inheritance from our distant ancestors has made us: fearful and resentful, and unable to change. We will never escape war because there are limits to how far we can put our origins behind us. Most evolutionary psychologists would probably agree. We are still lumbered with the brains of our Stone Age ancestors which is why evolutionary psychologists argue we are so maladapted to the world in which we live. We are still tribal; we are still governed by the same fundamental impulses and desires. We still pray to Gods we think worth praying to. We are still fiercely territorial when it comes to the crunch.

For that reason, evolutionary psychologists tend to have little patience for the rational actor model, which presumes that individuals make economic choices aimed at maximising material payoffs based on all the available information of the time. The model is not wrong in presuming that people do indeed try to be rational, at least most the time. The problem is that we are not as clever as we like to think, and often we have great difficulty identifying what is in our true interests. Different ideas about reality also explain very different styles of behaviour. Some of us are more fearful of failure than we are of achieving success; others will be willing to take a leap of faith into the future, even at some risk to themselves. Our decisions are often based on irrational heuristics and biases of which we are not always consciously aware. And we are frequently given to unwarranted optimism: we think we will succeed even in the face of evidence that we won't. And if one way of being rational is to learn the lessons of history, we appear to be chronically incapable of doing so. These characteristics of human nature are no different today than they were back in the days when our ancestors gathered around a campfire to tell each other stories.

This is where Hobbes comes out on top. Fear is the primal emotion of every species, not only our own. In his book *Beyond Words: What Animals Think and Feel*, Carl Safina marshals compelling evidence that most animals experience the same range of emotions as we do. These are the emotions of shared brain structures and shared chemistries, originating in a shared ancestry. 'They are the shared feelings of a shared world' (Henderson, 2017: 169). And of those many emotions, fear is the strongest. In 2006, researchers from Brown University discovered that even when we are sleeping, parts of our brain remain alert, looking out for potential threats (Watanabe and Tamaki, 2016: 1190–4). As Hobbes recognised, fear is asocial: you do not need to be a social animal to experience it. And in every species, it is focused on the fate of the body. We humans enter the darkness on the day of our birth. In the words of the Roman poet-philosopher Lucretius, a baby comes into the world, 'like a sailor cast forth from a fierce wave ... unable to speak' (Nussbaum, 2018: 18). Its anguish is focused on a body over whose fate it has no control. But as the child grows up to recognise family members its anguish abates. Later in life, even though we live in a world where our destiny will never be entirely of our own choosing, we can overcome our fearfulness by creating social networks that secure us and make us less anxious about the future. And no networks have been more effective than the family and the tribe.

We have to be careful, however, when using the latter word these days. Anthropologists avoid it if they can, and it is usually advisable to avoid the minefields that academics like to lay for the unwary. So, let us talk instead in the most generic terms about social groups. Selection at the level of groups promotes altruism and co-operation, but there is a bitter price to pay. In reducing in-group conflict, it amplifies inter-group conflict leaving us, writes Edward Wilson, 'enmeshed in perpetual conflict' with outsiders (Wilson, 2017: 37).

As social animals, we still continue to benchmark ourselves against outsiders, and perhaps not surprisingly, the most successful groups tend to be more fiercely exclusive than others. According to the neo-Kantian thinker Christine Korsgaard, the author of *Self-Constitution* (2009), this is how we constitute ourselves as rational agents. Our subjective self is largely constituted through relations with people like us. The more features we recognise in others as constitutive of ourselves, the more pronounced is our 'constitutive integrity'. In identifying 'otherness'—the different, the uncanny, the strange—we come to understand ourselves much better. There would seem to be no escaping that logic (Korsgaard, 2009). And don't for a moment imagine that experts can escape from this trap. A recent article in *Scientific American* challenged the assumption that well-informed people can break with tribal orthodoxies by weighing evidence more carefully and reaching truly dispassionate judgements. Unfortunately, learning and education encourage us to hype up the inherent virtue of our own group, and in some cases, such as with religion, to claim that we alone possess the 'truth'. Many of us choose to use our reasoning abilities to find evidence that supports our own group view and to dismiss all other evidence that contradicts it. We are still prone, the article explained 'to putting tribe before truth' (Kahan, 2018).

All of this may be true, but that doesn't mean that we are faced with a binary choice. To believe that we will never escape the violent state of nature requires us to accept that biology rules our lives, and that we are driven by nothing more than basic instincts. To believe that war is a purely social invention requires us to believe we are prisoners of culture and that there is nothing more to us than socially conditioned desires. Rousseau chose to believe that we were corrupted by the invention of private property. Unfortunately, history doesn't bear out the claim. What he didn't grasp—or wouldn't—is that violence is the cause of social inequality, it is not the symptom. Greed leads us to dispossess others, and history is a constant struggle between the 'haves' and 'have-not's'. This belief in our original innocence, of course, is part of a long tradition of wishful thinking. The idea that we were once ignorant of all sin, even the original one, is striking evidence both of our deep-rooted belief in our own fundamental goodness, as well as our rather touching susceptibility to believe in stories that we still think are worth believing in.

This thesis has long since disintegrated along with the optimistic Enlightenment mood that it captured. Apart from which, as we now know and our ancestors didn't, evolution ensured that as we humans became more sedentary and the population grew there was a selection pressure for less within-group aggression, which was translated into such paedomorphic features as smaller skulls, jaws and teeth compared with our earlier hominid ancestors. Later civilisation produced its own changes, including the ownership of property, which, contra Rousseau, was not 'unnatural'; as a toolmaking species, given to talking about our fate and future, we were bound sooner or later to leave our hunter-gatherer past behind us. It was also inevitable that once we learned to domesticate other animals that we would also try to tame ourselves: by breeding out some of the passions that were bred in by natural selection. And we've been domesticating ourselves over the millennia by breeding out hyper-aggression and breeding in greater social intelligence. We have tried with mixed success to reduce emotional impulsiveness and innate aggressiveness in all walks of life through socialisation in the home and through education.

In addition, even the earliest people evolved codes of behaviour such as taboos against incest. Our social conventions are a natural outcome of our desire to establish rules. Back in our distant past small groups began to develop social norms and conventions to define the group's goals. Those goals were internalised by other members and in time the group developed a 'moral code' of right and wrong behaviour. In developing independently of others, these codes tended to reinforce the in-group versus out-group mentality (Tomasello, 2016). And this made it increasingly difficult sometimes to recognise our common humanity. The fewer shared values between two groups, writes the sociologist Helen Fein, the more likely the members of the out-group will find themselves beyond 'the universe of obligation' (Fein, 1993: 48).

To sum up, there is no straightforward divide between nature and culture: each reinforces the other. Besides which, according to Richard Wrangham, a British primatologist based at Harvard, both Hobbes and Rousseau missed the point: we are both violent and peaceful at the same time. What made us less violent than some other primates, such as baboons, is that we started to punish reactive aggression. We ruthlessly pursued people who struck out and lacked self-control, who killed others on a whim, or simply because they had been insulted and were out for revenge. All this took a long time of course, but this is why, very early on, we also sanctioned capital punishment, and in the international sphere one particularly lethal kind of collective violence: war which was often justified before or after the fact for wrongs that had been visited upon us by others (Wrangham, 2019). The trouble is that *Homo sapiens* is a contradictory species—it is good at making love and good at making war, as both overpopulation and the threat of nuclear extinction illustrate all too vividly today.

One Small Sacrifice

We are also—and this is critical—willing to defend the tribe, and yes sometimes even the Truth with our lives. War would be impossible if we were not willing to make sacrifices for each other. We tend to think that war is all about killing, but that is only part of the truth. If it is not always as easy as we may think to persuade a human being to kill another, it is even more difficult to persuade one to put his life on the line. The great exception has always been a kinship group. The Inuit off the Alaska coast live a particularly precarious life. When they go hunting, they can be swept away by an ice floe or capsized by a walrus. And when they go whaling in small open boats, the boats often get up-ended by the whales whenever a harpoonist gets in too close for the kill. Because of the risks, the crews always consist of close kinsmen. No-one but a close relative, say the Inuit, is likely to dive into the water to rescue you. Blood in this case really is thicker than water (Dunbar, 2012: 16). The story confirms a famous thought experiment by the British biologist J S Haldane, who hypothesised that if you dive into a river to save a man from drowning, you are likely to incur a 10% chance of drowning yourself. If he's a stranger, it's simply not worth the risk. But if he's your brother, carrying half your genes, trying to rescue him probably is well worth it—from the point of view of the genes, of course. Kin selection in other words has the power to evoke altruistic behaviour.

Of course, the argument relies on group selection, a theory that is hotly contested even among evolutionary psychologists. But sometimes we have to take sides, and for me group selection is the most convincing explanation for why we are altruistic.

Even among primates, social behaviour is governed by basic rules, such as who has priority in access to food. These rules are good for the group because they produce social order. The cultural transmission of such social behaviour has been observed in all primate societies; the difference in humans is that when we break the rules we can articulate right from wrong—we can feel guilt or shame and internalise such feelings at an early age. We know anti-social behaviour when we see it, and we can boost social cohesion by behaving well. It was Darwin who first suggested that some members of the group can shorten their lives or reduce their chances of reproduction or both if the advantage that their sacrifice provides the group gives sufficient advantage over other competing groups. The altruism gene can spread—group selection argues—through the population of the group by mutation and selection (Wilson, 2019: 81). The sacrifices we make—the small advances in human cooperation—have probably come from random mutation as much as social or moral engineering.

'Few die well that die in a battle', we read in Shakespeare's play, *Henry V*. Yet dying has always been a central selling point of war. It is not the killing we tend to remember, but the fact that so many soldiers are willing to put their lives on the line, and it is not hard to find the reason for it. Shakespeare's famous 'band of brothers' doesn't actually require consanguinity; it's a brotherhood nonetheless, and since the Second World War it has been the prevailing explanation for group cohesion in combat. The idea was first put forward as an academic thesis by S L A Marshall in his seminal book *Men Against Fire* (1947). It was later taken up by popular historians, the most celebrated of whom was Stephen Ambrose whose book *Citizen Soldier* (1997) was the inspiration for Steven Spielberg's TV series *Band of Brothers*. It is also a principal theme of many novels. The deep friendships that soldiers forge with one another is one of war's minor keys of grace.

At West Point, they still read Stephen Crane's *The Red Badge of Courage*. Crane himself never saw a battlefield in his life, yet he managed to convey the reality of war purely through an active imagination. Crane's novel is revered for its engaging portrait of a young soldier Henry Fleming who is a reasonably intelligent but callow youth—the type that seasoned soldiers encounter in every war. He is a young man with a head full of Homeric myths and a heart full of heroic yearnings. Curiously for a young man who had never been near a battlefield, Crane had a special empathy for the rank and file. And he used them to see beyond the rhetoric of bravery to the fear that even the bravest soldier eventually is forced to face. Every soldier who has seen combat knows the capriciousness of fate and remembers those who have lost their lives to it.

But there is one way of mitigating both fear and anxiety, and Crane's novel is a celebration of it. We are caught up in Henry Fleming's wild swings of feeling from fear to guilt and his gradual awareness of his own 'kinship' to his comrades is central to the story and its telling. 'He felt the subtle band of brotherhood more potent even than the cause for which they were fighting. It was a mysterious fraternity, born of the smoke and danger of death' (Crane, 1994: 26). What Crane intuited entirely from his reading, we know today to be scientifically correct. Neural-scientific research tells us that the process that drives us to join groups or teams is very real. Groupish-ness has a neurological origin. Using the intra-nasal administration of the hormone oxytocin, experiments have shown that we become more co-operative with other in-group members, as opposed to members of an out-group, when fear levels are high. Shared emotions really can give a unit a common sense of purpose by activating neural areas of the brain usually associated with fear. Using functional magnetic resonance imaging, we can now see how bonding with the 'band of brothers' actually works. A neural network that includes the *nucleus accumbens*, popularly known as the 'pleasure centre', is responsible for generating the desire to be part of a

group. That is not how novelists, or for that matter most soldiers, tend to think, and of course it is what they think that
shapes their behaviour in battle.

If you doubt this, then read Sebastian Junger's award-winning
account of his time as an embedded journalist with a combat unit
in Afghanistan. Months after returning to New York, he met up
with one of the infantrymen he had got to know closely.
Unfortunately, the man had become one of the 'walking
wounded'. Like many other returning veterans, he had difficulty
forcing life into a new shape. He was clearly suffering from burn-
out, both emotional and psychological. His life had become one
of wild mood swings fuelled in part by too much alcohol. He was
also suffering from anhedonia, an inability to experience pleasure. But as he told Junger, when soldiers drink themselves into
oblivion it's not always to forget the bad stuff—the horrors they
have witnessed in the field—but it is more complicated than
that. 'We drink because we miss the good stuff'. Clearly some
men miss a world in which trust is at a premium, the trust that
soldiers invest in each other. For a few—the born warriors—
combat is the kindest experience of all for it offers 'that profound
and mysterious gratification of protecting another person with
your life' (Junger, 2010: 232–4). I think in this context of
Michael Frayn's answer to his own question: what does it mean
to 'lay down one's life' for a friend? 'In such total blackness there
must be light that we cannot see because its brightness blinds us'
(Frayn, 1974). The unarticulated is often the inexpressible or
ineffable which speaks to us all the more persuasively because
what is really important is often left unsaid.

The Artificial Ape

There are many reasons why our chimpanzee cousins haven't
managed to invent war, but let me just highlight one. They don't

have weapons. When a group of chimps sets upon another it can often take up to twenty minutes to finish him off with their fists. Armed with a weapon, even the weaker of the two parties can end the fight in no time at all. It is true that chimps have been observed to kill each other with a stone, but they cannot throw one very far. Throwing a stone at another person may seem a rather basic task, but it really isn't. It's as complicated as it is for a modern baseball player throwing a fast ball at 95 mph (Stephenson, 2013, 26). Of course a pitcher doesn't ask himself how likely a ball is to respond to the force and direction with/in which it is thrown or the likely action of gravity or friction of the air any more than a spin bowler would in a game of cricket. But both make instinctive calculations based on experience and training. Even throwing a stone requires an understanding of its likely trajectory and the distance that you want it to travel. And that requires a brain like ours.

We too, of course, once killed each other with rocks. 'Breaking heads and cutting throats' was Lord Byron's minimalist definition of war. Many of you may believe that the very core of war is distilled in these very few words; but think again. We gave up beating a head in with a rock at some point in time, though as late as the *Iliad* Homer tells us that, in the absence of any other weapons to hand, the great friend of Achilles, Patroclus, kills a Trojan soldier called Esylaus with a stone. By then we had been using spears and bows and arrows for several thousand years. And they were useful not only in war. Armed with a bow and arrow, a human can stalk his prey alone. Armed with a rock or club, his best hope is to work with others—driving game into an ambush for example. This is probably how we killed most of the megafauna that we hunted down to extinction thousands of years ago, including the last mammoth elephants which were still roaming the Siberian wastes a few hundred years before the siege of Troy.

Probably the main explanation for the frenzy of killing that marked the disappearance of the mammoth elephant and the giant fauna that we hunted to extinction even earlier is that we were able to develop killing skills so quickly that we were able to kill simply because we could. Cultural evolution is faster than natural selection and cultural variation is faster still. Culture allowed our ancestors to out-evolve all other animals. It took millions of years, for example, for the canines of sabre-toothed cats to become as large as they eventually did. But it took only 20,000 years to go from the Aurignacian bone spearheads of our human-Neanderthal ancestors to the more deadly Solutrean point that resembled the canines of sabre-tooth cats and may have killed in a similar way—by exsanguination.

We are a tool-making species, and archaeological evidence of the past twenty years finds the first tools were fashioned into weapons millions of years ago, long before *Homo sapiens* entered the picture. Palaeontologists still evade calling weapons by their real name, such is the force of political correctness. But we are not, writes Timothy Taylor, talking about finding appropriate twigs for extracting termites from termite mounds, like chimps; we are talking of the painstaking modification of fine-grained igneous rocks into sharp-edged forms whose principal job was to part flesh from flesh and bone from bone (Taylor, 2010a: 377). And over the centuries we have gone in for the less painstaking mass production of weapons.

The skeletons found on the battlefield of Hattin, where in 1187 a Crusader army was ambushed with catastrophic results, yield disturbing finds. One skeleton lacks a lower arm, which clearly had been severed by a sword just below the elbow. The same man had been wounded in the head and three times in the neck. His body also shows a glancing cut to his cheekbone and a fatal blow that cleft his skull apart. That was the killer blow— the one that cut his life short. All these wounds were probably administered by a sword, but the men who fought at Hattin could have been killed in other ways too: by a spear thrust, or by an arrow. Centuries later, they would most likely have been dispatched by a cannon ball or a bullet. And instead of incurring the risk of cloven skulls and shattered spines, their bodies might have been blown apart. Their death would have been faster and possibly less painful, and it might have involved much less hard work for their killers. But then the bullet in the heart is only part of the story. Crusader knights may well have waded quite literally in blood, both that of their enemies and their friends, but they were spared the fate of many soldiers in the gunpowder age. The most common type of debris removed from the flesh of wounded soldiers was bone and teeth from their neighbours in the ranks, a fate that most historians usually prefer to pass over (Keegan, 1993: 90). Flesh did not fare well in a hail of iron. What the Europeans found especially disenchanting about the industrialised battlefields of the twentieth century was also the horror of mutilation. When, during the battle of Verdun (1916), a group of soldiers took a direct hit, the result was surreal in its horror: the barrage left a great hole in the ground. 'Sticking out of it, symmetrically... were legs, arms, hands and heads like the bloodied cogs of some monstrous capstan' (Ousby, 2002: 66). The choice of the Unknown Soldier, a poor wretch whose body had been the most disfigured and the most completely broken, was emblematic of what industrial warfare had become (Tooley, 2003: 192).

At some point, probably early on, we began to turn tools into weapons. Both have been called 'the extra-somatic means of adaptation for the human organism' that allows us to enhance our innate somatic (or body) strength beyond what would seem naturally possible (Taylor, 2010b: 19). But it is a complex process. Enhancing our strength also rendered us biologically weaker. It became impossibly hard work for a man to kill another with a stone. Even in the last 10,000 years we have lost 10% of our skeletal robusticity. Even Otzi, the Iceman, hidden from the world for 5,000 years until his body was discovered in 1991, had bones stronger than most of us. This was the biological consequence of tool-making. When it came to the use of cognitive tools, however, we see an opposite outcome. As our bodily strength declined, our intelligence increased. We turned our minds into a tool, which over time enabled us to go in for making bows and arrows, then rifles, and most recently rockets.

This is another critical difference between humans and chimpanzees. Chimps can of course bash each other on the head with a stone or a rock; the fact that they use stones gives them, in the eyes of some historians, a back entrance to the Stone Age! Archaeology as a subject of study now embraces any species that produces a material signature on history. And what it tells us is that it would be quite wrong to imagine that our species is somehow more evolved than other primates. Not true. We have simply been evolving on a different branch of the family tree. Evolution is still occurring in both of us, and we both use tools. But when chimps use a stone to crack a nut or an improvised stick to lever insects out of a tree trunk, in no case is there evidence that they have ever thought of modifying the structure of either the stone or the stick to improve its function. Chimps in Senegal have been observed thrusting sticks into the hollows of trees to kill bush babies, but they have never been observed to practise thrusting, and they have never turned a stick into a spear. And of the many reasons why, one is especially important. They lack a developed sense of causation. By the middle of the Stone Age, there is evidence of our ancestors using hafted tools, tools that are composites of components joined together. Joining quite different pieces together requires a clear concept of cause and effect. And that was a long time ago. When it comes to chimpanzees, there is only one conclusion to reach—they have reached a 'technological ceiling'. 'Sadly, the preparation of a suitable rod for termite-fishing is about as far as it can go' (Allen, 2004: 206).

Humans possess another advantage involving our minds as well as our brains. Once we recognise the usefulness of a weapon, we constantly strive to improve it. We are an intellectually curious species. Michael Tomasello found that when an experimenter stopped playing a game with a child, the child would try to re-engage the experimenter. When the same thing happened with a chimp, it would immediately lose interest in the game being played (Sloman and Fernbach, 2017: 116–17). We are also willing to share knowledge with others. What we are doing is connecting our minds together, and tools help us to do this. Tomasello has described this ability as 'shared intentionality'. We are curious when we see someone else using a new technology or employing a new technique. Or to put it another way, we are given to asking questions about what the future looks like whenever we meet someone who might have reached it first (Wong, 2017: 22).

Now, when you think of tools you probably confine your thoughts to inanimate objects like a stone, or a spear or a bow and arrow. But what made us so adept at war was that we began using other animals as tools. Think of them as the excluded constants of human history. Aristotle (in)famously described human slaves as 'talking tools'—tools, of course, that were not allowed to talk back. But we have domesticated and enslaved many species that can't engage us in a conversation. And although it is only recently that we have begun to recognise how much we are inextricably intermixed in each other's life story, it is clear from our history that we are pre-adapted by evolution to co-operate with other animals. What co-evolutionary history tells us is that human behaviour is shaped by such processes. There is even a theory that we may have also learned the social skills that we needed to cooperate with each other from observing the behaviour of wolves. Wolves, after all, take care of each other's cubs, feed the old when they can no longer take part in the hunt, and never leave another wolf behind, just as the US Marine Corps boasts of never leaving behind one of its own men (Flannery, 2018b).

Whether or not we learned our social skills from wolves, it would appear from the archaeological record that we began to work with them 20,000 years ago. It is now conjectured that men and wolves may have hunted down megafauna like the mammoth together. Two very different species, observing the strengths and weaknesses of each other's hunting methods chose to hunt together. Wolves could outrun men and corner an animal herd; humans could finish them off from a safe distance with a spear. In time some wolves came to the camp side for food—those who were less aggressive and less fearful of humans than the rest. Eventually they became dogs. And they were selected, almost certainly not for their intelligence but for being socially more adept at interacting with us. Intelligence probably followed on from domestication. For example, unlike a wolf, a dog can follow a human being who is pointing at an object—it knows that the gesture reflects a thought and that the person concerned is communicating a thought worth sharing. Unfortunately for wolves, we have spent thousands of years hunting them to extinction with a degree of hatred that we usually reserve for each other.

Another example of co-evolution is our use of the horse. From the abraded teeth of horse skeletons it would appear that we first slipped a rope into a horse's mouth almost 7,000 years ago. Horses are what Ulrich Raulff calls 'converters' that helped us to unlock the energy of plants and made it available for our use. As draught animals they were 'oat-powered engines'; a single horse could deliver roughly seven times the power of a man. The great paradox of human–equine collaboration of course, is that we domesticated a mammal whose first instinct when approached in the wild was to flee from us; we literally had to capture horses and break them in, as we still do at a rodeo. But because they are herd animals, we were able to exploit this trait by transforming their instinct to flee into directed movement against another group of men. Horses also allowed us to expand war's scope, making possible such ambitious endeavours as empire-building (Raulff, 2007).

The central point is this—human agency has been enhanced for at least the last 10,000 years by our relationship with our tools, which is why Bruno Latour insists they should be of interest to sociologists as well. For what we understand as the 'social' represents more than a bonding with other people; it also constitutes an association between human beings and the tools they use. Technology and society have evolved together; they cannot be divorced from each other. Ask yourself this question: if we did not have a hammer to hammer in a nail, or if we tried to run a company without book-keeping, if neither actually made a difference, could we talk about human agency at all? Agency, adds Latour, is what 'allows', 'determines', 'permits', 'facilitates', 'renders possible or impossible' (Latour, 2007: 77). It enables us to boost performance. Today, there is another fast-developing body of knowledge called 'materiality theory' that examines how objects enable actions, how intelligence extends into the realm of 'things', and how that world, in full circle, structures our own culture.

There have been many different stages in this story of co-evolution. One of the first involved the use of cognitive tools to manipulate other people. We call it Machiavellian intelligence, and it is part of the basic toolkit that we share also with other primates. Another involved the great civilisations of the ancient world, which could only function thanks to such tools as accounting (taxation) and writing (bureaucracy). A third was the machine age, which gave machines a form of social life for the first time. The most recent phase for Latour involves the transition to the post-human. We are already becoming more machine-readable. The computers we use every day may one day be able to gauge our moods as well as they already monitor our interests—the websites we visit (Latour, 2007: 58).

And this fact is likely to transform the face of battle once again. The commander of tomorrow will be able to consult read-outs of the emotional moods of the soldiers under his command. And those soldiers in turn will be wearing exoskeletons that will gauge their psychological and physical condition as well as monitor their emotional states. Already, drone pilots operating from sealed cubicles in Nevada have their biometrics read, so that they can be 'switched' off or out of the system if they are getting over-stressed. One day we may also be able to go much further. In *The Science of Fate*, the Cambridge scientist Hannah Critchlow discusses an experiment that was carried out in 1985 by the neuroscientist Benjamin Libet. His subjects were asked to flex their wrists at a time of their own choosing. Using electrodes to measure their brain and muscle activity, it was shown that the subconscious instruction to move that issued from the motor cortex came first, the conscious instruction later. In other words, the brain decided when to act before communicating the decision to the conscious awareness of the subject. Perhaps, at some point in the near-future, a commander may even be able to grasp what a soldier is thinking before the soldier is even aware of his own thoughts.

Men Behaving Badly

The great change, if not necessarily a game changer, is that the commanders of the future will have an increasingly large number of women as well as men under their command. Since the 1960s, war has ceased to be gendered in the way it once was; it's no longer an all-male affair. Starting in the early 1990s, all branches of the military have been open to women including combat units. And although the numbers in proportional terms are small, the process of integration is continuing apace. What might be called the de-gendering of war is now far advanced.

This would have confounded our ancestors. For them, war was largely fought for and by men, sometimes for the possession of women. The most famous conflict in the history of Western civilisation begins with the 'abduction' of a woman, Helen of Troy. And the story of the *Iliad* begins with a dispute over another, Briseis, a prize seized by Achilles although she merits a mere ten mentions in the poem's 15,693 lines. The public face of war has always been male. Even when women's names do appear in the *Iliad*, they almost always appear next to a possessive generative: Andromache is always 'Hector's wife; Helen is always the prize that was won by Paris, or in the case of her former husband Menelaus, the prize to be won back. When women do appear in the poem, they appear as the context in which the men act out their lives. When Hector returns to Troy in the sixth book of the poem, he speaks with three women: his mother, who asks him to pray; Helen, who invites him to rest; and Andromache, his wife, who urges him to remember when he next goes into battle that he is a father and husband as well as a warrior. 'Two possible worlds stand facing each other and each has its own arguments', writes Alessandro Baricco, but we know which world will win out (Baricco, 2008: 153).

The apparent marginalisation of women might elicit a simple answer to my question 'Why War?'. 'I don't ask "why" because it's mostly the same', writes Margaret Atwood in her poem 'The Loneliness of the Military Historian' (1995). 'Wars happen because the men who start them think they can win' (Freedman, 2012: 17). But this explanation, though seductive, is far too trite. It is true that all but a few warriors in history have carried the Y chromosome, but historians since the 1960s have been writing women back into history. So why can't we also write them back into war?

Let's begin with one similarity between ourselves and other primates. Primates often fight each other for mating rights; back in the distant past so did humans. In an excellent study, Jonathan Gottschall brings into play readings from anthropology and evolutionary biology to show that Homer's world fits a common pattern: too few women and too many men have often led to conflict between neighbouring tribes. For thousands of years, the main cause of war was women—their abduction and rape, and the conflict between suitors, even the failure to deliver a promised bride (Gottschall, 2008). There is a striking passage in *The Odyssey* about the fall of Troy which illustrates that sexual slavery was the fate of many women whenever a city fell to the enemy:

> At the sight of the men panting and dying there
> She slips down to enfold him, crying out
> Then feels the spears, prodding her back and shoulders
> And goes bound into slavery and grief (Heaney, 2007).

Even today, writes Seamus Heaney, almost 3,000 years later, the callousness of the spear shafts on the woman's back and shoulders survives both time and translation (Heaney, 2007: 166). 'It's a woeful thing for women unripe, before the marriage rites, to tread this bitter journey from their homes', wrote the playwright Aeschylus: 'I would say that the dead are better off than this' (Tritle, 2000: 89).

Did our male ancestors ever question how much war victimised women? We have precious little evidence if they did, but we do have a play from fifth century Athens, *The Lysistrata*, a bitterly ironic take on war by the playwright Aristophanes. This extraordinary work was just one of many to come out of the Peloponnesian War and the great crisis that it precipitated in the Greek world. It led the Athenians to question everything they had taken for granted, including the fate of women in wartime. We must remember that Aristophanes wrote a comedy, not a tragedy, so whatever self-questioning he engaged in was constrained by the need to entertain his audience. And he was probably aware of the power he wielded in the act of writing—only men were permitted to write for the stage. But the play is still remarkable nonetheless for showing women going on a sex strike. Protesting about the killing, they stop sleeping with their husbands and lovers.

In a famous confrontation with the Magistrate, Lysistrata reminds him of some uncomfortable home truths. For one thing they pay the main price in war: it is their sons that go off to fight; it is their husbands who get killed. To the fate of being outsiders in a society geared for war, wives were often condemned to finding themselves outsiders within the confines of a marriage that might once have been happy. They had to live with men who, when they did return home, were often indifferent to themselves and those around them. Just because a veteran of the wars returns in person does not mean that he was the husband he was when he left home. And Lysistrata nails down the argument I think by highlighting another cost—men can always find young women to marry in their old age. If prematurely aged on account of widowhood, women were usually not so lucky. In other words, women and children have always been war's principal collateral damage.

Of course, women are not the only example of a subordinate social group within a dominance hierarchy. Young men, too, throughout the centuries have found themselves subordinate to their fathers and even remote ancestors whose honour they have often had to fight to uphold or restore. It is the subtext of *Hamlet:* 'through the ghost of the unquiet father the image of the unloving son looks forth', as James Joyce puts it in *Ulysses.* For the hapless young prince is forced to acknowledge a debt to his dead father that he is reluctant to honour, and which will eventually lead to his own death. But although women were subordinated, we shouldn't ignore the many ways in which they were able to construct lives beyond oppression. Culture often ensured that even if they did not take part in combat, they were not reduced by this. It would be entirely wrong to think that they were entirely marginalised; their role was far more interesting. Denied political power, women were forced to exert influence in whatever ways that were open to them: social or sexual, claiming in different ways the right to be recognised and heard. As Ralph Ellison reminded us in his novel *Invisible Man*, outsiders have a voice as well, even if it's on 'a lower frequency'.

The problem is that many evolutionary psychologists have tended to focus on adult men and their role in hunting and fighting. Much less attention has been paid by historians to nurturing and caring, although there is now an impressive body of work on the critical importance of home life in the evolution of empathy (Boehm, 2012). One reason why our cognitive intelligence is greater than that of other apes is probably because we take so long to grow up. A baby gazelle can outrun a predatory cheetah within several hours of being born; a human child cannot even crawl across a room for the first six months of its life. Paradoxically, this may have helped us develop our intelligence. We have been able to blend adaptation by genetic mutation with adaptation by learning; we have managed to evolve by using software not just hardware. The upshot is that we have been able to adapt much more rapidly to selective pressures. And grandmothers have been as important as mothers in this process.

Apart from killer whales, we are the only animal to outlive its own fertility. In our great leap to the top of the food chain, post-menopausal grandmothers were crucial in passing on two generations' worth of knowledge. And conditioning started in the home. In *Three Guineas*, Virginia Woolf identified a unique pathology: throughout history men have needed to see themselves magnified in the eyes of women—mothers, wives and partners. Shakespeare's great warrior Coriolanus may address his submissive wife rather dismissively as 'my gracious silence', but his own mother is another proposition altogether—she has brought up one warrior and intends that her young grandson shall be just as bloodthirsty as his father. As she says of him approvingly, 'He had rather see the swords and hear a drum than look upon his schoolmaster' (*Coriolanus*, 1.iii: 55–56). Grandmothers and their daughters were central to war—they did not belong to a world set apart from that of the male members of their families.

So, to the big question. Was the gendering of war biological or cultural, or was it the product of both? What is the explanation for the fact that women were excluded from war in every state and every culture: sex or gender? Biology was certainly central. War has always been exacting, physical work—*ergon*, (work) the Greeks called it, and it involved the slashing of bodies, often for hours at a time. Though we mustn't forget that occasionally women did go to war. Greek mythology imagined a female warrior race called the Amazons who went so far as to dislocate the limbs of their male children so that they would be forced to do manual labour in the home, or work in the fields. They were of course a male invention, one that encoded a range of sexual fears and fantasies. Nevertheless, like many myths it was grounded in history. Intriguingly, recent archaeological digs in the southern Ural steppes have found burial mounds with female warriors, as tall as men, some with old wounds from violent encounters, buried with weapons which they had clearly used in life. Historians like Herodotus knew the Amazons were not a figment of an overheated imagination; they were real. But they were the product of nomadic societies not city-states or the civilisations of the ancient world. What the Greeks couldn't grasp because they didn't know about natural selection was that they gave a huge selective advantage to tribes where women were able to fight and defend themselves (Mayer, 2014).

Then there were the 'accidental' female warriors who were pushed or pulled into fighting by circumstances though probably very few have survived erasure from history: Boudicca and Joan of Arc are two famous exceptions. One was seeking to avenge her own rape and that of her daughters by Roman soldiers; the other was impelled to put on armour by 'voices' she heard telling her to save France from the English. Today she might be dismissed as a cross-dressing schizophrenic, but her example inspired her countrymen to fight on. And then there is Nur Jahan—the favourite wife of Jahangir (the man who built the Taj Mahal), who personally led an army to rescue him from rebellious noblemen. And we shouldn't forget women pirates like Mary Read and Ann Bonny, and the greatest of all, still largely unknown in the West, Ching-Shih. Widowed in the early nineteenth century, she took over her husband's fleet of 1,500 ships and controlled more of the South China Seas than the Chinese do today.

All of this is far from the way the Greeks viewed the world. In their day, the survival of the state depended on a simple biological imperative. Since life was short and survival at birth precarious for both mother and child, women had to start on the production line as soon as they were fertile. But Plato thought that had no bearing at all on their fitness to serve as soldiers. In the world of farming, after all, both male and female guard dogs were equally efficient. It followed that any good education system should be able to produce both male and female soldiers as well. To the objection that different people had different innate abilities, Plato argues that people are obviously differently inclined but that an inclination had nothing to do with an innate ability.

But before rushing to embrace Plato as a proto-feminist, you should read the *Republic* more closely. If you do, you will find that his argument is this: there is nothing women can do that men cannot do as well, indeed infinitely better. Secondly, he argued that women could only become warriors by a radical change in their nature—by turning them away from generation and motherhood to warfare and death. He didn't think you could train out these 'natural' desires, but he did believe that some women had 'manly souls in female bodies'. In other words, their 'masculinity' could be nurtured by education. Plato finally came down on the side that there were 'manly' women just as there were effeminate men. Not very politically correct, to be sure! But then he lived in an age that didn't believe that gender is more complicated than binary division and that biological sex is far more complex than the societal norms of his day had people believe.

There was another biological explanation volunteered by the Greeks. It can be found in a passage from Thucydides' *History of the Peloponnesian War*. In the course of the fighting in Corfu, he tells us that some women engaged in the fighting by hurling tiles from rooftops 'with a courage beyond their sex' (Thucydides, *History*, 3.74.2). The word he used, *paraphusin* means 'beyond their true nature' (Cartledge, 2002: 86). For the Greeks, true bravery was reserved for the battlefield, and it was displayed exclusively by men. The courage they were expected to display was deemed to come naturally to them: it involved intelligence and careful calculation of the odds. The bravery of women by contrast, might be real enough, but it was emotional and often reckless. Women simply couldn't be put on a parade ground. There is a famous story about Sun Tzu whose *Art of War* is still avidly read; you can pick up a copy in any airport bookshop. It is said that he once tried to get a gaggle of courtesans of the King of Wu to line up in formation and teach them the rudiments of strategy. But when they wouldn't stop giggling, he ordered an executioner to lop off their heads.

These days of course women do serve in the military and their numbers are increasing all the time. So, what has happened? Well, for a start we know much more about biology than our ancestors. We know that women in some respects are stronger than men though the biological differences between the sexes are real enough—you only need think of sporting competitions. Based upon strength and speed men have a 10–30% advantage. They also have greater body and muscle mass, bone density, and connective tissue. This is why the two sexes don't compete against each other with a few exceptions such as mixed doubles in tennis. But even that's not the whole story. Both sexes require testosterone for the health of their metabolism and liver functions. It is not restricted to men, even though a lot of myths have arisen about the so-called 'male hormone'. But even the advantage it is deemed to give men in sport can be questioned. For there is no relationship between testosterone and explosive strength, and there is even a negative relationship between testosterone and stamina over a long distance. A 2004 study of professional cyclists found that they tended to have low testosterone (Karkazis, 2019). There are even occasions in sport when female athletes have displayed greater stamina, both physical and mental, than their male counterparts. Scientific studies of gender endurance are few, but the latest evidence is interesting. Physically, the more efficient storage of glycogen may favour women. And a lower centre of gravity—they are not as tall as men—may help them cover longer distances and make them more resistant to fatigue. But the deciding factor may be gender: women are less reckless, less eager to prove themselves, more concerned with survival, and simply more organised. They are less inclined to throw themselves into a situation before thinking through the consequences of their own actions (Osborne, 2019).

In fact, recent research suggests that, given the chance, young girls will embrace risk as readily as boys; the fact that they usually don't has less to do with a woman's sex than her upbringing. Gender norms are slow to change; girls are encouraged by their parents to be risk averse (Blakely, 2019). In the workplace, women are still discouraged from applying for jobs that use words such as 'aggressive' and 'ambitious'. However, when one company changed its advertisement to focus on other qualities such as 'enthusiastic' and 'innovative', the proportion of female applicants rose from 5% to 40% ('It's a man's world', *The Economist*, 20 April, 2019: 58).

But what of the old feminist argument that men really are temperamentally more suited to war? That they tend to be more risk-taking and status-seeking than women, and generally more competitive; that women seem to be more interested in sustaining relationships and working with other people; that boys tend to be more interested in computer science, and that this hasn't changed even in countries where women have equal opportunities to compete in that field. In a word they have different life priorities. Many feminists would reject these arguments as dated, and to be frank, patronising, and perhaps with good reason. What might be called 'unfinished business' for feminists, the arrival of women in the armed forces is merely the logical conclusion of the eruption of women into jobs previously reserved for and by men. Women first came onto the front line in the Battle of Britain (1940) when they came directly under fire when radar installations were attacked. The following year they were deployed in anti-aircraft and searchlight batteries, although they were not allowed to fire the guns. The public did not want them involved in combat, although 300 were killed or wounded in the course of the conflict (Tombs, 2014: 702). The Soviet Airforce had an all-female fighter squadron in the Second World War, which was disbanded immediately after the end of hostilities. And women were assigned specialist functions in the army, as machine gunners and snipers in which roles they were enormously effective (Krylova, 2010). They then disappeared from the picture until the North Vietnamese began recruiting women to treat wounded comrades and dig artillery trenches and even guard captured US pilots whose planes had been shot down. One of the most renowned—a woman called Ngo Thi Tuyen, when finally tracked down by the historian Karen Turner in 1995, was found to be in a sad state: physically and mentally scarred and bitterly resentful of the fact that after the war had ended the women who had served in the field had been cynically airbrushed out of history (Turner and Hao, 1998).

Women are now in the military for good as they have long been in the case of guerrilla warfare and modern terrorism—think of the female Tamil Tigers in Sri Lanka or the Chechen 'Black Widows', who were sold as suicide bombers after their husbands had been killed. When it comes to states, however, the real reason women have been able to carve out a role for themselves is that the character of war has changed, too. In his post-apocalyptic novel *Toward the End of Time* (1997), John Updike depicted a war between the US and China that involves highly trained young men and women in sealed chambers of safety typing an endless stream of codes and commands into computers (Updike, 1997: 286). Physical labour is no longer as central to war as it once was; war is becoming more cerebral and less visceral as it becomes increasingly specialised. It now demands what Mark Pagel calls 'a more domesticated set of abilities' such as mental agility (Pagel, 2012: 131). Though don't expect women to remain sitting behind the screens. Some will be taking part at the cutting edge, in Special Force units. Hollywood, as usual, may have stolen a march on history. Consider the heroes of recent movies—Tris in the *Divergent* series and the members of the all-women army in *Black Panther*—the Dora Milaje, not to mention the towering warrior Brienne of Tarth in the HBO series, *Game of Thrones*. True, these may all be characters from science fiction and fantasy, but that is where the rational often meets up with the oneiric (the realm of dreams and nightmares). At their best both genres allow us to estrange ourselves from the world we know, the better to grasp what makes us who we are.

And, if you do so, you are likely to reject the argument that war embodies a toxic masculinity, or that women who choose to join up remain prisoners of the very patriarchal system they themselves continue to uphold. All this assumes that war is the original invention of one half of humanity. But we should also remember that throughout the centuries, women haven't lived lives of emotional disconnect; many wanted and did live a value-laden existence, as valued members of a community. They too have celebrated the virtues of social solidarity and patriotism. Far from being passive victims, women were often agents of their own fate in so far as the patriarchal system under which they lived allowed. You can always argue that they were conned into complicity with men, a complicity which served the interests of men, not their own. On that reading of history, war becomes a story of misplaced loyalties to country or cause. But isn't that far too cynical a take? If today many women are attracted to military service, they should not be dismissed as cogs in a ruthless machine of sexual exploitation. If you regret the fact that they have taken up arms, then at least recognise that, like men, women too can be perversely human.

2

CULTURAL MECHANISMS

We have talked a lot about the instincts that we are born with, which are hard wired into us by natural selection, including an instinct to kill our own kind when circumstances dictate. But we also have cultural instincts—instincts to learn, copy, emulate and even outdo others. The instinct, for example, to write a novel like *War and Peace* or the instinct to film it—in the case of the Soviet director Sergei Bondarchuk, the desire to outdo the rival version of Tolstoy's tale by capitalist Hollywood in the 1950s.

We are not the only animals to have cultural instincts. Let's go back to the behaviour of seagulls. Their calls to each other are purely biological. But other birds, like parrots and song-birds, are capable of vocal learning, listening, rehearsing and perfecting the calls of their parents. It was the biologist Peter Marler who discovered that songbirds enter adulthood able to sing songs that may be unique to themselves. We too are born with the ability to speak, but what we choose to say, and the language in which we choose to say it, shapes our life and determines who we are. We have an instinct, in other words, to create culture (Fitch, 2012).

There are two things to grasp here. The novelty of being human is that, like songbirds, we learn from observation, which is a vast improvement over the repetitive but largely instinctual building and shaping processes of other animals. That novelty was of course itself a product of the Darwinian cycle enhanced by the swifter cycle of cultural evolution, in which the reproduction of the technique wasn't passed on to offspring through the genes but transmitted among non-kin conspecifics who picked up the trick of imitation.

But there is also a cybernetic process at work, for it is culture that allows us to develop some of the genetic predispositions with which we are born. The human body is full of possibilities that require cultural organisation for them to become manifest and concrete (Sennett, 2008: 277). And over time, the cultural artefacts we have created, such as a novel like Tolstoy's and the cinema which translates it onto the screen, have extended our emotional range even though our biological instincts are much the same as they were 200,000 years ago. Our ancestors then had fewer cultural instincts that allowed their biological capabilities to be fully realised. At the point where animal instinct fails, culture takes over and functions as an acutely human form of instinct (Ford, 2007: 8).

Take the example of language. Language is based on grammar that allows you to communicate your thoughts. It is utilised by people in real time thanks to their memory for words. It is implemented in the left cerebral hemisphere of the brain, which co-ordinates memory, word meaning and grammar. It develops in the first years of a person's life. It evolved to help us go beyond the low fidelity transmission of behaviour. Over time we were able to pass on the use of tools, and so go far beyond mere observational learning (Pinker, 2002: 70–1). You could also throw the historical development of language into the argument; in the case of Europe, from Latin into the romance languages and all the way to the development of a global electronic media today that made possible Donald Trump's infamous tweets.

Finally, the value we attach to war is almost entirely cultural. This may explain why we have never evolved an aversion to it as we have to incest. All primates avoid incest—some often leave the closed family circle at the point of sexual maturity, but only in human societies has it been transformed into a taboo. Interestingly, there is no taboo against war. There is no injunction to be found against it in the Ten Commandments or any other moral code that has come down to us over the ages. *Ecclesiastes* indeed celebrates the fact that 'to everything there is a season, and a time, to every purpose under the heavens ... a time to kill, and a time to heal... a time to love, and a time to hate; a time of war, and a time of peace' (*Ecclesiastes*, 3: 1–8). To be told on the highest authority that war has its own intelligently designed place in our life story is sanction enough for many.

And yet, of course there are plenty of injunctions against war. Think of the many proverbs that tell us that war is bad for our physical and psychological health. 'War is death's feast'. 'Who preaches war is the Devil's chaplain'. 'In war all suffer defeat including the victors'. And most famous of all from St Matthew's Gospel: 'He who lives by the sword dies by the sword'. The rhetoric is ubiquitous, but the reality has always been very different. One of the reasons that there has been no taboo against war is that religion has often sanctioned it. And one of the earliest tales we have about war puts religion at its very heart.

Krishna's Answers

Imagine that you are standing in the dusk on a vast Indian plain, looking across at an endless horizon at two competing armies forming up for a battle the next day. It is the eve of a great battle in Kurukshetra, which is now in the modern Indian state of

Haryana. Two warriors converse, in what is possibly the most famous conversation in Indian literature, and one that is thousands of years old. The conversation can be found in one of the great Vedas, the *Bhagavad Gita* (a 700 verse Sanskrit script that is part of the great Hindu epic the *Mahabharata*). Its date is still contested, as too is its authorship, which is usually attributed to Vyasa, a man who, like Homer, may never have existed. Imagine you are overhearing the greatest warrior Arjuna and his charioteer who is actually the God Lord Krishna in disguise. They are discussing the cost of a war that is being fought to determine which competing set of cousins will win the throne. Arjuna is a troubled young man. He is seriously conflicted about the thought of the human cost of the battle. He is horrified when he imagines the roster of deaths that may include his granduncle on whose lap he had played as a child and the teacher who had made him into the greatest archer in the world.

Arjuna is so fearful of losing his moral compass that he is moved to ask: why war? He is nothing if not persistent and fires off a series of questions that he hopes will prevent him from having to fight the next day. Unfortunately, Krishna is an intellectually resourceful god and won't be out-argued. Why must he fight, asks Arjuna first? Because we can't put friendship first. We have to act not for ourselves but for a higher purpose. When Arjuna still demurs, Krishna ups his game. A higher purpose may not be as persuasive as a personal challenge. Isn't Arjuna a man, and doesn't his honour—his manliness—require him to fulfil his duty? When this too fails to do the job, Krishna falls back on metaphysics. Sure, you may kill a man including a friend, but you can't imperil his mortal soul. When that too leaves Arjuna unconvinced, Krishna goes in for the kill—to be human requires we take sides. We have to make choices and stand by the choices we make. There is no value in equivocation.

What's telling about the story is that Arjuna, like Achilles, makes his own choices; they aren't made for him by others. He isn't part of a chain of command; he doesn't have to obey rear echelon offices who, safe behind the lines themselves, put their men in a position to be killed. He really does exercise personal choice, or does he? For when Krishna later reveals himself to Arjuna as a god, he tells him that the outcome of the battle has already been decided. But, at least, upon entering the fray Arjuna will achieve spiritual enlightenment. Fight, he must, for that is his destiny. But he will earn release from Karma if he surrenders all desire, including the desire for fame (Armstrong, 2006: 364).

In his book *The Argumentative Indian* (2005), Amartya Sen recalls how as a high school student he'd asked his Sanskrit teacher whether it would be permissible to say that Krishna got away with an incomplete and unconvincing argument. 'Maybe you could say that', the teacher replied, 'but you must say it with adequate respect'. Sen is suggesting, rather diffidently perhaps, that Arjuna's decision to fight was over-determined by a defective intellect—he left himself open to Krishna's less than intellectually compelling arguments. This is why, although the *Bhagavad Gita* is one of the great poems in world literature, reading it is always a melancholy pleasure because we are still providing the same answers that Krishna does to Arjuna's question: why war? Men still appeal to 'manliness' and their reputation, and states to their honour (now rendered as 'credibility' in these unpoetic times). We still justify going to war by insisting on the need to be counted and take sides. All the arguments are related to the way we behave, which we try to control through codes of conduct and philosophies of life which differ from culture to culture.

The Vedas are one of the few surviving artefacts of a once great civilisation which left behind no ruined cities that you can visit, and which founded no kingdoms or empires. What it left behind instead was a unique literature that lives on even today in the Indian imagination. Arjuna's conversation with Krishna is historically important, above all for introducing us to the cultural mechanisms that have fuelled war since the beginning, and some of which continue to fuel it still, such as calls to manliness, honour and in this case, to a religious construct, karma. And it is rendered more immediate by poetry, which has always given war a poetic charge. These are what Tinbergen called 'mechanisms' that fuel biological behaviour. If you prefer another term, then I would suggest 'cultural enhancers', a term coined by the zoologist Mark Pagel. Cultural enhancers strengthen beliefs, transmit information and increase social cohesiveness. Pagel likens them to a class of performance-enhancing drugs. In war, he remarks, they may strengthen your resolve and give you courage before a battle. They needn't produce any direct product such as a better spear that might directly affect one's chances of survival. Instead, they usually heighten emotions, thereby influencing the way that we behave, which is why occasionally that can make all the difference between victory and defeat (Pagel, 2012: 134). Nevertheless, writes Pagel, let's not overstate the case. Cultural mechanisms or enhancers largely reinforce the biological reasons you are fighting. Drugs may well improve your performance in a foot-race, but they are not the reason you are taking part in the race (Ibid: 159).

Storytelling

Athletes run for a reason: reputation—to write themselves into the record books. The great poet Pindar wrote a series of odes celebrating the courage of great warriors and the accomplishments of the great Olympic athletes of his own day. The *Olympian Odes* have survived because they stress the joy of victory, and the exultation of competition. But victory is always fairly won. Even in today's world of steroids and stamina-enhancing drugs, we still insist in the Olympics on human striving within the limits set by nature.

We can only celebrate greatness by telling each other stories. And here is one story of how storytelling came about. In Greek mythology, we learn from Plato's dialogue *Protagoras* that there are two Titans, who are brothers, Epimetheus and the better-known Prometheus. The Gods instructed Epimetheus to assign qualities to all animals. Thus, he made gazelles swifter than lions, but lions much stronger. But he also gave humans the finer qualities. He made us eusocial—totally dependent on each other, and in our dependency, able to love, care and empathise with others (Amis, 2009). But Epimetheus was also forgetful, and by the time he got around to us, he had run out of other qualities to assign including what is the most important of all for survival, ingenuity. It was left to his brother Prometheus to give us writing and memory and later to steal fire from the gods, which allowed us to fashion weapons and go to war.

We still remember Prometheus for giving us one gift that is priceless, the gift of fire. Once we mastered the use of fire, we were able to cook meat, and this really did make a vital difference. It broke down food into easily absorbed sugars and provided the nutrients and the energy required for further brain growth. Cooked food gave us a larger brain size. Our brain cells may be no larger than those of chimps, but we have far more of them. Fortunately, we no longer had to spend hours every day munching away. We could specialise in root-gathering and tool-making, child-rearing, and of course hunting. Above all, cooking gave us a focus. Fire provided not only warmth and protection but also a focus for social life. And as larger social groups emerged, it became dangerous for others to stay outside the group. Loners were fire-less, shelter-less, and homeless and would not have survived for long. Sociality really did become a survival tool. Prometheus' gift changed everything. Sitting around a campfire and sharing a meal, we began telling each other stories and forging social bonds and thinking about the future. Fire quite literally gave us 'food for thought'.

We are still essentially, a storytelling animal. We live our lives according to a narrative structure including the long period of childhood that our species experiences. This is a period when children listen to stories and play games which require imaginative play. The complexity of the world that a child is introduced to is challenging. One of the ways to make sense of that complexity is to internalise it as a story. Stories, in other words, are a default mode through which we organise our observations of reality. We have been trying to understand the world through storytelling since we first sat by the campfire and told tales. Who are the campfire elders today, asks Mia Levitin? The TED talkers and the Moth-yarn spinners, the Pixar story-boards and Netflix producers, and the YouTube and podcast personalities of the day (Levitin, 2019: 24).

Storytelling began with our hunter-gatherer ancestors. In the night-time conversations of one of the few now left in the world, the Ju/'hoansi (!Kung) who are to be found in southern Africa, about 40% of the time is taken up with telling tales of heroic acts by the ancestors (Wilson, 2019: 124). At some point, however, our ancestors made a quantum leap; they began to re-enact some of the stories they spun. The first musical instruments we've discovered date back 42,000 years to a group of people living in the Swabian Jura in Germany. They accompany the first carvings we have of imaginary creatures and human beings. Some archaeologists believe that they are the first example of theatre; members of a group would have brought these representations to life. In the darkness of the cave, the carvings of creatures would have been illuminated by fire. The audience would have been transported as a result to another time and dimension. Theatre is important even in its crudest form because it promotes the skills of imitation and gives full range to the expression of emotional thought (Flannery, 2018a: 186).

Fast-forward to the ancient Greeks, who were the first people to write plays and create the theatre in the form we know it today. One of the plays was *The Sack of Miletus* (511 BCE), a drama which depicted the recent Persian occupation of the Greek city. It proved so emotive, we are told by the historian Herodotus that the audience burst into tears. The author Phrynichus was fined 1,000 drachmas for reminding them of a disaster that was too close in time and memory. It is an excellent example of how the reality of war is often illuminated through the prism of literature.

The ancients, we are told by historians, were not given much to introspection, but there is an extraordinary veracity in war that strips many a man of his conventional covering and brings him face to face with himself. The theatre too, was intended to challenge the audience to come to terms with the world and in so doing to enlarge the field of its thoughts. What the great tragedies like Sophocles' *Ajax* or Euripides *Trojan Women* investigated was the impact of war on the city and its citizens. Plays allowed the playwright a unique opportunity to voice public concerns about how war had possibly coarsened the political discourse or led the state to countenance immoral deeds out of 'necessity'. They showed how war can lock you in a cycle of revenge but how revenge can often be deeply moral when it is born of the desire to keep faith with the dead, taking up their cause where they left off.

Phrynichus himself paid his fine and moved on with his life, and apparently never looked back. We know that he later went on to produce *The Phoenician Women* (476 BCE), a play which this time celebrated an event that the audience found much less distressing, the defeat of the Persians at the battle of Salamis (480 BCE) some years earlier. He is an important figure in Greek tragedy even if none of his plays have survived. He is credited with introducing a separate actor as distinct from the leader of the chorus, thus laying the foundation for theatrical dialogue. Some also credit him with introducing female characters into the play, though they were played on stage by men, many of whom would have been war veterans. In his book *Tragedy, the Greeks and Us*, the New York philosopher Simon Critchley makes much of this point. The actors in ancient Greece were 'not flimsy thespians who had majored in performance studies with an abstract interest in social engagement, but soldiers who had seen combat' (Critchley, 2019). Many in the audience would have done so too.

Now storytelling is one thing, reading quite another. Long before the Greeks invented tragedy, we had begun to transform some of the stories we told into literature. And for that we needed writing which changed the way we thought about thinking and did far more: it changed the way that we began to think. We are what we read, writes Maryanne Wolf: 'the secret at the heart of reading is the time it frees for the brain to have thoughts deeper and deeper than those which came before' (Wolf, 2008: 202). Reading, she explains is not an instinctive skill—it's not genetic in the way speech is. It requires us to translate the symbolic characters we see on the page into a language we understand. And the technology we have employed to practice the craft, from the papyrus roll to the printed book, has in turn, reshaped the neural circuits inside the brain. Reading really did change us. It allowed us to divorce a statement from its author and take it out of context and reflect upon it later. It permitted a quite different kind of scrutiny of the truth.

The first written text that we know of, *The Story of Gilgamesh*, is a poem about war and a great warrior called Enkidu. Written on clay tablets and discovered only in the nineteenth century, the final version of the poem dates to around 1,200 BCE. The invention of printing thousands of years later allowed these stories to be circulated among an ever-larger number of readers. Eventually, a new literary form, the novel, allowed us to connect with fictional characters more intensely than ever before. For the first time, it was possible to inhabit another person's life. Generations of readers have found other heroes to inspire them: Henry Fleming (*The Red Badge of Courage*); Robert Jordan (*For Whom the Bell Tolls*); Jack Aubrey in Patrick O'Brien's series of novels set in the Napoleonic wars. They don't have to be classics or set texts; most war books don't last the course. But whether a work of fiction is good or bad, we are what we read. For in fiction, people who we would never encounter in real life are often revealed to have inner lives not entirely different from our own. The poet T S Eliot tells us that we read novels because in real life we meet so many true friends. But there is a downside to this, of course. We embrace certain fictional characters to whom, being figments of our imagination, we are entirely invisible ourselves; we may well love them, but they can't return our love. It is a particularly cruel form of unrequited passion.

When photography arrived, we found ourselves locked into the lives of other people even more effectively, although sometimes, if we were not looking thoughtfully enough, we could be locked out. The camera created a world in which both the living and dead co-exist and can often communicate. The cinema was arguably an even more powerful medium. Hollywood's latest iteration of the warrior, its Marvel Comics superheroes, are merely a throwback to Enkidu and his friend Gilgamesh. Computer games are the most recent way in which we communicate with each other. Through games such as the *World of Warcraft*, we can be interactive members of the same team. Game players recognise each other best perhaps through the games they play.

There is a perfectly good scientific explanation for how story-telling works. Whenever we are told a story, chemicals like cortisol, dopamine and oxytocin are released in the brain. Cortisol assists with memory formulation and embeds the story in our minds more deeply. Dopamine helps regulate our emotional responses and keeps us engaged; it explains, for example, why we want to know the identity of the murderer in a 'whodunnit' and why in television serials we hate cliff-hangers. And oxytocin is associated with empathy. We empathise with our heroes; often we not only identify with them, but even wish to become them. Even the most hardened sceptic, after reading a book or watching a movie, may be haunted every so often by his own exclusion from the story.

The neuroscience of storytelling is intriguing for another reason. It tells us that biology is not all-determining and that the old idea that the more cultured we became the more we could put biology behind us is simply not true. Cultural artefacts such as the novel encourage us to empathise with others, thanks to brain chemistry. The novel allows us to inhabit another life. The same is true of TV soaps today. What literature does is expand our emotional range by enabling aspects of biology that otherwise would have remained dormant. Video games too, release chemicals such as dopamine and oxytocin which bind us to a fictional world, and in some cases can lead to an addiction to the game being played. For many players, the fictional world is more real than the 'real' one they inhabit day-to-day. All of these are examples of the different ways that culture brings out biological instincts which might otherwise remain dormant.

The Myths We Live By

Why do we create fictional heroes? The answer is that they connect us to a mythical past and myths are important for the power they give us to create archetypal figures. We read in the *Odyssey* that the gods wove adversities for men so that future generations would have something to sing about. Over time, the 'truth' of the tales has been rendered more powerful, not more precise, and more moral than empirical. For myths don't find their most powerful expression in literal belief; they exert their greatest power by providing us with archetypes or role models.

Homer told a story about one of the greatest of them, Achilles. His story is not the only one; many others have been lost but nobody has told a more compelling one or got us to recognise why it still matters that his story is still worth telling. Surprisingly, even though ignited two and a half thousand years ago, the allure of Achilles has not yet flared out. 'We came to Fort Lewis afraid to admit we're not Achilles, that we're not brave, that we're not heroes' (O'Brien, 2003: 45). So remarks one of the characters in a story by Tim O'Brien while chatting to a friend as they both sit cleaning their M 14 rifles and talking poetry and going back, as so many aspiring warriors in the West have, to the archetypal Western hero. Even today, some soldiers cannot read the *Iliad* without finding phantom traces of their own life. Homer's epic continues to be translated; there have been at least eleven translations in English in this century alone. In 2009, Robert Fagles was invited to West Point to read out some passages from his recent translation of the poem to the cadets. Some of them found themselves deployed in Afghanistan the following year and took part in a campaign called *Operation Achilles*.

Let me be the first to admit, however, that war as depicted in the *Iliad*, is not like a real war. It is more reminiscent of basketball, a game that depends on an outstanding individual, someone whose outsize talent can carry the weaker players. And in the poem, the outsize player is Achilles. But then Achilles is an archetype—a rendering of the perfect warrior. Does it really matter that we know he never existed? Not really. In his book *Fictional Worlds* Thomas Pavel argues that there is no fixed boundary between the real and the fictional. Fictional characters can possess a reality of their own. They may not inhabit our world, but they still have a place in it even if it is not easy to define. On the conscious level, we know perfectly well that Achilles never lived, and the Trojan War, as related by Homer at least, never took place. But on the unconscious level, our fictional heroes can impact on our psyche nonetheless (Pavel, 1986). Remember that we too live largely fictional lives. Our friends are a captive audience before whom we enact an idealised version of our life. They are willing to take us at our own estimation of ourselves—that is why they are our friends. So, why should we not want to be someone else, or to become someone we are not? Video-game players find it is easy enough to step out of the virtual world and back into the analogue one.

Achilles is a challenging role model, all the same. He is an unusual hero, for he is a person for whom others don't exist. Like many narcissists he is always in danger of drowning in his own reflection. He also suffers from an emotional intemperance that often wreaks havoc on those around him. He is the hero many warriors would most like to be but also fear they might become. Which prompts me to ask: is the magic beginning to fade? Ours is an age, after all, that prefers to debunk the glamour and extol the quotidian. And it's difficult when reading the *Iliad* to warm to all the killing. Alice Oswald's recent rendition, *Memorial* (2011), is striking precisely because she relates the poem's 'bright unbearable reality'—its litany of the war dead most of whom are little more than names but who live and die unforgotten. Perhaps that is why, at the US Naval War Academy in Annapolis, students who study the *Iliad* as part of their assigned reading profess that they would rather be Hector, albeit 'a Hector who *wins*' (French, 2003: 158).

Because Achilles is such a difficult hero these days to embrace, we have difficulty understanding the message of the *Iliad*. A case in point is Wolfgang Petersen's movie *Troy* which is meant to be based on Homer's tale. One critic confidently announced in *Slate* that the movie stays true to Homer's grim message: 'for all the heroics of these legendary warriors the Trojan War was a grotesque and needless waste of lives' (Mendelsohn, 2004: 48).

Reviewing the movie in *The New Yorker*, David Denby told his readers that in the end the Greeks didn't win anything worth winning. The bitterness of loss is all that remains, a bitterness we're told that is the underlying theme of Homer's tale, except again, that it really isn't (Ibid). Don't we still remember Achilles because his life is worth remembering? For fame is what he fights for and wins in exchange for a brief life, the easily forgotten down-payment on success.

Surprisingly, however, these misreadings do not appear to have downsized the brand. Perhaps that is because our archetypal heroes are constantly reinvented to suit the times. That is the compelling nature of myth. In fact, we have been strip-mining the *Iliad* from the beginning, and with every new translation of the poem, the story is brought into even sharper focus. The English poet W H Auden, in a lecture on Shakespeare's play *The Tempest*, which he delivered at the New School for Social Research in New York in May 1947, suggested that when literature becomes mythical—when its heroes take on a life of their own—words are not that important. Even the means of communication don't matter very much, whether our fictional heroes live through the medium of a novel or an epic poem or even a comic strip. Every era is always inventing new stories for its mythical heroes or projecting them into new circumstances where they take on a life of their own (Auden, 2002: 296–7). And even if figures like Achilles are super-heroes, unlike our Marvel comic heroes today, they are intensely human. A flawless Achilles would be a much impoverished and shrunken figure. What links the modern world with the pre-modern past, what explains why the young Anthony Swofford took the *Iliad* to the Gulf in 1990 as he prepared for war, and why the young ex-Dartmouth graduate Nate Fick was influenced by the classics to join up and fight the next Iraqi war, is the fact that our mythical heroes are intensely human, which is why we keep a place for them still in our hearts.

Swofford wrote a book about his experiences, *Jarhead*, which was later turned into a film; Fick recounted his wartime experience in a memoir, *One Bullet Away* (Swofford, 2003; Fick, 2005).

If they read at all, most soldiers tend to read popular fiction which is often underwritten and overworked, and its characters sketchily drawn. In most war fiction, the characters tend to be disappointingly two-dimensional, they are there mostly to serve the needs of the story, and it's the story that counts most. These are works that, unlike Tolstoy's, won't survive long because they are too time-locked in the moment in which they were written. But beyond the Western world poetry is still important. The Oxford scholar Elisabeth Kendall has found that even today in the desert tribes of East Yemen, poetry is very much alive among the young men who are called upon to recite poems at formal gatherings, the young men who radical Islamists aspire to recruit for their *Jihad* against the West. The leaders turn to poetry because their radical visions of the future cannot be put in plain terms. Visions of a future Caliphate are enhanced by the beauty of Arabic, its distinctive rhythms and patterns. And the fact that Arabic is common to all Arabs alongside the colloquial languages most actually speak has sustained a notion of Arab unity that inspires hope for many, including those who dream of one day re-establishing the Caliphate. And when they are not reading and composing poetry in areas like Yemen where the oral tradition is still strong and where locals have limited access to the internet, they read the Quran which has the great advantage of being considered by Muslims to be the literal word of God (Petter, 2017) The same is still true of the Old Testament for many Israelis. During the Second Intifada, many Israeli women found comfort in singing psalms (Sloan-Wilson, 2008: 133). War and poetry have always been inextricably interlinked.

Even so, in the Western world poetry may have had its day as a cultural mechanism. In the West, the punishment we inflict on our warriors seems to be twofold. We tend to strip war of its poetry and subject the warrior to scrutiny without the protection that poetry provides. Isn't it the power of Homer's poetry that allows Achilles to live with his contradictions so completely?

The Historian's Craft

'Churchill was the price the British people paid for reading history' (Taylor, 1969: 489).

It is said that a myth is a story about the way things never were but always are. History is about how they were—once and of course might be again. And like epic poetry, history began with a discussion of war, and historical narratives, thanks to a kind of cybernetic loop, have continued to fuel it ever since. Indeed, the very first work we have from the ancient world is by Herodotus, who set out to tell a story—a story about a historic struggle between two peoples, the Persians and the Greeks. 'Daddy, what did YOU do in the great War?' is one of the best-known British recruitment posters from the First World War. And it is remembered for its distinctive tone of emotional blackmail; it played quite successfully on the guilt of not volunteering for military service. It showed a clearly embarrassed father, cruelly interrogated by his young children, one of whom is playing with the kind of lead soldiers that H G Wells had encouraged children to play with in order to get war out of their system while they were still young. The counterpart in the ancient world can be found in one of the quotes from Athenaeus' *Parodies of Xenophanes*. 'As you lie stretched on a soft couch by the fire in the winter season... where were you when the Persians came?' (Millett, 2013). The Greco–Persian Wars were in fact the central theme of the very first work of history in the Western world, and what is so striking today is their contemporary appeal.

A striking example is Zack Snyder's movie, *300*. The movie came out in 2006 and generated US$500 million in box office receipts, which made it one of the top hundred money earners of all time. It was based, as they say in the industry, on a 'true story'—the desperate but defiant resolve of 298 Spartans (anorak moment: two were actually absent from the battle) to stand firm at Thermopylae against an invading Persian army which so outnumbered them that they knew that they wouldn't be returning from the battlefield alive. At Thermopylae, the Spartans found themselves in the crosshairs of history. Theirs was of course a warrior society. What was expected of every Spartan male was a willingness to die for the community. And Spartan women really did demand of their husbands and sons that they return home, either on their shields (borne aloft as heroes), or with them (so that they might fight another day). Feminists might dismiss them as members of a subaltern class who were suborned by a patriarchal code, but the fact that men knew that their deeds would be celebrated by their wives and kept alive in a textual afterlife in the memory of their sons allowed them to die in one register in the comforting knowledge that they would continue to live on in another.

The film *300* was popular at the time for a reason: it seemed to suggest that the 'ancient' conflict between East and West had been played out again on 9/11 when terrorists from the Middle East attacked Washington and New York. But the movie also sparked another example of the timeless battle between the historical past and those who claim the right to tell it. Some objected that the Spartan line-up at Thermopylae looked like a Gay Pride outing: the Greek government even brought a case against the film to UNESCO. The Iranian government was furious as well at the depiction of Xerxes, the Persian king, as a cross-dressing freak of nature, a rendering which ignored Aeschylus' depiction of the King in his play *The Persians* as a great if flawed man (a true tragic hero). It was in fact quite a remarkable portrayal, when you come to think of it, given the fact that the play was written much nearer to the battle of Salamis, which the play celebrated, than we are today to the events of 9/11. Even so, the American historian Victor Davis Hanson, the movie's historical adviser, later defended the historical veracity of the screenplay. Sure, there were corny lines, but two of the 'corniest' were lifted directly from the ancient sources. 'Come and take them', the Spartans responded when ordered by the Persians to hand over their weapons. 'Then we'll fight in the sun', they also replied when warned that the Persians would discharge so many arrows that they would blot out the light. Both are literal translations from two separate accounts by Herodotus and the later Greek historian Plutarch (Hanson, 2010). Hanson in fact, makes a good case for the movie. Where he is on more dubious ground is to insist that Thermopylae was represented by Herodotus as a 'clash of civilisations', a contest between 'western individualism' and 'eastern centralism' or 'collective serfdom'. It wasn't, though this version of events probably struck a chord with an American audience that had been told by their President that the War on Terror was 'civilisation's fight against barbarism'.

Of course, let's recognise that until very recently most historians were highly selective in their recording of events; they also had the final word. Unfortunately, few individual voices have come down to us from Cannae (216 BCE) or Hattin (1187) compared, for example, with Waterloo (1815) or Gettysburg (1863). We still know next to nothing of the experience for the rank and file before the end of the nineteenth century when in Europe reading and writing became mandatory in school. Thanks to the absence of sources, we are denied the kind of direct insights into war that soldiers themselves have been able to offer since 1914.

And historians helped to ennoble war in another way—by identifying and writing up its great battles. Stripped of its battles, isn't military history rather boring? If you take away the moments when everything seems to hang on an afternoon of fighting, then war loses much of its lustre; all you are left with are you not, is the violence and the anguished voices and the harrowing narratives of slaughter? We have preferred instead, to imprison war over the ages in moments of historical significance which may be ahistorical—victories on a battlefield don't always explain why wars are won. History would have taken on a very different shape without its forgotten guerrilla struggles against imperial rule. All of which is true enough, but it is also largely beside the point. Battles, let us admit, make for dramatic storytelling and exploit the historians' need to spin a story worth telling. Without them the narrative sails would be hard to hoist.

Discovering the 'story line' of any society (say the Greeks' 'fight for freedom') of course, requires a great deal of back projection. And everything depends on the story you wish to tell. We remember the defeat of Persia as a great victory for freedom because that's the story Herodotus chose to relate. The later Roman historian Dio Cassius, writing hundreds of years later, tells us that the Persians themselves came up with a very different version. They announced to the world that they had invaded Greece, burned down Athens and taken thousands of prisoners who were subsequently sold into slavery. In other words, they had taught the Greeks no end of a lesson. In the wider world beyond Herodotus, the victory over the Persians was also often portrayed in much cruder, prosaic and explicitly sexual terms. When Persia wasn't portrayed as a woman, it was painted as an effeminate man. On one Greek vase from the 460s, we find a Persian bending over, ready to be penetrated by a naked Greek man who approaches him, an erect penis in hand. As Kenneth Dover remarks, this expresses a simple but direct message: 'We've buggered the Persians' (Hall, 1993: 111). It is not a message that would have resonated with our Victorian forefathers.

But then again, don't let the nay-sayers claim that our ancestors were entirely gulled by historians who chose to represent war as an epic contest of historical forces, or moral values, or heroic deeds. Yes, many would argue that war is a classic case of the Emperor without his clothes, and that in the nakedness revealed there is a great deal less than meets the eye. But wouldn't that represent a cheerless desire to rob the cognitive experience of being human of any existential awe? History is epic in quality because it exaggerates the possible. The tales we spin are fascinating for a reason—they show that the impossible can be attempted. An army outnumbered in battle can win (Marathon); a people can take to an element dominated by the enemy, in this case the sea, and prevail (Salamis); a small band of men can prevail against an invading army (Plataea). These examples show the sheer scope of human possibility. They alert us to the magnificence of the human spirit in times of stress; we can exult in any triumph against the odds. And never forget that it is we who insist on giving life its epic quality. Our common instinct for reality, wrote the philosopher William James, 'has always held the world to be a theatre for heroism' (James, 2003: 281). War not only enhances the drama of history, it also contin-ues to shape the memories of those who were there, long after the fighting. 'Remembering we forget / much that was monstrous', wrote the anti-war poet Siegfried Sassoon who bore witness to the horrors of the Western Front; 'we forget our fear /...and / discern the mad magnificence whose / storm-light throws / wild shadows on these afterthoughts' ('To one who was with me in the war'). *The mad magnificence*—in these three lines Sassoon struck what, for a confirmed critic of war, must have been one of the most painfully honest notes in his life's work (*The New Statesman*, 22 May 1927, see Collected Poems, Sassoon, 1949).

Sassoon's patriotism never really flagged even when he lost faith in the war. And one of the historians' main contributions to fuelling our fascination with war has been to tap into another of our biological instincts: to be part of the tribe. The very earli-est inscription on a monument to the fallen in battle to have

survived was published only in the summer of 2010. It com-
memorates the Athenians who fell at the battle of Marathon, and
it is 2,500 years old.

ERECHTHEIS
Fame, as it reaches the furthest limits of the
.... sunlit earth
shall learn the valour of these men: how
they died
in battle with the Medes and how they
garlanded Athens
the few who undertook the war of many
Drakontides
Antiphon
Aphsephes
Xenon
Glaukiades

The survival of the Marathon casualty list is due entirely to
the historical interests of an Athenian millionaire, Herodes
Atticus, who lived in the second century CE and was a tutor to
the Emperor Marcus Aurelius. Otherwise, we know nothing
much about the billionaire although we know surprisingly a lot
about Marathon thanks in part to the monument he appropri-
ated. He had it installed in his country house in the eastern
Peloponnese. What's important about the inscription is that it's
a 'first'—the first to celebrate the sacrifice for the tribe—in this
case a Greek city-state, by perfectly ordinary men, some artisans,
others peasant farmers who died side-by-side fighting a common
foe. The Athenians were proud of their victory and the sacrifice
by men who, equal of course in the eyes of the enemy, were on
that day equal in their own eyes too. In this case the word 'few'
really does mean what it says. No one knows how many Persians
died at Marathon, but we do know how many Athenians—only
192, but they made all the difference (Thonemann, 2011: 10).

But there is catch of course. This is not the truth of war, it is the truth of the authorised version. And it has led so many young men through the ages to an early death, as W B Sebald writes of the battle of Austerlitz (1805) in a moving passage which I will quote at length.

> We try to reproduce the reality but the harder we try, the more we find the pictures that make up the stock-in-trade of the spectacle of history forcing themselves upon us: the fallen drummer boy, the infantryman shown in the act of stabbing another....the invulnerable Emperor surrounded by his generals, a moment frozen still amidst the turmoil of battle. Our concern with history...is a concern with pre-formed images already imprinted on our brains, images at which we keep staring while the truth lies elsewhere, away from it all, somewhere as yet undiscovered (Sebald 2001: 101).

As Sebald gets his hero to ask in the novel, 'might it not be that we also have to keep appointments in the past' (Ibid). Often these appointments keep us from moving forward; they prevent us from standing secure for our future. And in the course of the last century, they sent millions to their death for it was thought that only through conflict could a people honour their ancestors and repay an unrepayable debt.

A scathing attack on such thinking can be found in one of the essays that form Nietzsche's *Untimely Meditations*. Nietzsche was particularly critical of nationalist historians for wanting 'to conserve for posterity the conditions under which we were born'. In wanting the history of the nation to 'ring true', they were inclined to judge its worth by its success or failure in battle. War was the Big Bang in which the nation came in to being. Battles were thought to provide a people with its life blood, its foundational myths and semi-mythical heroes such as Serbia's Dušan and Russia's Alexander Nevsky. As a result, they tended to write off entire ages or epochs as low or high moments in a country's past. Wasn't it only thanks to the sacrifices and accomplishments of their ancestors that the nation existed at all? 'One thus recognises a debt that constantly grows greater' (Nietzsche, 1995: 67). In the immediate aftermath of Germany's defeat in 1918, Hermann Hesse complained that the state had belittled its children, crushing their spirit and keeping them in place by comparing their dull and uninspiring lives with a magnificent past that had been distinguished by the bravery and self-sacrifice of their ancestors (Hesse, 1985: 58). It was this belittling that formed the principal theme of Eric Remarque's famous First World War novel *All Quiet on the Western Front*, a classic story of youth betrayed. In urging them to join up and serve the Fatherland, their schoolmaster had also betrayed his own vocation to guide them into adult life.

Even today history continues to imprison people in its deadly embrace. For today's Russians, the Great Patriotic War (1941–5) is still central to the national myth, just as at the time it served the purpose of restoring self-respect to a country that had been traumatised by Stalin's purges. What the war did was to reawaken a sense of community; it was the first time, in Solzhenitsyn's words, that the Russian people were 'close to each other'. There is another story to be told about the war, of course. How the Gulag inmates, being the most patriotic, were sent to clear the minefields; how machine gunners opened fire on anyone who tried to desert; how the commanders in the early days of the fighting often sent soldiers into battle without guns. And then there were the unnecessarily high losses as Russian generals sent into battle millions of solders, often untrained, some without weapons with a complete disregard for human life ('They come like sacrifices in their trim / And to the fire-eyed maid of smoky war / All hot and bleeding will we offer them'. Shakespeare, *Henry IV*, IV). The memory of the war continues to hold a troubled society together and not just because the regime exploits it. It doesn't need to. The enthusiasm is real enough. As

Catherine Merridale discovered when she interviewed the surviving veterans in the 1990s for her book *Ivan's War*, they 'knew the way they liked the war to be—their favourite writers were war writers but no Soviet book on war ever mentioned panic, self-mutilation, cowardice or rape' (Smith, K., 2019: 31). These of course are air-brushed out by patriotic historians. 'What happens to great events', asks Svetlana Alexievich in her book based on interviews with the damaged veterans of the Soviet Union's last war in Afghanistan (1979–88): '...they migrate into history while the little ones that are most important for the little person disappear without a trace' (Alexievich, 2017: 18).

In the West, however, it would seem that we are now far less inclined than we were to invest our faith in political leaders who urge us to go to war. Here, too, as a 'cultural enhancer', history is perhaps beginning to lose its appeal. During a trip to the National Portrait Gallery in London, the Romanian philosopher Emil Cioran was shocked by the contrast between the virile faces of earlier generations and the bland and unheroic features to be found in contemporary life. Gone was the arrogance and passion in the eyes of Elizabethan statesman and Victorian men of commerce. Britain's empire had been built by war, by its sailors and military adventurers. It had been lost by a new generation who were less interested in power than they were in 'correct' behaviour. The English were no longer a nightmare for anyone. They had become a post-modern people. Struck by the change, he concluded his account by formulating a new principle of history: 'only at the price of great abdications does a nation become normal (Cioran, 1984: 53).

Barbarous Philosophers

'Barbarous philosopher! Come and read us your book on the field of battle' (Rousseau, 2002).

It was while serving in an army barracks in Bangalore that Winston Churchill began reading books systematically for the first time. It was only at the comparatively late age of twenty-two, or so he tells us in *My Early Life*, that the desire for learning came upon him. He had always liked history at school and decided to begin with Gibbon, before moving on to Macaulay. He already knew by heart (as did so many children of his generation) the *Lays of Ancient Rome*. He then took a leap and progressed onto philosophy, beginning with Plato's *Republic* and ending with Schopenhauer and Darwin's *Origin of Species*. For Churchill, this was a preparation for life. He learned for the first time that 'ethics' did not mean 'playing the game'; it concerned more than just knowing the things you ought to know, it also included the way you ought to know them. His greatest discovery was the 'Socratic method' which was 'apparently a way of giving your friend his head in an argument and pronging him into a pit by cunning questions'.

Does the 'Socratic method' really help you in war or is it best confined to American law schools? Do philosophy and war mix? You might be forgiven for thinking the answer is no. The Roman historian Tacitus tells his readers an amusing story about the now forgotten philosopher Musonius Rufus, who is remembered if at all for teaching Marcus Aurelius philosophy. Marcus is one of the emperors we still remember for his *Meditations*; the work of his teacher hasn't survived. But at one point in his career Rufus was afforded a rare opportunity to address the troops on the frontier. It was not a great success. He was widely ridiculed and even threatened with violence and would have been trampled on—or so the historian tells us—had he not 'listened to the warnings of the quieter soldiers and the threats of others and given up his untimely wisdom'. In Plato's *Philostratus*, we are told that another philosopher Dio was able at least to quell a mutinous army with a quotation from Homer (*Lives of the Sophists*: 488). On this occasion, poetry won out over philosophy.

To be sure, ideas, by virtue of their very abstractness, don't often appeal to soldiers. They are often considered to be too removed from reality in the field to be of much use; they can get you killed. But philosophy isn't alien to our nature; we philosophise all the time without recognising it. The 'Socratic method' is enlisted to get us to question our standard assumptions; it is useful in a law court for that reason. It is not only continuous with the everyday but also with mathematics and the natural sciences, which, like philosophy, use logical and other reasoning. And what would war be without ideas? The Chinese sage Sun Tzu, after all, asked his readers to treat war as a problem of intelligence. He tells us that war is a necessary evil, so wage it only when you must, and do so quickly because the longer you fight the more likely you will be destroyed by it. It is evil, not in any moral sense, but because it disturbs the Dao, the harmony of the universe. It's necessary because of the wilfulness of human beings. Necessity is the one force that can make people risk their lives and justify their deaths in battle. And if you subscribe to a philosophy of limits you are unlikely to be undone by pushing your luck too far, like Napoleon in 1812. And you don't need a Chinese sage to tell you this. In Napoleon, the philosopher Kierkegaard saw a man who had succumbed to vertigo. 'Frenchman on their march across the Russian steppes where the eye seeks in vain for a point at which it can rest... trickle like dry sand through the fingers'. For him the march was a metaphor for the perils of limitless ambition (Fenves, 1993: 35). Condemned in his last years to exile on St Helena, Napoleon found it impossible to deal with a world that he was not in the daily business of shaping.

The *Art of War* is still popular because it's deceptively short. My students tend to gravitate towards it for that reason. But the marketplace of ideas is continuing to change. We live in an age of pop intellectualism and big buzzy ideas condensed into short books or tailor-made TED talks. Cadets in military colleges no longer get their ideas just from the military classics, but also from contemporary blogs, think-tank papers by today's leading strategic thinkers and, yes, occasionally even from TED talks. All these are cultural enhancers for a new age.

And 2,000 years later we are still asking some of the questions Plato asked, such as what is 'knowledge' and what is 'justice'. And we are still coming up with the same answers to the same questions. For example, most philosophers have argued from the first that there is something else that shapes the way we think—power, passion, and desire—and that these have to be in place for us to think at all. The human desire for power, which has taken us to the top of the food chain is not the result only of our intelligence but of our primate evolution stimulated by storytelling (and sometimes narrative overload). We appear to have a wired-in need and ability to construct models for describing our world. But we must always be wary of taking them too much to heart. Theory and practice can often come apart; at critical times in war, they often tend to.

By the time the international system we recognise today took shape, another 'cultural enhancer' had taken centre stage. It was called theory. Some ideas are under-theorised, and a few don't demand a theory, but theories tend to add a spurious scientific credibility to the reasons people want to go to war. And towards the end of the eighteenth century in Europe, theory was woven into the texture of war in a way that philosophy never had been by becoming an object of study in military academies. This was much to the annoyance of many military historians who tend to regard theories as lifeboats—welcome as a ship is sinking but liable to sink themselves if they take on every exception to the rule. Historians tend to focus on the anomalies in life, its unintended consequences and inconvenient complications. No historian worth her salt would be foolhardy enough to cram these into a single formula. However, social scientists often do.

The principal theorist of war in the Western world remains a Prussian army officer, Carl von Clausewitz. His book *On War*—though dense and at times unreadable—is still on the syllabus of military academies. And it is there for a reason. For Clausewitz set out to translate experience into theory, and close observation into practical advice for practical men. His book aimed to translate what we call 'tacit knowledge' (what we know from observation and sometimes have known for some time) into 'explicit knowledge' (what we have later found from science to be true). It was also the first major work on war to engage in second-order reflection; it was especially concerned with the nature and status of theory itself (Von Clausewitz, 2007).

When reading any work, one must ask, should we be interested in a writer's life as well? I rather like Czeslaw Milosz' observation that 'biographies are like shells; they don't tell you much about the mollusc that lives in them'. Finding the right balance between an author's life and work is often a challenge. The temptation to tilt in favour of the work is strong because many authors worth writing about have not led particularly interesting lives. This is certainly true of Clausewitz even though, first and foremost he was a soldier. Unfortunately for him, if fortunately for us, he missed out on most of the major battles of the Napoleonic wars such as Jena (1806) and Leipzig (1813), the famous 'Battle of the Nations'. After the war, he was side-lined and banished to be Director of the Prussian Military Academy, where he was not even allowed to share his views with the cadets. His military career proved so unrewarding that towards the end of his life he had no option but to write his way out of it.

Inevitably, however, his life as a soldier fed into his writing. And what he had witnessed was how Napoleonic France had been defeated by the forces of nationalism. The future he intuited belonged to the nation-state. This is not to say that patriotism and nationalism are not very different, and the territorial imperative needs no theorising—the defence of one's homeland has always been a dynamic of life. In 1917, the poet Edward Thomas was asked why he had enlisted. Scooping up a handful of English soil he replied, 'literally for this'. In his book *Where Poppies Blow*, John Lewis-Stempel contrasts this love of the English countryside in his countrymen's imagination—a land of rain and wind, oak and beech, rolling hills and perpendicular churches, a rural idyll, a pastoral imagined community with the Germans' preoccupation with dark gloomy forests. What does this call to mind if not *The Lord of the Rings?* Tolkien fought at the Somme (1916) and was traumatised by the experience. In his epic tale, he contrasts the peaceful Shires, the land of the lovable Hobbits, with the industrial wasteland that harbours the Orcs. No prizes for guessing who the English are.

But then the English imagination was largely visual, not ideational. It traded in images not ideas. And it was as an idea that nationalism was particularly dangerous. In the world of action, wrote Ernest Barker on the eve of the Second World War, 'apprehended ideas are alone elemental and the nation must be an idea as well as a fact for it to become a dynamic force' (Barker, 1969: 42). And one of the defining themes of the nationalist debate was that the modern nation had to be equal to the metaphysics of its own being. In the early 1930s, the young Cioran looked forward to the day when his own country would escape its 'sub-historic destiny' and transcend its condition as a 'second-hand country'. 'Our entire political and spiritual mission must concentrate on the determination to will a transfiguration in the desperate dramatic experience of transforming our whole way of life' (Cioran, 1995: xvii-xxv). Not only did a nation have to have the trappings of nationhood, such as a distinctive language and an ethnic group to which its speakers belonged, it also had to have a grand stage to awaken its people to their destiny, and what could be grander than war? Nationalism as an idea was especially dangerous when a society found itself transitioning into a nation-state. For it was the transition that bred resentment for past humiliations, whether imagined or real, and which ignited passions that were difficult to control. The danger inhered in the yearning for a nation which was still incomplete. 'We have made Italy but not Italians', Mussolini declared famously. In that declaration, he gave voice to the nation-building imperatives of war. His desire to complete the project was at the heart of Italian fascism. The drive for war in these years was not a political phenomenon so much as an existential need.

Nationalism became more dangerous still when it was conjoined at the end of the nineteenth century with another dangerous idea, social Darwinism. War became more of an existential experience than perhaps ever before because it was judged by some writers to be the ultimate expression of a community's vitality in the great struggle for existence. People came to believe that evolutionary genetics showed that we were fundamentally asocial animals though we are not: we have evolved to be eusocial. The problem with metaphors such as 'the survival of the fittest', one of the most pernicious, is that they took on a life of their own outside the claims of Darwinism itself. The metaphors often worked against the grain of what Darwin himself had tried to explain, namely that cooperation, not conflict is the determining factor in human existence.

What the social Darwinists simply ignored was the theory of mutualism or symbiosis. In his second book, *The Descent of Man*, Darwin had gone to great lengths to point out the general difference between qualities which could allow a social group (such as a nation) to survive over many centuries, and those that might keep a single individual afloat for his lifetime. The struggle for existence for groups could be better described, not so much as a battle for survival, as a struggle for mutual dependence. We have discovered since then that simple organisms, for example, can live together in a state of mutual dependence; take the example of bacteria in our guts from which we benefit just as much as do they (Midgley, 2002: 140). Another example is the eukaryotic cell—one with a true nucleus—which came about by the co-operation of two or more prokaryotes—cells without nuclei. Co-operation is the great source of innovation in evolution (Goodwin, 1994: 166–8). And history, too, shows that when things get complicated, co-operation usually comes to the fore because it makes all other interactions possible.

Unfortunately, despite the carnage of two world wars, nationalism still remains a potent force in much of the world today, and there will be many countries that may one day choose to go to war again in its name. Its rhetoric, writes Michael Ignatieff, continues to 'rewrite and recreate the real world, turning it into a delusional world of noble causes, tragic sacrifices and cruel necessity' (Ignatieff, 1993: 193). He was writing about the wars in the western Balkans, which followed the collapse of communism and killed nearly half a million people and displaced many more. We are still likely, he concludes, to remain prey to 'the lure of fantasy' for some time to come. Bad ideas don't always evolve into better ones; they merely keep re-appearing. And nothing is likely to supersede our yearning for community. Unfortunately, it is still the most contingent factors of our identities—class, race and nationality that still loom the largest in our collective imagination.

Ways of Seeing

One of the things that makes us human is our obsession with images. Art is a cultural mechanism, too. And to understand why this is so, think of one of the many differences between chimpanzees and ourselves (Dutton, 2009: 7). Dennis Dutton reminds us that although a chimpanzee can paint if given a canvas and a paint brush, we can only talk of the picture it then paints as 'art' because the trainer removes the paper at the right moment. Otherwise, the chimp would continue to apply paint until there is nothing left on the canvas but a perfect absolute blank—like the captain's map in *The Hunting of the Snark*. Chimps, moreover, never return to look at their achievements; they have no interest in their impact on others of their kind, nor for that matter, their impact on us. We humans, on the other hand, have an instinct for art, and that instinct can be harnessed in the service of war. An instinct is an ability that culture turns into a capability. To harness it requires not only intuitive talent, but also learned skills. The great paradox is that a great work of art can transcend the instincts that make it possible. Most artists are driven by an inner compulsion to communicate an emotional state, or merely to entertain others. For 65,000 years, we have been producing pictures, daubing them first on the walls of caves, then later, on canvas, and most recently projecting them on the big screen.

But here's the thing. We know that words can get you killed. But what about images? Can they propel a story or merely embellish it? Can an image get you killed, too? The two are very different. What makes an image antithetical to language is that it has none of the elements usually associated with good story-telling: a sense of time passing, the changing and often conflicting moods of the main characters, and, above all, a story well told. Words are persuasive for that reason. Homer moved his readers by making war subliminal, even ecstatic. The trick was in the language, its exuberance, and beauty. He rooted war in a very human world, a world of argument, contention, rivalry and emulation. Once the killing is stripped away, Homer's tale speaks to very human ambitions and rivalries. Sure, there is darkness in the story, but you will also find much nobility. We can bring this up to date if we think of the traumatised veteran of Virginia Woolf's novel, *Mrs Dalloway*, who joins up in 1914 'to save an England which consisted entirely of Shakespeare's plays'. Or consider Willa Cather's Pulitzer prize-winning novel *One of Ours* (1922). Its hero Claude Wheeler has a strongly rooted conviction that 'there was something splendid about life, if he could but find it'. He joins up when the US enters the First World War and dies fighting bravely for France, a country he knows only through books. He dies 'believing his own country better than it is and France better than any country can ever be'. As Cather adds wryly, 'he had hoped and believed too much' (Glover and Silkin, 1989: 523). Thanks to what he had read in books.

To truly grasp the emotional impact of both literature and painting as a cultural mechanism, we need to invoke Nietzsche's claim that the Greeks 'spiritualised away the cruelty' of life through the medium of epic poetry. We used to do this through the medium of art; today we do so through the medium of film. If you read history closely enough, he argued, you will realise that human cruelty is so great and so timeless that it does not lend itself to serious ethical reflection. It is pointless to ask, for example, whether war is good or bad, or for that matter whether its cruelty is pointless. Yes, life is distinguished by cruelty and pain, but that is the painful reality and there's nothing much we can do about it except perhaps to conspire with it. Relieved of having to judge the world morally, we can live life to the full. In the Bronze Age, the warrior elite had been protected 'by the hand of Homer who with artistic deception had consecrated the unspeakable ugliness of war' (Ahern, 1995: 42). Haven't we been trying to disguise the ugliness of war ever since, and isn't that one of the factors that drives it? Don't we still anaesthetise ourselves to death by employing euphemisms such as 'the Fallen'? Isn't that why, Nietzsche asked, 'almost everything we call "higher culture" is based on the spiritualisation of cruelty, on its' becoming more *profound*' (Ibid: 31). It's not a position, let me add, that is beyond criticism, besides which the profound is not necessarily the valid.

So how exactly did the artists of their day 'spiritualise away' the cruelty? Let's take one of the earliest examples of representative art in Europe at the height of its achievement (fourteenth to nineteenth century). Picture a battle between two city states, Florence and Siena. Picture the Battle of San Romano, though it wasn't really a battle—it was more of a skirmish that took place just north of Florence in 1432. Had it not been for the rendering of the scene by Uccello it would have been long forgotten. The painting has kept it alive. It shows two evenly matched forces in the field dominated by the Florentine leader Niccolò da Tolentino seated upon an oversized horse and wearing not a helmet but an enormous hat, a fetching turban. Uccello's picture is at once complex and audaciously simple in its composition. In the background we see archers reloading their crossbows and men waiting to engage each other to the death, but all the action has been squeezed into the foreground. Both the commander and his horse have a disproportionately large presence. The battlefield that Uccello painted is really nothing more than a vivid stage set on which war is depicted as a form of pageant. And where is the blood? The mangled bodies? The dead horses? And the sheer chaos of conflict? They are nowhere to be seen. Uccello, wrote Wyndham Lewis, 'formularized the spears and aggressive prancing of the fighting men of his time until every drop of reality was frozen out of them' (Glover and Silkin, 1989: 121).

One explanation for this was technique: Uccello's obsession with linear perspective, a new discovery that one writer calls 'the cognitive style' of an entire era, its 'period eye' (Baxandall, 1972). It created the mathematical illusion of space. Everything had to be symmetrical, which war rarely is. The masters of Renaissance perspective showed vast battlefields and armies on the march. Think of the massed ranks of soldiers marching into battle in Albrecht Altdorfer's *Battle of Alexander at Issus* (1529).

War was transmuted by a kind of alchemy into theatre and spectacle which in turn gave it a kind of fullness of life even though the viewer lived that life at one remove. Artists made their subjects figures of classical tragedy and gave war a mythic dimension it has subsequently lost. To be frank, most of the paintings depicting war simply lack the psychological depth that went into the great religious pictures of the day; they don't invite us to focus on the emotion of the scene, unlike the close-ups of the suffering Christ or the grieving Madonna. But the fact that they are not psychologically complex doesn't detract from what they were intended to achieve: to impress us with the splendour of the scene. Often a thin line anyway separates the aesthetic from the monstrous.

Uccello's painting was also driven by the narrative he was paid to illustrate. Remember who was doing the commissioning, and more importantly why—an Italian mercenary like Uccello's patron, or a hereditary monarch or later an anonymous state bureaucracy? Before the twentieth century, paintings of historical events took their character from those who commissioned them, and some of the most powerful pictures were commissioned by brutal and clever men, by *condottiere* like Nicolo da Tolentino himself who was as hungry for intellectual and cultural fame as he had been in his prime for military power. In a world 'un-patrolled by God' writes Jonathan Hale, war was governed no longer by Providence or fate but human ambition (Hale, 1985: 32). Greatness was measured by success on the battlefield. Fast-forward two hundred years to a painting by a relatively unknown artist, Jan van den Hoecke's *The Cardinal Infante Ferdinand at the Battle of Nordlingen*. Both the Cardinal and King Ferdinand II of Hungary take up more than half of the painting. It was painted to glorify war and especially the person who mattered most—the ruler whose honour had to be projected and promoted at all costs if he was not to fade into the dark and out of history.

Of course, times change and so too do the requirements of propaganda. And, as propaganda, art told a story that the modern state found useful, too. For art can also move us and awe us, by stimulating revolutionary or patriotic sentiments, or both at the same time. A particularly vivid example is the picture of *Napoleon Crossing the Bridge of Arcola* (1826) by Horace Vernet; another is *The Charge of the French Fourth Hussars at the Battle of Friedland* (1891) by Edouard Detaille. As propagandists, artists spun a heavily redacted tale. They wanted to show the French revolutionary armies animated by revolutionary ideas. In his novella 'Billy Budd', Herman Melville wrote of 'those wars which like a flight of harpies rose shrieking from the din and dust of the fallen Bastille'. Often, the reality was disappointingly different. Antoine-Jean Gros' depiction of *Napoleon at Arcola* (1797) shows the young general, flag in hand, storming the narrow bridge under a hail of Austrian bullets. But historians now tell us that the bridge was in fact taken from the rear because the men under his immediate command refused to cross it, and in trying to rally them Napoleon was rudely thrust into a ditch and nearly drowned.

Most artists of course, never saw a battlefield, and therefore never painted from first-hand experience. Most were followers, not leaders, and their work remained safely devoid of anger or rage, or even basic sympathy for the victims of war. They rarely chose to speak out on behalf of those who have remained voiceless down the ages: peasants conscripted against their will, refugees fleeing their homes, women and children dispossessed of a future by the loss of husbands and fathers. Their voices were suppressed; they were not licensed to speak. Even when every so often artists did show the horror of war, they did so with the same fatalism with which they showed the plight of the poor. A notable example is a series of etchings by Jacques Callot, *The Miseries of War* (1633), which laid bare the punishments meted out to the common soldier for desertion, and their inevitable post-war fate, as they were forced to eke out an existence in hospitals or the home or were reduced to begging by the roadside. But peasants didn't study art, and the educated classes who did were probably horrified to see that in wartime the marginalised often seized the moment to exercise the only freedom they knew: the freedom to kill their masters. In war, there are often moments of chaos when the people subjugated by circumstances, both political and social, can reassert control. In one of Callot's pictures we see three peasants, two armed with a pitchfork, the third with a club bursting from their hiding place and beating to death a bearded soldier.

Goya took this further in his series of etchings, *The Disasters of War* (1809–20). There cannot be any mistaking the message here. Nothing is held back including harrowing scenes of famine and torture. And there is a radical departure—the introduction of women and children into the picture. We see a group of women executed by a firing squad, another fleeing from the enemy. We also see several graphic scenes of rape, and this really is a first in the history of war—scenes of women fighting back. What is more radical still is that Goya shows that evil is everywhere—it is just as much in the hearts of the defenders as it is the aggressors.

Even so, it is notable that the artist never exhibited these paintings in his lifetime. It was only in the First World War that the rank and file appeared on the page or on canvas, allowing them in the process to finally step forward into the light of history. And for the first time, artists painted scenes that should have discouraged anyone who had thought of joining the colours. For what some of them chose to show was another 'first' in war—the aftermath for the survivors. The word 'aftermath' was originally an agricultural term to describe a new growth after the harvest. What Europe 'harvested' in the First World War was 20 million injured soldiers, twice the number of those who never made it back. Think of the mutilated men in Otto Dix's painting *The Card Players*, who are trapped in bodies beyond repair, or Heinrich Hoerle's even more striking and hideous *Cripple Portfolio Plate 8: Friendly Dream* which shows a quadruple amputee staring in horror at a vision of hands and feet in plant pots, all waving cheerily at him, and by association at us. Contemporary critics lauded these painters for what the Germans call *Schonungslosigkeit*—an unsparingness that made emotional closure impossible for a spectator with an ounce of imagination.

Yet it was precisely at this moment that the great artists abandoned representation for abstraction. And when painting turned its back on the representational, it was in effect freeing itself from the dangerous real world where moral judgements are made (Burgess, 2018: 243). In his lectures on *The Philosophy of Fine Art*, Hegel had already anticipated this. Art, he argued, had once been the highest form of social experience. By the time he was writing, this had ceased to be the case. We must not misunderstand what he was actually claiming. He was not claiming that great works would not be produced in the future. Nor was he predicting that artists yet to be born would have nothing to say. Indeed, he believed that art would continue to be perfected as a medium. But he insisted that it would no longer be the place where people looked for the highest values. Art would become entertainment. Indeed, he already thought it had (Danto, 1986: 114).

In fact, the last major painting about war to have had a major impact on our collective consciousness was exhibited in 1937. In *Guernica*, Pablo Picasso set out to show the deliberate bombing of a town in the Spanish Civil War, an operation that was intended by Goering as a birthday gift for Hitler's forty-eighth birthday. He showed an atrocity, but the bombing was meant to be an atrocity from the beginning. It was not an unintended consequence of war. The victims were not 'collateral damage';

they were the intended target. Even today, the painting has the power to evoke the horrors of war, provided, of course, you know what you're looking at. As the bombs plummet, one woman flings her arms up in a despairing attempt to stop them; a mother, cradling a dead child in her lap lifts her head and parts her mouth to scream. But any of these scenes, from the gutted animals to the screaming mothers might have been representative of other events from the hideously recognisable twentieth century, a century that for many people was all about dodging a bomb or a bullet. Picasso's picture might also have been an equally haunting depiction of the death camps or the century's man-made famines. The painting might not be about war at all, though it captured a universal truth about every war in its use of fragments and broken images. In later years, however, it required a knowledge of art history to know what the picture meant.

> It stood as a handsome backdrop for pick-ups at the Museum of Modern Art, or a place to meet a date, like the clock at the Baltimore Hotel. And it was sufficiently handsome in its grey and black harmonies to have ornamented the kitchen cupboard in a sophisticated apartment I once saw, where soufflés were concocted for bright and brittle guests who no more than the hostess realised what the gutted animals and screaming mothers were agonising above the Formica (Danto, 1986: 3).

Harsh words indeed, by the American philosopher Arthur Danto.

It didn't matter. For long before the death of representational art, painting had been superseded by photography. How we see the world is like everything else historically situated; it relies a lot on the medium through which we understand the 'real world'. Photography reshaped our understanding of war; one might even say that it had been waiting to be photographed from the beginning. 'I have seized the fleeting light and imprisoned it' was the boast of Louis-Jacques-Mandé Daguerre in 1839 after successfully producing the first daguerreotype. And light is what it's all about—freezing a moment in time. As Susan Sontag wrote, 'no-one would dispute that photography gave a tremendous boost to the cognitive claims of sight, because—through close-up and remote sensing—it so greatly enlarged the realm of the visible' (Sontag, 2003: 115). It did so in the case of war by bringing its subject into the light; it cast light on a practice which was almost as old as history itself; above all, it brought to light some of its horrors for the first time.

None of the greatest of war photographers have ever tried to glorify the battlefield; even if they had wanted to do so, the medium made this difficult, if not impossible. For the power of photography, writes John Berger, depends largely on our imagination. 'What it shows invokes what is *not* shown' (Berger, 2013: 20). What is not seen is partly constitutive of the overall picture. It invites you to imagine even greater horrors which may have been witnessed but have gone unrecorded. In doing so, photography leveraged us into new territory. Moreover, unlike a painting which shows us that something like that can happen, a photograph shows that it did. And photographers were to be found in the front line themselves, often running the same risks as the soldiers. 'If your pictures aren't good enough, you're not close enough', remarked Robert Capa whose photos of the Spanish Civil war made him famous. The lightweight Leica camera allowed the cameraman to be on the front line for the first time. It was dangerous work: 135 photojournalists lost their lives covering the Vietnam War. One of the most famous, Don McCullin, survived a mortar explosion, but he still managed to take an iconic photograph of a man dying next to him whose luck, unlike his own, had just run out. Capa was not so lucky. He was eventually killed when stepping on a mine in 1954 while covering the war in French Indo-China.

Pictures of maimed and shattered bodies allowed the war photographer to weaponise art for the first time, to ambush the public visually. In highlighting the cruelty of war, photography made a mockery of the heroic stories that people had learned at school. Photographic technique helped enormously in that transformation. Suppressed horizons, birds' eye and worms' eye views, and close-ups became relatively common. Low camera angles, cluttered, out-of-focus foregrounds leading to deep, sharply focused backgrounds; subjects caught unawares, mid-gesture; the juxtaposition of two unrelated images. These and other devices created a sense of life captured at the very moment of conception. Through the alchemy of time, more than a few of the most well-known war photographs were transmuted into historical images that have fixed the events they captured in the collective imagination. You have probably seen Capa's dying Republican soldier and McCullin's traumatised Vietnam veteran whose solitude is all the more striking for being shared and most poignant of all perhaps, one of war's many non-combatants, a young girl fleeing from a napalm attack in the Vietnam War. They all appear as history's extras, minor players shoved to the front by a photographer who has given them a brief starring role. These images are more powerful because we are confronted with faces staring back at us. In staring back at them, we can't help asking what they might have told us about their experience if we had bothered to ask them, or if we had stayed long enough to listen to what they had to say.

All of which is undoubtedly true, but perhaps surprisingly, photojournalism has never at any time threatened to break war's hold on our imagination. No war in history has ever been brought to an abrupt end by an image, even on television. The Vietnam War did not come to an end because of photos of children set aflame by napalm; it was brought to an end when the politicians recognised that they faced a strategic endgame. In the days that followed the First Gulf War (1990–91), the world's television cameras broadcast the picture of a hopeless oil-caked cormorant caught in the spills that followed the Iraqi torching of Kuwait's oil wells; it became a registered trademark which communicated that these days the consequences of war extend far beyond the social realm; they can also have a devastating impact on the environment. But the image didn't linger for long in the memory, and thoughts of the consequences of the First Gulf War didn't prevent the outbreak of a second.

Besides which, the images that had the most impact were transmitted by a much more powerful 'cultural enhancer': cinema. It is the ideal medium for war, in part because war itself is so cinematic in scope. Some of the great battles of the past, we might say, foreshadowed or prefigured Hollywood. Violence and sensationalism are entertaining, let's admit it; both cinema and epic poetry are cut from the same cloth. In the 1920s, the Czech writer Karel Čapek observed that the people sitting in movie theatres basically were the same as those who twenty-five centuries earlier had sat around the Homeric bards 'and listened to heroic songs, to how the Achaeans and Trojans chopped one another up'. Despite all its flaws, he added, cinema had the same advantage as the *Iliad*—it is epic in scale (Carey, 2005: 37).

And cinema has always been especially effective at conveying the aesthetic of war as no other medium has. However hideous for most of the combatants and non-combatants who find themselves caught in its slipstream, war has always had an aesthetic appeal. Of the thirteen full-length films made by one of Hollywood's greatest directors, Stanley Kubrick, six deal directly or indirectly with war. He never got to make the film on the life of Napoleon, but from the published screenplay it would have been one of immense spectacle. Has any era of history, asked Kubrick, been more colourful than the Napoleonic with its serried ranks of soldiers locked in battle, blowing each other to kingdom come? Later he admitted that there was indeed a disparity between the 'sheer visual beauty' of the scene and its human consequences, but claimed that 'it's rather like watching two golden eagles soaring through the sky from a distance; they may be tearing a dove to pieces, but if you're far enough away the scene is still beautiful' (Daseler, 2018: 10). The Sublime, writes Terry Eagleton, 'is the most typical of all the aesthetic moods allowing us to contemplate hostile objects with absolute equanimity' (Eagleton, 1991: 123). It is interesting to imagine how Kubrick would have filmed the burning of Moscow. But then, arson has always had its appeal. The novelist Stendhal, who took part in Napoleon's Russian campaign, left the city of Smolensk for Moscow 'illuminated by the finest fire in the world'.

For these, and many other reasons we shouldn't underestimate the role cinema has played in shaping the imagination of young people. 'I keep thinking about all the kids who got wiped out by seventeen years of war movies before coming to Vietnam', wrote Michael Herr in *Dispatches* (Herr, 1977: 67). He remembered how many young men would try to re-enact war movies when they knew a TV crew was in the area, filming the war as it happened. 'They were actually making war movies in their heads, doing little guts-and-glory leatherneck tap dances under fire' (Herr, 1977: 169). And what they knew about war before they experienced it at first hand is what they had learned from watching the exploits of their movie heroes. In Philip Caputo's *A Rumour of War*, there is a revealing passage that displays his growing realisation that he enjoyed war, perhaps too much.

> 'C'mon Charlie, hit me you son of a bitch' I yelled at the top of my lungs. 'Ho Chi Minh sucks. Fuck Communism. HIT me Charlie'. I was crazy, I was soaring high, very high in a delirium of violence... I was John Wayne in *Sands of Iwo Jima*. I was all Aldo Ray in *Battle Cry* (Caputo, 1999: 21).

Back in 1961, many West Point cadets said that they had been enthused to join the military by the films of John Wayne (van Creveld, 2008: 314). In the 1990s, many of them were enthused by the movies in which Sylvester Stallone played another iconic hero of the hour, John Rambo. The only problem is that Rambo is a one-dimensional action figure who stars in a less than compellingly reductive vision of war as pure violence. His kill count is high: over 130 people in the first three films in the franchise, and there is no end to his ingenuity—his victims are garrotted, blasted, stabbed and strangled, blown up by mines or grenades and other more inventive explosives, shot by bullets or arrows, incinerated by flamethrowers, bludgeoned or beaten to death, tossed off precipices and thrown out of aircraft. Rambo is nothing if not an authentic modern warrior.

The franchise has been criticised for delivering spectacle rather than insight, for drawing the viewers' imagination to the extremes of violence on screen. What is lost between the extremes is the middle ground, the intermediate space known as life. In that regard, cinema has cheapened the franchise since John Wayne's day. Or has it? For Wayne never served in the Second World War unlike many other Hollywood actors, but he made a fortune out of playing war heroes on film sets where no one was ever in danger of actually being killed.

The young Ron Kovic too, was inspired to join up by the movie version of a real-life soldier Audie Murphy. Hollywood screened his memoirs *To Hell and Back*. He never forgot the scene of Murphy (the most decorated soldier in American history) playing himself, blasting away into the German lines. But Kovic himself had a bad war. He returned home a paraplegic and his own book *Born on the Fourth of July* became a virulently anti-war movie. Except for the fact, concludes another disillusioned veteran Anthony Swofford, it is difficult for any movie to be really anti-war.

> Vietnam War films are all pro-war, no matter what the supposed message, what Kubrick or Coppola or Stone intended. Mr & Mrs Johnson in Omaha or San Francisco or Manhattan, will watch the

films and weep and decide once and for all that war is inhumane and terrible, and they will tell their friends at church and their family this. But Corporal Johnson at Camp Pendleton and Sgt. Johnson at Travis Air Force base, and Seaman Johnson at Coronado Naval Station, and Special 4 Johnson at Fort Bragg, and Lance-Corporal Swofford at 29 Palms Marine Corps base watch the same films and are excited by them because the magic brutality of the films celebrates the terrible and despicable beauty of the fighting skills (Swofford, 2003: 7).

In *Jarhead* (2005), the cinematic version of Swofford's experience in the First Gulf War, we see him watching Francis Ford Coppola's epic film *Apocalypse Now* and cheering wildly with his friends when the helicopters burn up a village. In Sam Mendes' Hollywood version of Swofford's original book, the thumping soundtrack of rap and T-Rex adds to the sensory bombardment. Overhead, US bomber pilots fly missions with the heavy metal music of Van Halen pumping through their head-sets. What is this if not a compelling example of Steven Pinker's argument that the cliché that life imitates art is often true because the function of some art is for life to imitate it? (McEwan, 2006: 38).

Holding onto Reality

Evan Wright, who accompanied a reconnaissance unit of the US Marine Corps to Iraq in 2003 doesn't mince words. Its members came from a culture whose metaphysic is shaped by the entertainment industry. Many were on more intimate terms with video games than they were with their own parents. 'I was just thinking one thing', he records a soldier saying, 'when we drove into that ambush: *Grand Theft Auto: Vice City*. I felt like I was living it when I seen the flames coming out of windows, the blown-up car in the street, guys crawling around shooting at us, it was fucking cool'. And 'cool' is what the military-entertainment industry has made war for many young soldiers experiencing it for the first time. 'Iraqis think we're cool', said another soldier, 'because we're so good at blowing shit up' (Wright, 2004: 5).

'Blowing shit up' on the screen is a great preparation for the real thing, whatever these days we mean by the word 'real'. What makes the world of video-gaming so different from that of the cinema is that the players are stakeholders—they have skin in the game. Twelve million people subscribed to *World of Warcraft* at its peak. The game is known as an MMORPG—a massively multi-player online role-playing game. It is a team exercise that requires inter-personal skills, the ability to work with and relate to other players. For its players, the game fulfils a need intrinsic to being human: a sense of achievement. It does this by simplifying the virtual world while at the same time offering them a chance to escape back into the real world. The first British ISIS member to blow himself up in Iraq left behind a message claiming that he had been inspired to join up after playing endless hours of the game *Call of Duty*. He turned everything he had learned about on-line culture and tools of the trade into what one journalist called 'a macabre version of online dating'. 'You can sit at home and play *Call of Duty* or you can come here and respond to the real call of duty... the choice is yours', he tweeted before he boarded a plane and left for the battle front (Carlin, 2018).

In fact, military video-gaming has been profoundly influenced by 9/11 and the War on Terror (Payne, 2016). Shorn of the real experience of war however—the killing of civilians and incidents of post-traumatic stress—there is a stark difference between visual realism and actual reality. A common criticism of games like *Soldier of Anarchy* and *First Battalion* is that they allow the players to treat the battlefield as just a 'kill-box' in which the rules of engagement can be relaxed precisely because all there is to do is kill the enemy. It is body counts, not hearts and minds that matter most; kinetic exchanges, not what the US army calls 'courageous restraint' is the order of the day. Most games represent war as an egregious form of entertainment, and if you find it too entertaining you can lose your moral compass quickly enough. This was true of one gamer of *America's Army* who, whenever he logged into the servers of the game, typed in the names of American service personnel who had been killed in action the previous day (Chan, 2010: 274).

H G Wells' manual for war-gaming, *Little Wars*, showed us that our desire to immerse ourselves in other worlds is a very old one, and that it begins in childhood. What he offered in his book is what he called 'a homeopathic remedy for the imaginative strategist'. Here was the thrill of battle without the violence. If he had had his way, he added, he would have prancing monarchs, silly scare-mongers, excitable patriots, even professors (like me) locked up in 'a cork lined room and left to fight it out to their heart's content'. Well, one day it may be possible to leave the war enthusiasts among us to fight it out not only on screen, but also in an immersive reality world where, locked behind a computer screen, they will be able to engage in acts of visceral violence with little harm to themselves, and more importantly, anyone else.

For virtual reality (VR) is becoming more 'real' every day as the technology keeps improving. We are seeing great advances in depth (resolution) and breadth (the number of human senses that VR taps into). Nothing for the moment has as much depth or breadth or invites as much engagement as the physical world. But this is probably changing. Realism in VR is increasing all the time as resolution does, as contrasts deepen, and high-fidelity sound sharpens. According to its cheerleaders, it also can enlarge our experience of the world by infusing new significance into our thoughts and feelings; it can also transport us to places we will possibly never visit and that many won't want to, though others will. Many of us 'must have a desire for the rush of adrenalin, for the smell of napalm in the morning....the great game, tin soldiers made real' (Nikolaou, 2007). Virtual reality already offers 'a burst of fluorescence that spoils the darkness of ordinary life and reveals another more luminous reality' (Borgmann, 1999: 189). Are these claims over-inflated? Perhaps, not. We can feel more fully alive when we move in virtual space, writes Jaron Lanier, the computer scientist who is credited with inventing the term 'virtual reality'. And he insists that we haven't seen anything yet. 'It will amplify our *character* more than any other media ever have'. Why the attraction, he asks? It makes physicality more real, especially for those who like to live on the edge. But it does more—it a technology that exposes you to yourself. It allows you to expand your unconsciousness. When everything changes, you are still at the centre, experiencing the present more intensely than in the real world. In other words, he adds, it fosters self-awareness and thus allows us to live more intensely. 'VR is the technology that ... highlights the existence of your subjective experience. It proves you are real' (Lanier, 2017: 56).

What would Wells have made of VR, I wonder, not to mention immersive virtual reality which will enable its denizens to inhabit a battlefield that may be as real as any that soldiers today face—minus of course the negative side effects: mutilation, trauma and death? VR is already promising the coming of the hyper-real, the moment when reality collapses into its simulated version, at which point it may become impossible to distinguish the representation from the real thing. Indeed, which world will be more 'real' for its players? The mundane physical world with its limited opportunities, or the virtual with its more vivid characters and greater intensity? William Gibson, the man who coined the term cyberspace did so after watching some kids playing video games at an arcade in Vancouver. 'It seemed to me that what they wanted was to be inside the games, within the notional space of the machine'. Later, he added that it seemed that the real world had completely disappeared for them (Gleick, 2018: 306). For where this may eventually lead, read Eric Cline's *Ready Player One*, which imagines a virtual oasis where people can love, work and play, removed from the 'real world' into which they have been born. Although this vision won't be realised for some time, companies are already investing billions of dollars in the physical and digital infrastructure that will eventually bring that world into being. But when that world becomes real and people can fight wars in it, how long will it be before they lose touch totally with reality? How long will it be before they find themselves quite incapable of feeling the urgency of the questions Tolstoy addressed in *War and Peace*?

3

ONTOGENY

War, as we've seen, has its origins in our emerging humanity and is fuelled by cultural mechanisms that cater to our cultural instincts as well. But we also have a history which no other species does. The word Tinbergen used was ontogeny, a word that came naturally to an ethologist. It is a concept that describes the origin and development of an organism usually from the time of fertilisation of the egg. When scientists use the term, they talk of the development of a single individual or system from fertilisation to maturation. And anthropologists use the term to describe the process through which each of us embodies the history of our own making. And then there's the ontogeny of social behaviour, the process of becoming social, the process by which a child becomes an adult. Whatever its idiom, there is variability both in the process and the outcome. Childhood is not only genetic; it is prolonged in some cultures, but not in others. Back in the days when I was at university in the 1970s, it was thought that in Europe it was an eighteenth century invention.

Michael Tomasello places a special emphasis on human childhood because unlike, say, young chimps, human children cooperate early on and seem to understand common ends. They're not smarter than young chimps—they have better social skills. Children are born into a social world of adults and other children and grasp the rules quickly enough. They begin imitating others at a very early stage and start to develop emotional intelligence which allows them to interact with their parents. The ability to learn about one's social environment requires social collaboration and cultural learning. They start developing all these as early as the age of three. By the age of six, they start modifying their behaviour in order to 'fit in'. Culturally, they learn to bootstrap that understanding of their physical world. Ontogeny, in other words is the process by which we become human.

What makes us genetically unique, however, is that we also have a history; we live in historical time. We are historical beings. History is what defines our humanity; we are a species in constant flux. 'Become who you are' was Nietzsche's great challenge—we are in a constant state of becoming because we are plastic in our possibilities. Of all animals, we are the ones that display an unbelievable degree of behavioural plasticity and the reason is simple—our genetic under-determination is itself genetically determined (Gellner, 1984: 515). Of the seven species of ape, we are the only one to have successfully incorporated artifice into its way of being. Only we have escaped being governed entirely by the Darwinian dynamic of natural selection; only we have an extra-somatic means of adaptation (Taylor, 2010a: 19). It is called culture, and it is largely technological in nature, whether the technologies we are talking about are languages, cities or machines. Culture is part of our evolutionary heritage, and it is what makes us an incomplete species, for we need technology to realise our potential.

It wasn't until the nineteenth century that we discovered how we had evolved, but we have known for a long time that things change. And we haven't needed written texts to record history.

Our Neolithic ancestors re-enacted the past of their ancestors in caves. Aboriginal songs dating back 7,000 years tell stories of the great deluge, the coastal inundation that saw sea levels reach their present level. We probably were the first hominid species to develop a sense of time. The fact that Neanderthals buried their dead suggests that they too had an understanding of time passing, but we haven't found a single one of their tools that has been improved upon. Indeed, many archaeologists treat the early Palaeolithic as if it had no history as we would understand—change. The radical break comes with the appearance of *Homo sapiens* and language. Language allowed our distant ancestors to feel unmoored from the present, to imagine themselves living in a past, perhaps a supposed golden age, and it allowed us as recently as only a few centuries ago to also live in the future, the default mode of the modern era. What language gives us is a sense that things can be otherwise—it gives us verbs with subjectives and conditionals that allow futures to be explored. But the downside is that the possibility of changing social rules or orders may encourage defection from one group to another, as well as fuel factionalism within the same group. The result may be greater conflict thanks to a rise in fixed belief-systems or, most damaging of all, 'group think' (the tendency to fall in line with a group's often mistaken understanding of a situation).

The Father of Everything

'War is the father of everything. Some it makes gods, some it makes men; some it makes slaves; some free'. If the pre-Socratic philosopher Heraclitus is still remembered, it is for this dictum that has survived both time and translation. He was, according to tradition, a melancholic man, who was called 'the weeping philosopher' because of the sadness induced in him by human folly. He was exiled to Ephesus where he left no school behind him; he seemed to be largely uninterested in the dissemination of his ideas. He left us 120 fragments which are obscure—it is now thought deliberately so; he wanted only his wisest readers to understand him. His elusiveness was designed to be non-negotiable. Nevertheless, he lived at a pivotal moment when a group of men began to seek natural rather than supernatural explanations for the world around them. They began asking more demanding questions about the natural world and tried to establish an investigative framework for their questioning—we call it philosophy.

Metaphors, it has been said, can give a thought a sudden lift—like the flare of a burner in a hot air balloon. And what most people still remember about Heraclitus is his metaphors such as 'war is the father of everything'. They get us to think new thoughts, and to see likenesses we have not registered before. They are also part of the universal language we speak, and they are universal because they are a consequence, writes Edward Wilson in *Consilience* (1998), of the spreading activation of the brain during learning. They are for that reason 'the building blocks of creative thought' (Watson, 2002: 771). They make things vivid in a way that the non-metaphorical use of language may not. In claiming that 'war is the father of everything', Heraclitus was talking in general about how history changes human life. And he was reaching for a metaphor his readers would have found all too familiar. For war was the principal force in shaping political life, not only for the Ancient Greeks but almost everyone else. If you don't believe me, imagine history without its Crusades or fights for liberty, or its revolutions and revolutionary wars. Imagine it without its heroes fighting against injustice or its subject peoples battling against imperial rule. The fight for independence is still a major narrative for many nations including the United States. Mao Zedong's image still gazes down on Tiananmen Square.

History is the story of constant change. Think of it this way. Human societies are complex adaptive systems. A society is made up of different 'parts' that interact with each other and produce complex and often unpredictable behaviour. Growing complexity is the story of history. Which is not to say that it is not full of fits and starts and occasional reverses, but the direction is clear enough to most historians. You can, if you wish, apply a concept of development without smuggling in normative assumptions, if by development we mean, not Progress, whatever that may be, but increasing complexity. Indeed, it's far more credible to claim that history is not progressive but directional, and what makes it so is our capacity to learn, to adapt to our environments and to learn increasingly quickly as the world becomes ever more complex.

Behind the flux of history Heraclitus saw an intelligent structure at work: war changes life in many ways, but it is also changed by the changes it brings about. What he grasped about war was its ever-changing character: it promotes change and becomes increasingly complex over time. This explains his most famous formulation: we can't step into the same river twice. The reason for that is that by the time we do we have changed too. In other words, change and stability co-exist. War is unchanging in its nature, but every time we bring to it new ideas or technologies, every time we take another step into the same river, its character changes once again. War never remains the same, but it is never transfigured out of recognition either; it remains war whether you are fighting with composite bows or hacking into another country's computers.

A Small Talent for War

Stepping back from the flow of history we can discern a story. It began slowly. The battlefield melees photographed by the

Harvard-Peabody expedition in New Guinea in the early 1960s had remained unchanged for thousands of years. Had H G Wells' time traveller travelled back to the island's pre-history, his trajectory would have been his own point of departure. But once the first empires arose in the Middle East around 5,000 BCE, things began to change significantly. The Assyrians, for example, were the first empire to develop a modern-style general staff which they needed to put large armies in the field on a routine basis. The hoplite warfare of the Greek city-states a few centuries later gave way in time to the mass armies of the Hellenistic age. Cavalry gave the feudal levies of Europe a decisive advantage until the invention of the longbow. The mass conscript armies of the last century mimicked the assembly-line production of late capitalism. Today cyber-warriors locked away in their sealed cubicles direct attacks on digital networks.

Nonetheless, what is of significance historically is that despite all the changes in military history that I have just elaborated, or more pertinently perhaps because of them, war has remained a constant throughout history. Just think about it. Slavery has waxed and waned in different eras. It was first introduced in China for the first time by the Shang dynasty, and in India by the Indo-European invaders who turned slaves into a caste. In the Mediterranean world, the Romans ran a huge commercial slave market which then disappeared only to be followed centuries later by the Atlantic slave trade at the end of the fifteenth century. Today it has reappeared, though in different forms such as sex trafficking and bonded labour in South Asia where children are sold into servitude by their parents to pay off their debts. Most recently, slave auctions in the so-called Caliphate established by ISIS were advertised on Facebook. Alas, slaves are for many of us members of an out-group, and accordingly many people apparently feel no moral constraint to feel their pain or even sympathise with their plight. But compared with slavery, war has been central to every mode of life we have created so far. It is common to every culture and every era; it transcends both time and place.

Let me illustrate this by sprinting quickly through the historical record from the time our ancestors fought the very first recognisable 'battles' to the point today where we are taking war into low earth orbit and perhaps one day even beyond. I am fully aware that I am reducing the history of war to its bare narrative essentials; an approach that may come at the expense of depth but not, I hope, direction.

The first transition—the greatest historical leap of all—was from the primate stage of evolution to one that was recognisably human. What is interesting is that we think human nature is made up of a genetically endowed set of needs, desires, preferences and impulses that all interact with each other. Our nature, so we believe, has evolved since the Pleistocene Age which lasted for more than 1.6 million years. Selective pressures in time created the people we are today. They brought out our co-operative instincts and abilities, including coalition-building. It was also probably in this period that we began to turn on each other for the first time, quite probably because this was also the period when we went in for imaginative mapping, including the territorial division of property. We developed an intuitive sense of numbers. At 40–60,000 years ago, beginning first in Africa and then later in Western Europe, our ancestors also developed an artistic sensibility for the first time, as well as a concept of religion. This gave rise to a highly developed sense of justice which reminded people of the injustices visited upon them by others. Add to this a heightened awareness of the challenges posed by out-groups, which came about at precisely the moment we learned to throw objects, including spears (Barkow, Cosmides and Tooby, 1995: 375–424). It was a combustible mix.

Anthropologists call the first social groups 'bands', and they were the very first political system to be devised by *Homo sapi-*

ens. The archaeological evidence suggests that most humans still lived in them as recently as 11,000 years ago (Diamond, 2012). War for them was associated less with people than the situations in which they found themselves. Conflicts were powered not by dreams or ambitions, like Alexander the Great's personal pursuit of glory, or for that matter even the interests of a dominant political class. In bands, leaders persuaded others to follow them into battle for less all-encompassing ends, mostly for local and immediate advantage such as a grab for resources. And they relied not on power but on their own authority and charisma. Morton Fried tells us that in such societies, leaders don't give commands; they don't say: 'Do this!'. They don't give orders. They make statements such as: 'if this is done it will be good' and usually the person who makes the claim is also expected to engage in the task at hand, usually forfeiting his authority if things don't turn out well (Fried, 1967: 83). For that reason, such leadership as charismatic leaders do provide tends to be transient.

What did the battles of this period look like? Forget the colourful encounters between opposing armies that we read about in most history books. The American anthropologist Martin Harris describes a battle between two hunter-gatherer groups in northern Australia in the 1920s that was witnessed by a contemporary anthropologist. Having agreed formally to fight the next day, the two sides met at a pre-arranged time of day. The older men shouted out grievances against specific members of the opposing war party, but since the old men did most of the spear-throwing they tended to miss most of the time. Not infrequently, they hit some innocent non-combatant or one of the screaming old women who weaved through the other side's ranks yelling obscenities at everybody and whose reflexes for dodging spears were not very good (Harris, 1978: 35). It may seem a rather farcical encounter, but a lot depends on definitions. Does war really require a sophisticated form of organisation, the mobilisation of a large group, effectively an army in all but name?

The aboriginal battle described by Harris is, you have to admit, a pretty colourless affair. What's more, it displays no strategic or tactical innovation, no attempt to outwit an enemy, or even to deceive him. Primitive warriors were not so much heroic as stoic, in part because their encounters with the enemy tended to lead nowhere fast. What's lacking in this period of history is 'humanity'. As Hobbes maintained, the state of nature had none of those mechanisms such as art and history that have animated war in the past. In the state of nature, human faculties may be harnessed, but they are rarely awakened. But if in our worldly-wise eyes this way of fighting may seem very basic, it still has all the elements of what we understand war to be. It involved two sides who fought by certain agreed 'rules', however rudimentary. It was fought with weapons, however crude. The question, however, is: was it particularly deadly?

We mustn't run ahead of the evidence, though many historians have a tendency to do so. Steven Pinker, who is firmly in the Hobbesian camp, believes our distant ancestors were a murderous bunch. Death rates in prehistoric times as a percentage of population were far greater than in the twentieth century—the so-called century of 'Total War'. As Lawrence Keeley shows in *War Before Civilization*, prehistoric conflicts were deadly, measured by the percentage of deaths within a population, and just as ruthless as modern war, measured by the killing and maiming of non-combatants. Many archaeologists dispute these findings. Some insist that war was simply absent from most of our existence; it is a product of the agricultural revolution (Fry, 2013). And they don't take hostages—witness the opprobrium heaped upon Jared Diamond for his book *The World Until Yesterday* (2012) for taking the same line as Pinker. Pinker would argue no doubt that he and others are being attacked by agenda-driven archaeologists who are not willing to accept that our distant ancestors were a violent lot. However, aren't historians supposed to see further by cutting through the ephemeral surface textures to the deeper rhythms and meanings of history, if they are there to be found? Aren't they required to see through their own stories when they no longer carry much conviction? What happens when the evidence changes but your former worldview persists? What happens if you fail to face up to the full implications of recent scholarship?

All of which is very true, but then again, the story Pinker wants to tell meets with some objections along the way, the chief of which is lack of evidence. Another is that his own findings are open to question. One archaeologist Brian Ferguson, reviewing evidence of twenty-one of his pre-historic battle sites in his best-selling book *The Better Angels of Our Nature* claims to have found that in four cases Pinker has counted the same site twice. Additionally, he accuses Pinker of cherry-picking cases with unusually high casualties, claiming that they are deeply unrepresentative of pre-history in general. War began sporadically out of war-less conditions; we are not hardwired for war, we learn it (Ferguson, 2013).

We confront a familiar problem in the writing of history—the historical record as interpreted by historians and archaeologists provides us with different answers to the same questions. Ultimately, the non-expert is to go with his gut. And I choose to take sides with the neo-Hobbesians. To suggest that our hunter-gatherer relatives were peaceful ignores the fact that we were fighting other hominid species hundreds of thousands of years ago; that we probably made *Homo erectus* extinct thanks to superior weaponry, and the same may even have been true of the Neanderthals as well. The jury is still out. In the end, I am inclined to side with Richard Wrangham and Dale Peterson who claim that we are 'the dazed survivors of a continuous five-million-year habit of lethal aggression' (Wrangham and Peterson, 1996). As the Harvard archaeologist Steven LeBlanc adds, 'anthropologists have searched for peaceful societies much like Diogenes looked for an honest man' (Shermer, 2016: 205). And they have been just as frustrated in their search. To quote the Israeli historian Azar Gat, 'the range of evidence from across aboriginal Australia, the only continent of hunter-gatherers, strikingly demonstrates that deadly human violence including group fighting, existed at all social levels, in all population densities, in the simplest of social organisations, and in all types of environments' (Gat, 2018: 58).

The second major transition in history involved moving out of the hunter-gatherer stage of existence to agrarian societies, a transition that may have been prompted by a warming of the climate that led in turn to higher plant growth, a more sedentary existence as well as the domestication of plants and animals which allowed more people to live off the land. By 8,000 BCE, people in the Near East were cultivating plants and herding animals. In the New World, which was always out of step with the Old thanks to its geographical isolation, the development of agriculture between 7,500 and 3,500 BCE turned the nomads of the Americas into sedentary farmers. According to Aztec mythology, it was Quetzalcoatl, the Plumed Serpent, who was the first to discover the first grain of maize; he succeeded where all the other gods had failed. After that, there was no turning back. Farming may have been back-breaking work, but some historians insist that it was 'the window of opportunity' that we needed to make history and which we jumped through as soon as we could (Cook, 2003: 7). Others insist that we were pushed through it kicking and screaming (Smail, 2008: 197). But the transition was self-reinforcing. Industrial societies do not regress back to being agrarian ones, and agrarian societies rarely, if ever, regress back to a hunter-gatherer mode of life.

Unfortunately, Neolithic man failed to do consequence management; he did not foresee that increasing dependence on a single source of food would in good years of surplus tempt neighbours to steal it, compelling us in turn to start building walls and perpetually mounting guard against marauders (Harari, 2015: 87). The transition from a hunter-gatherer to an agrarian world also probably saw the return of the original primitive alpha male, this time with members of dominance hierarchies maintained by predation. Theft, murder and random acts of violence were probably common until Hobbes' 'social contract' kicked in—a metaphor for the state which regulated violence by monopolising it. This was all very different from the hunter-gatherer era of history which was more egalitarian. Before the transition, chiefs had to persuade; with the invention of the state, they could now command.

There is little agreement among historians or archaeologists on when the first battles of the agrarian period were fought, and the riddle of why they were fought still remains unanswered. The earliest site of what looks like collective killing is at Nataruk, west of Kenya's Lake Turkana. At least twenty-seven individual bodies have been identified, many of which suffered from extreme blunt force trauma to the crania and the cheekbones and arrow lesions to the neck. Stone projectile tips are still lodged in the skull and thorax of two men. What makes the find (in 2012) important is that it has all the hallmarks of a planned attack. What makes it historically significant is that it predates the agrarian age. Before its discovery, the world's earliest known full-scale battle site was generally thought to be that at Jebel Sahaba on the Upper Nile which dates back about 11,000 years, to a time when agriculture was still in its infancy. The victims were preponderantly young males whose skeletons showed multiple bone fractures. The cut marks on the bones all attest to organised violence. Twenty-one victims had a total of over 100 projectile points, a remarkable example of overkill. So, for many archaeologists, Jebel Sahaba is the earliest large cemetery in the archaeological record—the first real evidence perhaps of organised and sustained warfare. But it begs the question, do we date war to the rise of fixed territories, as marked by the presence of cemeteries for example, or is violence just more visible in the archaeological record once cemeteries appear?

It is hard to exaggerate the cultural jump in war that came in a few thousand years later with the first civilisations and empires. They really did change everything, in particular because they saw the transition from 'emergent warfare' to state warfare, although the change did not occur overnight. If we had surveyed the world on its eve, for example, could we have predicted the eventual emergence of state-centric warfare? Probably not. We are not dealing with a computer game designed by a programmer, but with an emergent phenomenon. But knowing what we do, could history have turned out differently? The answer, again, is probably not. It was not an evolutionary anomaly but our destiny as a species towards even greater social complexity.

Among its many drivers, two especially stand out. If we are to sharpen our focus, we need to grasp how every historical transition has seen the harnessing of two forces: energy and information. In the case of energy, for much of history human labour has been the raw material of growth. Workers provided opportunities to boost output. The states that arose in the first 1,000 years of recorded history did so in the basins of three rivers, the Euphrates, the Nile and the Indus. They were the great assimilators; think of them, if you like, as being very similar to the Borg Collective in the *Star Trek* franchise: an alien race which assimilates ruthlessly every other that it encounters. Most ancient civilisations too, assimilated people and turned their new acquired human capital into energy. Warfare in Mesopotamia from 3,500 BCE for the next two millennia involved, not so much the conquest of territory as the herding of people into state structures against their will, to ensure they were put to work. There were irrigation ditches to dig, fields to tend and temples to construct. Many of Babylon's legal codes concerned the punishment of escapees and runaways. Defeat and enslavement produced in Babylon 'a kind of servile cosmopolitanism'— think of the Israelites who were forcibly removed there by Nebuchadnezzar (Greenblatt, 2017: 24). Fast-forward several centuries and we find one of the greatest slave raiders of all time, Julius Caesar. He invaded Gaul to reposition himself in Roman politics and to do that he needed money. After campaigning for seven years he returned to Rome with one million prisoners in tow who were sold into slavery, thereby transforming his fortunes and making him a billionaire overnight. Michael Mann has called some of Rome's wars 'slave-hunts'. That is not how our Victorian ancestors saw them; trapped in their time they saw Rome as an imperial power with a civilising mission, a people very much like themselves. Today we are much more sceptical—sometimes you have to nerd out and see reality for what it is, not what you would like it to be.

The historical trajectory I have just described inevitably involved almost perpetual warfare. The struggles of states against peoples or nomadic tribes recur throughout the historical record with astonishing regularity. If we take a long view, is it so remarkable that so many people chose not to be part of someone else's project? Stateless societies have spent thousands of years struggling to stay 'outside'. And these 'peripheral' ungoverned regions of the world were home to a dizzying array of different peoples who preferred to live transient lives, far away from any governing authority. As late as the Bronze Age they were still in the majority. It was 'a world of peripheries where states and cities rested like small islands amid a great sea of stateless civilisations' (Wengrow, 2014). Regrettably, the voices that reach us from these societies are largely mute. They had no Herodotus to record or celebrate their exploits, and no Thucydides to analyse their political life. Yet they endured far longer than most states. The historian James Scott suggests that orality and rootlessness and the absence of political organisation may even be understood, not as a deficiency, so much as a response to domination and a mode of resistance. The term 'barbarian', he insists, was not really a cultural category so much as a political one: it designated a population not administered by a state (Scott, 2017: 33).

Most of these groups have disappeared from history, but one which managed to escape state control longer than most was the Cossacks. Clausewitz was horrified by these 'pitiless, pony-riding nomads' who harried stragglers as the French army marched back to Poland, riding down soldiers who fell behind the main force, or selling them to peasants for cash, or stripping those who could not be sold in arctic temperatures to the bare skin for their clothes. But the novelist Isaac Babel who served with a Cossack unit during the Russo–Polish war (1920) saw in them a people of simple virtues: 'wild beasts with principles', he once called them (Babel, 1994: 347). They were opposed, for one, to all forms of authority; they had no kings. They chose their war leaders and judges and retained the right to dismiss both by vote. They looted on a large scale, but they also distributed the booty by lot. Most interesting of all, the readiness to bear arms gave everyone the right to a voice in the management of their own affairs.

If the acquisition of people was central to war, so too was the organisation of information. As Seth Lloyd writes, 'to do anything requires energy. To specify what is done requires information' (Christian, 2018: 78). These days the word is to be found everywhere. We think that the universe is probably made up of information. A few scientists even believe information-based concepts may eventually fuse with or even replace traditional notions such as particles, fields and forces (Calasso, 2019: 78). And then there is evolution, Darwin's 'big idea'. A hundred years ago we talked of evolution in terms of the 'survival of the fittest'; today we talk of it in terms of the 'survival of the best-informed'. Survival is now seen as a form of information-processing; life goes beyond crude strength to knowledge. The more successful a species is in processing complex kinds of information, the better it can adjust to a greater array of environmental challenges. What drives this evolution is increased computational ability. The human being is an information processor bound in a complex network with others of his kind.

As David Christian writes, the ancient civilisations that appeared in Mesopotamia 5,500 years ago were the most complex systems yet built. Information enabled cities like Uruk, probably the very first to tap into larger and larger flows of energy thanks to writing and literacy. Writing was the new technology that allowed the elite to keep track of the energy resources at their disposal. One of the largest archives from the Sumerian civilisation is that of Girsu in the state of Lagash—the texts that have been discovered there include ration lists given to temple personnel and receipts and accounts related to the state-run temple economy. Tablets found elsewhere are so numerous that many are still unread. Writing produced a more stratified, complex society, and greater complexity demanded in turn a class of scribes to document information, a class of bureaucrats to manage and a class of priests to ply their trade and do what they usually do so well—to keep everyone else in line.

As states grew in wealth and power so did their ambitions. Standing armies, writes Christian, 'were like the proton pumps that maintain an energy gradient across cell membranes' (Christian, 2018: 220–1). Soldiers pumped wealth from villages to towns, and thence to cities and governments, menacing enemies and subjects equally alike. Christian encourages us to see war in ecological terms. Wealth consists not of things but of control over energy flows that make, move, mine and transform things. The model way of doing this from the earliest days was to seize the wealth of your neighbours. Even then, argues Doyne Dawson, there was a 2,000 year gap between the rise of the first city-states in Sumer and the appearance of what he calls 'state-level warfare'—the warfare with which we are most familiar today, with large armies, decisive battles, wars of manoeuvre and mobility and logistic reach. The states of the Near East only began to go in for large scale empire building around 700 BCE. There followed an endlessly destructive series of armed conflicts in Western Asia which witnessed the rise of new empires: the Akkadians, the Hittites, the Assyrians, and the Persians. Each had their own distinctive weaponry: the Akkadians—the compound bow; the Hittites—the horse-drawn chariot; the Egyptians of the New Kingdom—bronze armour; the Assyrians—chariots, cavalry and siege engines; the Persians added warships to the list (Dawson, 2001). They were the very first people to take war into a new domain—the sea. For which, according to Aeschylus's play *The Persians*, they invited divine retribution. They had been given the East not the West by the Gods and so had overreached themselves in fighting at sea. It was the classic Greek line—hubris is followed inevitably by nemesis.

But there is also another, equally striking story to tell. When they were not fighting each other, the great empires of the ancient world had to contend with a far more serious challenge: invasion by the nomadic peoples of the Eurasian steppe. One of the central themes of history was the nomadic destruction of all the great empires beginning in 612 BCE when Scythian horse-men from the Ukraine helped overthrow the Assyrian empire. Sedentary societies were not as effective at using horses as the nomadic people of the steppes. And horses gave them speed. They could appear quite suddenly and retreat quickly into the hinterland. Living on the fringes of two great empires in the arid zone between the Arabian Peninsula and the Fertile Crescent, the Arabs knew how to navigate their way through the desert where they couldn't be pursued. Nomadic peoples were highly mobile because they were not weighed down by supply trains; they lived off the land. And, like hunter-gatherer societies, all adult males were warriors, compared with civilisations in which warriors were a specific cast, or caste in the case of India. Significantly, for example, there is no Turkic or Mongolian word for 'soldier'. And they brought with them skills that were impossible to replicate elsewhere such as mounted archery, a technique which could only be mastered by those who dedicated their life to it, though one civilisation—Persia—eventually mastered the art.

History is still haunted by the ghost of empires past; some of which continue inescapably to shape our imagination. One of the greatest legacies that the Roman Empire left behind was the trauma of its own decline and fall. Edward Gibbon didn't need to pile on the ruined landscapes—decline and fall underwrite every cracked pediment and toppled Doric column. In the Western collective consciousness, the barbarians were terrifying enough to write themselves into the imagination of our nineteenth century ancestors. In a famous novel, Joris-Karl Huysmans gave voice to what he imagined was a historical reality—he saw the horsemen gathering on the Roman horizon and imagined the alarm that they must have raised in the minds of the empire's citizens:

> On the banks of the Danube thousands of men wrapped in rat skin cloaks and mounted on little horses, hideous Tartars with enormous heads, flat noses, hairless, jaundiced faces and chins furrowed with gashes and scars, rode hell-for-leather into the territories of the Lower Empire, sweeping all before them in their whirlwind advance. Civilisation disappeared in the dust of their horses' hooves, in the smoke of the fires they kindled (Huysmans, 2005: 56).

It is a powerful passage, but its prose style is a giveaway—it is indicative of an age not so secure in its convictions, fearful of its own decline and ever watchful for the barbarians forcing their way back into history. 'What hope is there', asked Max Weber a few years later, 'if the Cossacks are coming'—a reference to the growing power of Russia.

We must add some historical caveats. Today, historians are a little less inclined then their forebears to talk of the 'barbarousness' of the invaders. They tell us that the nomads didn't 'prey' upon civilisations so much as they tried to deal with the imbalance of resources that stemmed from geography and climate change, and the fact that they lacked the power of settled societies to tax their citizens. And they were often the victims of climate change as well—the invasion of Northern Europe by the Huns in the fourth century was prompted by the climate-induced destruction of their traditional pasture lands.

Also, the problem with all big picture painting is that it requires a knowledge of the details from which it is constructed, and that is where the historians often fail us, for some of the claims they make of nomadic invasions are often difficult to sustain. Take the battle of Tours (732 CE) which has often been cast as a decisive defeat of an Arab invasion of Europe. This scarcely did justice to the facts. For the idea of 'Europe' hardly existed at the time, and the raid hardly constituted a full-scale invasion. The horsemen who surged out of the Arabian deserts in the seventh and eighth centuries were animated not by their new faith so much as a centuries-old tradition of raiding and looting, but this time on a far broader canvas that stretched all the way to India. The Berbers who invaded Spain and crossed over from North Africa did so for loot, livestock and slaves, and it's likely that many of them had only an imperfect knowledge of their own faith.

Historical insights are continuously undermining the old plotlines. Take an earlier battle, Chalons (451 CE) where, we are told by the Victorian historian Edward Creasy, the Huns were turned back, and Europe was 'saved' from barbarism. But the Huns were the great exception in the barbarian invasions of the fifth century for they soon disappeared from history. Most nomadic invaders discovered soon enough the truth of the old Chinese proverb: 'you can conquer a kingdom on horseback but to rule it you have to dismount'. The Huns never did get off their horses. Many other nomadic tribes like the Goths eventually did.

For some historians, the cycle of nomadic invasions was as distinctive as its signature: devastation; for others it was part of an inevitable and often positive historical pattern of challenge and response. Complex adaptive systems are called that for a good reason: usually they adapt to new challenges and changing conditions. Even when overwhelmed by foreign invasions or social conflict at home, or ecological failure like overgrazing or over-irrigation, societies usually don't revert back to their earlier mode of being. Instead they downsize. Around 900 CE, the Mayans, for example, abandoned their great cities with their massive temple complexes for a simpler way of life; they were forced to do so by environmental pressures. Nevertheless, the land continued to support the same number of people even if they were forced to reorganise themselves into smaller administrative units. Another example is Angkor Watt, which was abandoned in the fifteenth century because it could no longer sustain a growing population. But the land continued to be farmed. Downsizing was the answer—a move away from the giant Buddhist Mahayana temples that we visit today, to the smaller scale communal wooden halls of Hinayana Buddhism, which have long since disappeared (Cremin, 2018). But the very fact that societies are able to adapt by downsizing is a remarkable example of adaptability at work. So much so that a decline in complexity can be seen as a successful adaptation (Lewis and Maslin, 2018: 336).

The problem is that when societies adapt to challenges, they usually establish negative feedback loops which cause the output of a system to feed back into the system, dampening further change. The collapse of the Western Roman Empire is a case in point. The feudal kingdoms of Western Europe that replaced the Western Roman Empire remained agricultural; they didn't regress back to subsistence farming. But with the collapse of tax revenue as a result of lower growth, it was impossible for any state, even one as large as Charlemagne's, to maintain the kind of professional army that had been a feature of the Western Roman Empire, even at the very end of its life.

And so, we come to the third transition in our mode of living from the agrarian to the industrial era. Remember, but for fossil fuels we would never have made it out of the agrarian state. In the early nineteenth century, the world managed finally to escape the resource constraints we once thought were fixed. We developed the power to outsource muscle and motion to machines, thereby producing the greatest economic breakthrough in history. If the last 3,000 years of history were to be compressed into a single day, it would not be until the final minute that self-sustaining economic growth finally took off.

Nevertheless, contrary to popular opinion, the industrial revolution did not start with the steam engine. As Nietzsche once wrote, close observation will usually reveal the dovetailing where a new building grows out of the old. 'This is the task of the biographer: to think about the life in question, the principle that nature never jumps' (Nietzsche, 1986). The industrial state wasn't jump-started; it was foreshowed by a new relationship with the land in seventeenth century Europe, sometimes called the 'commercial revolution', which unleashed unprecedented market forces. Increased incomes were reinvested in colonial projects and trade which both helped to produce a global system of commerce. The Industrial Revolution was also foregrounded in a revolution in finance at the end of the seventeenth century. John Brewer talks of the rise of a new entity: the 'military–fiscal state'. In Britain, the invention of the national debt enabled the state to spend far beyond the tax base without bankrupting itself. This financial revolution enabled a formerly middle-ranking power to emerge as the dominant player in the international system. In a long succession of wars between France and Britain, the British eventually prevailed thanks to their innovative financial thinking. By monitoring public expenditure very closely, both Parliament and the Bank of England created a 'virtuous cycle' of spending that was the basis of British naval power for 200 years (Scheidel, 2019: 383). And war in turn helped power the industrial revolution. Some writers, indeed, are of the opinion that Britain got the Industrial Revolution first because of its undisguised militarism (Satia, 2019).

The industrial state that followed in its wake was powered by several other positive feedback loops: coal production; the reinvestment of profits in new technology; and the relentless drive for profit, all of which transformed warfare too. Even before the industrial revolution, the Venetian Arsenal was the world's first assembly line and first 'industrial' shipyard which was able to launch a fully stocked ready-to-go to sea galley every day. When James Boswell, Samuel Johnson's famous biographer, visited the Arsenal and contemplated 'the great storehouse of mortal engines', he was struck by how calmly men could construct 'the instruments of destruction of their own species' (Boswell, 1991: 102). To sustain Nelson's navy fifty years later required enormous workshops for rope and rigging, copper makers in Wales who provided sheathing for the hulls of ships to increase their speed, and early steam-driven machine tools that made millions of light low-friction pulley blocks for the rigging. Iron works and cannon makers gave an English naval squadron more firepower in the age of Nelson than both sides deployed at the Battle of Austerlitz (1805) (Tombs, 2014: 405).

Max Weber once defined power as 'the ability of a group to achieve its aims and goals whilst others are trying to prevent it from realising them'. What changes over time is not the fact that people seek power, but what they do with it. Technology in general has had a persuasive power in war, for that reason. The industrial age created a pattern of thinking, or mentality, a machine-mindedness that encouraged the Europeans to think in terms of the unlimited possibilities of mechanical effort rather than the limitations of human labour. It also sparked a persistent search for a 'technological quick fix' which led John Ruskin, one of the most eloquent critics of industrialisation, to complain that war had become almost entirely 'a matter of machine-contriving' (Pick, 1993: 72).

It also transformed war into a business. The American Civil War was the first industrialised war and Ulysses S Grant can claim to be the first business general in history. Robert E Lee, his opponent, was of the old school, an inspirational general whose inspiration finally failed him. Grant was the first of the modern generals—a manager who relied most of all not on inspiration, but dogged determination. One junior officer wrote of him that he was 'a plain businessman', a general who believed that victory was secured by outgunning the enemy. Even today he is still remembered at West Point for calling war 'pounding'.

And in no time at all states began to think of people in cold statistical terms. Weapons designers preferred not to talk about the death of people, but 'lethal area estimates' and 'kill probabilities', as well as 'sensitivity and compatibility studies'—the procedures for making sure that a given bomb could be used in a given airplane. 'The era of the well-aimed shot is already behind us', lamented the German warrior Ernst Jünger, 'and deadly gas hovers like an elemental power over everything that lives' (Wolin, 1993: 128). Huxley's novel *Brave New World* still repays a visit with its vision of biological warfare. 'In the Kurfürstendamm and the eighth arrondissement, the explosion of the anthrax bombs is hardly louder than the popping of a paper bag'.

The history of war, to recapitulate, can be seen in terms of three factors. War powered human progress at the material level. Our modern lives, writes Ian Morris, are twenty times safer than those of our Stone Age ancestors (Morris, 2014). War helped us to forge states, and states gave us maximum security against outsiders. And states were chiefly in the business of war. According to the Stanford historian Walter Scheidel, there has not been a single advance in technology, finance or political organisation in Europe that until very recently has not been the result of intra-European conflict. Europe's success in getting the industrial revolution first owed everything to 'the wasteful and blood soaked nexus of ceaseless war' (Scheidel, 2019). In economic terms, everything is a trade-off, and the appalling cost of war in terms of lives lost or made miserable was offset by 'progress', material not spiritual. The problem is what is called the 'progress trap'—a development that looks like an advance can turn out to threaten the entire system, and Europe was almost destroyed by war in the course of the twentieth century. Scaling up technologies proved nearly fatal.

Generally that has been a problem throughout history. The state has encouraged a steady improvement in human performance—in the lethality of weapons, and their reach. Think of the progression from the spear to the bow and arrow; from the muscular power required by an archer to chemical power in the hands of a person with a gun; from the chemical power of guns to the nuclear power first made available by the splitting of the atom. Today, we are witnessing yet another change, from nuclear power to digital power, and the rise of a new domain in war: cyberspace. And now, for the first time in the history of warfare, the ability to inflict damage is no longer proportional to the capital investment. Computer viruses are the ultimate low-cost weapons. A computer code can disable any computer network anywhere in the world. And whereas a missile comes with a return address, a virus doesn't.

Every mode of being, in sum, throws up new technologies which in turn create new opportunities that may keep us almost permanently in the war business. Think of cyber-war, space wars, hybrid wars, and so the list continues. And extend your imagination a little further. In 2014, the US Office of Naval Research committed US$4 million to a program on 'anomalous mental cognition' in the hope of finding proof that one day it might really be possible to take war into an entirely new dimension: the psychic sphere. Indeed, Russia's military journal *Army Digest* claims that its soldiers have already developed telepathic battlefield skills that have allowed it to strike the first blow in a psychic arms race that has only just begun! (MacIntyre, 2019).

Breaking Bad: A Brief Cultural History

War is a universal phenomenon, but if it has a universal language, it is one that has many different idioms. It can be long or short, limited or total, defensive or offensive, just or unjust (in the eyes of its practitioners). Wars come in waves and phases; they can be spontaneous or planned; they can be destiny defining or historically unimportant (the shortest war in history lasted just under 30 minutes—the conflict that brought Zanzibar into the British Empire in 1890). Wars can also convey a variety of moods. They can be calculating or ferocious; they can be fuelled by the rational or irrational, by hatred and cynicism. But in all cases, they are culturally specific.

War doesn't have an essence. Only that which has no history can be defined in categorical terms, wrote Nietzsche. Clausewitz tried to find one: it had a tendency, he claimed, to escalate, but that is only part of the picture. The contemporary measurement of combat deaths is not very helpful either; since when does war have to involve combat? Or be kinetic? What we can identify however is a universal grammar of war which involves several gambits that transcend time and culture: attack and defence, retreat before regrouping; envelopment of the flanks, guerrilla warfare, which long predates the name the Europeans gave it in the Napoleonic wars. These have all been employed in battle through the centuries, from the ancient world to the present day. They have been taught, adapted, and re-designed in staff colleges and military academies.

Borrowing an analogy from Wittgenstein, we might claim that war is more like an extended family that displays recognisable similarities without necessarily having any single feature in common. This is where culture kicks in—every society has different ways of thinking about war which others often find surprising because it challenges what the anthropologist Clifford Geertz called their own personal 'web of significance'. From the time we are born, we are indoctrinated by our specific culture in the way we are told or think that things should be done; we are imprisoned by our cultural beliefs and inescapable prejudices (Geertz, 1973). And in the case of war, culture from the beginning has structured unique ways of fighting, in the process providing different societies with their own distinctive grammars, styles, and routines. And although the cultural histories of war may differ in the details, like any extended family they are also remarkably similar. They are the histories of people or civilisations that were forged in war and which harnessed it in turn for their own purposes—conquest, plunder, the projection of a universal message, or religious jihad, the cruellest act of religious devotion.

Military history shows that societies have distinctive grammars of their own. In this short essay, 'Some Reflections on Non-Violence', the noted British biologist J B Haldane made an extraordinary confession. Although he was committed to the principle of non-violence, he admitted, 'I am a man of violence by temperament and training. My family, in the male line, can I think, fairly be described as *Kshatriyas*'. Haldane came from a long line of Border people whose main job had been to stop the tribal peoples of the hills from raiding the cattle of the plainsmen. As a child, his father had encouraged him to read legends of the warlike exploits of the Scottish nobility. Unable, as his ancestors might have done, to take him to a battlefield so that he could experience war at first hand, he took him down a mine instead. In those days there was always an ever-present danger from poisonous gas, or cave-ins and explosions. So, when in 1915 he first came under enemy shellfire on the Western Front, his first thought was 'how my father would enjoy this' (Haldane, 1985). It was a sentiment that summed up both the man and his times.

Haldane found himself drawn to many of the virtues and vices of the warriors in the Indian epics. He was well aware that he might die in the flat, featureless fields of Flanders; nevertheless, he found the experience intensely 'enjoyable'. He was sustained, as it were, on a great wave of *dharma*. It is a difficult word to translate; it is often rendered as 'duty' or 'decency' or just good conduct. The dharma of a *Kshatriya* (a member of a specific warrior caste) required him to risk his life at a moment's notice. In Indian history we find little philosophical justification for war. It was grounded not in a unique belief system or ideology but a set of behavioural expectations that revolved around membership of a specific caste. Every caste had its own *dharma* that its members were expected to honour. On the Western front Haldane took the lesson very much to heart. 'This was the war as the great poets sung it. I am lucky to have experienced it' (Haldane, 1985: 169–70).

Haldane's essay is interesting in treating war as akin to a religious experience. He acknowledged the importance of that experience as mediated through the poetry of the great *Gitas*. And it was the distinctly unpoetic character of modern war that finally turned him into a pacifist. For modern war, he argued in 1956, was now characterised by the wholesale massacre of defenceless civilians on the ground or from the air. It could no longer evoke any of the *Kshatriya* virtues except courage. Robert Capa had another take. 'To me war is like an ageing actress—more and more dangerous and less and less photogenic' (Hersey, 1991: 149). Later in life, Haldane took his views seriously enough to decamp to India where he imbibed with enthusiasm the ideas of Gandhian pacifism.

Haldane was highlighting the natural counterpoint between culture and war. A case in point is the Indian way of war which Haldane admired so much. Unfortunately, so much of Indian history has been lost. Warfare in South Asia was often ritualistic; it was bound by strict rules and social conventions. Battles were regarded as tournaments. Armies were large, and archers were important. And of course, the caste system gave warriors a privileged place in society. Ironically, Indians have always been more fascinated by the caste distinctions between themselves than by what makes them different from their many invaders like the Mughals or more recently, the British.

And what is so striking is the fact that so many Indian rulers saw war in existential terms. The heroic has always been highly praised in Indian culture. Unlike China, whose emperors rarely went into battle, Indian kings were warriors themselves. The great warrior princes, whose careers blazed and then fizzled out, tried to follow Krishna's advice to Arjuna in the *Mahabharata*; each must live according to his own code. In 1673, Vijaya Raghava, the last king of a dynasty in the far south of India, threw himself, at the age of 80, into his final battle against the city-state of Madurai. When he saw the enemy soldiers raising their muskets to shoot at him, he cried out to their commander:

'Order your men to fight only with swords and spears. Do you want to know why? Because a man who dies from some lousy bullet shot from a distance has no hope of entering heaven'. The Madurai general duly fell in with the request; Raghava was dispatched with a sword thrust. There were reports that he was seen at that very moment entering the gods' temple at Srirangam some 40 miles away and merging into the stone image of the deity. Rather like today's Jihadists who think that by murdering people in the name of God they will enjoy the favours of seventy-two virgins in heaven, as late as the seventeenth century Indian warriors clung to the comforting belief that by dying in battle they would be embraced by the beautiful dancing girls of the gods. But then we are all prey, are we not, to wishful thinking? What is the purpose of the after-life if not to restore the balance; to offset the lives of those who have not been rewarded enough, or suffered too much in this?

What is so striking is that these attitudes can persist for centuries or lie buried only to reappear again in times of stress. A Western anthropologist who worked in north-eastern Sri Lanka at the height of the recent civil war discovered while living amongst the warriors of the Tamil Tigers that, like many Hindu warriors several thousand years earlier, they still thought of war as play—*vilaiyattu*. Combat was thought of as a game without fixed rules, rather like the game of dice, which in classical Indian thought is the main preoccupation of the God Shiva. As David Shulman writes, some of her interviews with the Tiger soldiers could have come straight out of the playful, often ironic verses of the *Mahabharata*, which also tells of soldiers dancing into battle (Shulman, 2018: 32).

Now, the social anthropologist Ernest Gellner claimed that humans present the picture of the most extensive behavioural variation of any species, but that every cultural community is characterised by powerful norms that are deeply held and difficult to challenge when they underpin a society's institutions, shape its world views and largely determine its religious beliefs. In the New World, things were very different. Take the Aztec way of war that didn't carry the inflections of the world beyond their own. Not only was the New World not in contact with the civilisations across the Atlantic, but, more surprisingly, it was not even in contact with others like the Inca thousands of miles to the south. Even so, what is striking in the absence of any relationship between the Old World and the New are the similarities between the two worlds. Organised political power was the salient feature of society. War was waged by armies that were divided into companies. Many of the weapons would have been familiar too: bows and arrows, swords and slings. But of course, the differences were also critical. The Aztecs had no guns: they had not learned of gunpowder from the Chinese. They also had no seaworthy ships, just canoes, rafts and reed boats. So even if they had known about the Old World, they could not have sailed there. They could not have 'discovered' Europe as the Europeans 'discovered' them.

And these points of contrast eventually proved fatal. The Aztecs had no cavalry. The Spanish brought their horses with them, and they made a difference. And then there were the non-material features. The Aztecs were largely ignorant of the history of the peoples who had preceded them. Without writing, historical memory fades fast. The Spanish conqueror Cortes might have been illiterate, but his advisers knew their military history, especially the accounts by Greek and Roman historians of their own encounters with civilisations very different from their own. And the Spanish recognised that war is a matter of knowledge, which is why military history is so important. We are expected to learn not just from our own mistakes, but also from the mistakes of others.

What the Spanish found most surprising of all was the ritualistic nature of Aztec warfare. Battles were great pieces of choreography. The main aim was not to kill soldiers, but to capture them in one-to-one combat. Weapons were deliberately designed to bleed and weaken an opponent, not kill him. At the height of the Aztec empire the English were engaged in a brutal civil war, the Wars of the Roses (1451–85). The death rate at the Battle of Towton (1471) was the largest in English history. In 1996, workmen at a construction site uncovered a mass grave which revealed bodies that had been hacked to pieces. One exhumed specimen known as 'Towton 25' had had the front of his skull bisected but not before his skull had been pierced by another deep wound, a horizontal cut from a blade across the back. How different was the Aztec way of war which aimed at the capture, not death of men? One historian puts it rather well: 'they were taking a sample of the opposing army rather than trying to wipe it out' (MacGregor, 2018: 191). The great warriors would often break ranks so that they could individually go in search of captives who could be taken alive; they would try to disarm them by a blow to the legs, by cutting a hamstring or smashing a knee. The aim was to bring them back home intact so that they could be sacrificed to the gods. Neil MacGregor in his book *Living with the Gods* (2018) argues that even ritual sacrifice in the Aztec empire was an attempt to mitigate violence, to ritualise it and bring it under control.

But there may be a more mundane explanation for why the Aztecs were surprised by the lethal single-mindedness with which the Spanish invaders fought. The peoples of the New World had never experienced the nomadic invasions from the Eurasian steppes. The real difference, suggests one writer, is that the civilisations of the New World never had to deal with the nomads who had preyed upon the great civilisations of the Eurasian world. And in the absence of nomads, battles in the New World lacked the ruthlessness and attendant lethality which the Eurasian tradition cultivated in Europe and China. The

Aztecs had not been exposed to the concept of efficiency in battle and paid for that with their lives (Dyer, 2004: 125). Or to put it differently, there was little selective pressure to drive evolution which is why they were still trapped in the Bronze Age when they first encountered the Spanish. If Cortes and his men had perished, another army of conquistadors would have followed them from Spain.

One of the great what-ifs of history is what might have occurred had the Chinese and not the Spanish discovered the New World. In theory, a Chinese fleet could have sailed past the Ryukyus, calling in on Japan on the way before setting out across the north Pacific, taking the route which Magellan took in 1521. Conquest, however, would have been unlikely, and the Chinese state would have had no interest at all in converting the Aztecs or the Incas to Daoism or Buddhism. For that matter they would probably have been less struck than the Spanish by the cleanliness of their cities (Cook, 2001: 1011).

Setting counter-factual history aside, what the Chinese did accomplish earlier on was extraordinary, culturally as well as technologically. For a start, of all the past's chief commentators on war, Sun Tzu is probably the best known and the most often quoted. Unfortunately, despite having one of the most famous names in the world, we know almost nothing about the author. We don't know whether his writing and his life meshed together. His personal life was lost in the chaotic times in which he lived (the so-called Period of the Warring Kingdoms). We cannot even glimpse him through the people with whom he interacted, more is the pity. But then again scholars in the twelfth century doubted whether he existed; he may have been one general, or several who lived at different times. There is no evidence of his involvement in the only battle attributed to him in 506 BCE. Sun-Tzu may not have been a person at all but a collection of ideas. We will never know for certain.

When it comes to war, every society produces its own 'business model' and China was no different. The socio-economic transformation of Chinese society in the pre-modern era saw the introduction of iron weapons, cavalry and distinctive infantry units. In turn, this required the expansion of the levy on peasants who were needed to man them. In fact, when added to the provisioning of horses and the forging of iron weapons, these demands would have taxed the resources of any agrarian society, even one as rich as Imperial China. No wonder then that in *The Art of War* you will find Sun Tzu writing: 'those who are adept in waging war do not require a second levy of conscripts nor more than one provisioning'. It is a classic example of how there are features of his philosophy of war that speak to the immediate concerns of his own day. Many centuries later, as the tax base expanded, China was able to put even greater forces into the field. The Sung dynasty (907–1276 CE) was able to maintain an army of 1.5 million soldiers—the largest standing army in history up to then. And the country remained the dominant technological power in war until the eighteenth century. Many of my Chinese students don't know this. Most would have difficulty naming more than a few of their country's greatest battles. Chinese emperors did not go on campaign. In China, the rhythms and cadences of major war and its battles are not deeply ingrained in the national imagination as they are in the West. The Chinese empire was run by bureaucrats steeped in Confucianism, and Confucian philosophers tended to downplay the heroic. The military classics that have come down to us— seven in all—encouraged their readers to see war as an intellectual exercise, involving stratagems and clever manoeuvres. This has misled historians into thinking that the Chinese put less emphasis on brute power than the Europeans. The reality is quite different—just look at the size of China today and compare it with what it was in the days of the Warring Kingdoms.

WHY WAR?

In a world of artificially intelligent machines, robots and hypersonic missiles you may well ask whether culture will still be important? I think it will. One of the great mysteries of history is why the Europeans, and not the Chinese, produced the industrial revolution. Back in 1248, for example, the English polymath Roger Bacon received a gift of Chinese firecrackers. He was able to reverse engineer the powdery substance which ignited explosively when lit and was able to pass on the formula in his epistle: *The Secret Workings of Art and Nature and on the Nullity of Magic* (Dolman, 2016: 30). Bacon predicted everything from rockets to cannons and in every case the Chinese got there first. They invented everything from the first machine gun to the first rockets. But they never really grasped the revolutionary nature of the technology certainly in the last decades of the Imperial era. Indeed, one of the guns that was captured by the British during the Opium War (1840–2) after the fall of Dinghai dated back to 1601. China feels that it lost its place in the hierarchy of world powers because it didn't have the industrial revolution first. That is why its leaders are so determined to come out on top in the next industrial revolution. Hence the artificial intelligence (AI) race with the United States, which has just begun. Whether you choose to call it AI or, as many prefer, 'machine learning', it is set to change the character of war profoundly, and this time China intends to be in the vanguard of the change.

So, to the last question: is there a Western way of war, too? The American historian Victor Davis Hanson thinks so and traces it back to the days of the ancient Greeks. John Keegan, the British historian who revolutionised the study of military history in his book *The Face of Battle* popularised the idea. And it provides an engaging theme—the fight for freedom. Battle in the Greek world, we are told by Hanson, was a contest between equals.

> Infantrymen marched out not to save their livelihood, not even their
> ancestral homes, but rather for an *idea*: that no enemy march uncon-

154

tested through the plains of Greece, that in Themistocles' words, 'no man becomes inferior to, or gives way before another' (Hanson, 2000).

If you really buy into the belief that the Greeks fought for the concept of freedom, then you may conclude that there is a critical connection between the West's own fitness—from its own reproductive point of view—and its contribution to the general fitness of mankind. The story persists to this day—it is a central trope of the *Star Trek* franchise where the Federation (a 'humans only club' according to Klingon lore) brings freedom to the further reaches of the Universe.

It is an idea that has a long back story, which can be traced back to Etienne de La Boetie's *Discourse on Voluntary Servitude* (1576). What was so important, he wrote of the Greco–Persian wars, was that the struggle represented not so much a fight of Greeks against Persians as a victory of liberty over domination (La Boetie, 2016: 6). The problem with such approaches is that they are largely a retrospective invention that take big battles out of the historical setting in which they were fought. They assume a default position, a supposed cultural norm—freedom which has been absent for most of European history but against which other ways of war are deemed to be inferior. They encourage us to take insufficient account of the achievements of others. Hanson has written a book called *Why the West Has Won* to show that superior thinking about war, technology and logistics enabled the Western powers to impose themselves on the rest of the world for 300 years. It would be equally possible, however, to write a book called *Why the West Has Lost* and to account for a long list of Western defeats at the hands of non-Western peoples: Carrhae (53 BCE), when the Romans failed to conquer Persia; Hattin (1187), where the Crusaders were trounced; Adowa (1896), where the Italians failed in their first bid to colonise Ethiopia; and Tsushima (1905), where the Japanese navy sank a European fleet (the Russian). None of these defeats were without impact on the way the defeated thought about themselves.

In the end, it is difficult to sustain the thesis that there has been a Western way of war which reaches deep into the past—as far back as the Greeks. Though, it is true enough that since the days of Machiavelli Western writers have engaged in a dialogue with the ancient world to better understand how their own age differs. In rediscovering many of the ancient classics, they did not attempt to copy them. The discovery inspired competition, not mimicry. Machiavelli himself was perfectly aware that the Roman army had been vulnerable to enemies such as the Parthians precisely because it had failed to devise a technological solution to the problems they posed. Sixteenth century Europe now had guns.

It is probably best, all things being equal, not to drop the concept of a 'way of war' entirely but instead to understand why it has such appeal. It aspires less to narrate a history than reverse engineer a culture in a vain attempt to discover its essence. It encourages us to identify immutable features of cultural identity when nothing that is historical is immutable. Nietzsche warned us famously against this. In *Twilight of the Idols*, he speaks of the challenge of what he called 'Egyptianism', which he thought was a characteristic vice of philosophers who were always trying to drain a concept of blood and 'mummify' it. And they did so by abstracting the concept from history, its ontogeny Tinbergen might have said, and reconstructing it as an abstraction. Euclidean figures and arithmetical truths have no history, but everything else does. 'Only that which has no history', Nietzsche argued, can be defined (Geuss, 2017: 188). I would suggest that many cultural ways of fighting exist and can be well documented, but others have nothing to do with history and everything to do with the needs of the moment. They are often summoned into existence when most needed by politicians. But this too is an excellent example of how the history of war as a subject of study can fuel our continuing interest in possibilities yet to be exploited. We look to the past for a reason: to redirect our attention to the present.

A Wrinkle in Time?

'Whoever lives for the sake of combat has an interest in the enemy staying alive' (Nietzsche, 1986).

When told of the nuclear bombing of Hiroshima, Churchill, resorting to a biblical analogy to express his feelings, described the bomb as the 'Second Coming in wrath'. Only a few years later, in the United States, children would be facing weekly drills which required them to scuttle under their desks so that they might survive a nuclear attack. Afterwards they would brush themselves off while the teacher led them in a song, usually 'God Bless America', or sometimes 'My Country 'tis of Thee'. Similar drills are held in many schools today, but they are intended to prepare children for mass shootings rather than bombs dropped by foreign powers. Violence in American life, in some shape or form, is rarely out of the frame for long.

We can place the atomic bombing of Japan in the larger context of the history of technology. We invented axes by 'chipping' or 'flaking' them out of large pieces of stone. We then went on to fashion spears, and then bows, which first appeared in the Neolithic period and which doubled the range of firepower. We continued to rely on muscle power for thousands of years. Then gunpowder took war into the chemical age. The invention of the atomic bomb was even more revolutionary for it broke with the past, with ballistics, chemistry and aeronautics, which can all be regarded as extensions of the gunpowder revolution. The bomb that was dropped on Hiroshima did not explode because of the blending of chemicals; it exploded because of the humanly engineered change in the very nature of matter (Appleyard, 1992: 22).

In the event, the bombers were not sent off to their missions, and the missiles weren't fired from land-based silos or submarines. Instead, the world watched Hollywood renditions of the apocalypse like *The Bedford Incident* and *Dr Strangelove*, or to give the movie its full title *Dr Strangelove, or How I Learned to Stop Worrying and Love The Bomb*. Hollywood's version of nuclear war was less admonitory than entertaining, perhaps, suggests Martin Amis, because the subject was so far beyond human comprehension that it resisted 'frontal assault'. What the movies suggested implicitly, for those awake enough to decode the subliminal message, was that Great Power war had reached the end of the line, an end apparently implicit at the beginning—in our own violent instincts that had now misfired and threatened to undermine the conditions of existence itself. One of the first expressions of that fear can be traced back much earlier to the ambition of Jules Verne's Captain Nemo to take to the seas in his state of the art submarine to sink the world's great armadas and thus war itself.

Of course, ontogeny strictly describes a development with an end result; history has no end state, or none at least that it is possible to discern. In ontogenetic terms, however, Hiroshima was presented at the time by some writers, not just as the logical end of industrialised warfare but also the traumatic end of a historical cycle that reached back to the origins of war. It was seen by the novelist E L Doctorow as 'a kind of *inoculation* and while this hypothetical benefit... cannot acquit those who ordered it of their moral responsibility for sufferings that were all too real, it does at best suggest those sufferings were not in vain' (MacGregor, 1998: 30). Had he lived to see it, the philosopher Hegel might well have read into the bombing of Nagasaki a few days later as an example of what he called the 'cunning of reason' at work; history moves in ways that often escape our understanding at the time. In this case, the atomic scientists effectively discredited modern warfare at the very moment of the Allies' greater success. 'Hiroshima opened the age of nuclear war; hopefully Nagasaki sealed it' (Ibid). As one of the characters in Don DeLillo's novel *End Zone* remarks: 'Nagasaki was an embarrassment to the art of war... I think what will happen in the not-too-distant future is that we will have humane wars' (DeLillo, 1986: 81).

Indeed, if we are interested in dialectical thinking, why not also invoke the work of Alvin and Heidi Toffler? In their book *War and Anti-War*, they argue that modern warfare had reached the 'point of dialectical negation'—history is going into reverse, and we are busy inventing weapons that minimise lethality (Toffler and Toffler, 1983: 163). And indeed, the militaries of the world are developing a new range of weaponry including acoustic devices that shatter windows, electromagnetic pulse beams designed to knock down an individual, and chemical agents that can act as calmatives. We will soon be able to take our pick from a range of kinetic, mechanical, chemical, biological, microwave and laser weapons that one day soon may allow us to even take death out of the equation.

But that belief too, depends on another questionable teleological myth, namely that every advance of civilisation represents an attempt by human beings in their dealings with each other to control their untamed animal impulses, and to sublimate and transform them culturally. The idea that we become more civilised, and violence decreases as a result, is to be found in Steven Pinker's book *The Better Angels of Our Nature* and its even more affirmative sequel, *Enlightenment Now*. What his critics would argue is that the history he relates does not necessarily reveal the process he wishes to demonstrate. Our behaviour may have become more transparent and to that extent violence brought under greater control, but there is no real evidence that we like each other any more than we did a few centuries ago. The claim is merely an article of faith, along with the belief that eventually religion will wither on the vine, for which there is no confirmatory evidence at all.

But what is certainly true is that there is still a nuclear taboo, and it has nothing to do with empathy for others. War, as Clausewitz told us, has a tendency towards what he called 'the absolute'; there is a tendency for it to become apolitical, to escape political control. The point is made in the movie *Crimson Tide*. Set on an American nuclear submarine as the world lurches towards war, the captain asks his Executive Officer whether it was a mistake to drop the bomb on Hiroshima to which he replies that Clausewitz would probably have thought so. For if the purpose of war is to serve a political end, its true nature is to serve its own ends. In a nuclear exchange, the true enemy would be war itself. That is why the politicians are frightened of its use.

Unfortunately, we are not out of the woods yet. The Americans are modernising their nuclear force; the Russians are developing a new generation of nuclear weapons. But neither they nor the Chinese will want to use them if they can avoid doing so. For the destructive power of nuclear weapons defies comprehension. A single Ohio-class ballistic missile submarine can carry twenty-four ballistic missiles each with eight 100 kiloton warheads. Each warhead is over six times more powerful than the bomb dropped on Hiroshima. Individually, nuclear weapons have the potential for mass destruction; collectively, a nuclear war could destroy the civilisation we have managed to build.

Looking back to 1945, we can understand why it seemed to many at the time as if war had outlived its evolutionary lifespan—that it had finally exhausted its evolutionary possibilities. Artificial intelligence and cyberspace suggest to the contrary, alas, that war is continuing to evolve in new and disturbing ways. Anyway it would be dreadfully grim to conclude, would it not, that what we will face in the future is what has happened in the past. If true, this might mean that we will be condemned to retreat further into it. War, claims Judge Holden in Cormac McCarthy's seminal novel *Blood Meridian*, 'was always there, before Man was, war waited for him. The ultimate trade awaiting its ultimate practitioner' (McCarthy, 2010: 127). Holden expresses McCarthy's own personal belief that we will never be rid of war because violence is embedded too deeply in our biological and cultural DNA (Evans, 2011). If there is an iron rule in the history of war, however, it is probably this: in constantly transcending the historical matrix in which it is born, it is able to exploit what is unchanging, our passions and emotional needs, our psychological dispositions and our constant search for meaning—that is how it has always functioned. War has always been an affair of the heart. And only when there has been a change of human nature might it become truly dysfunctional for the first time.

4

FUNCTIONS

So far, we have seen why war became part of our behavioural repertoire: how culture fuels it and how over time its character is subject to change. But how does it actually work? Before answering that question, let's consider another human practice—marriage. And let's begin by invoking a striking example of 'woke speak' which appeared in a letter in *The Times Literary Supplement* in March 2019 (Shane, 2019). Sure of her knowledge of history, which as it turned out was not very great, the author wrote in a review of the book *Love, Inc* by Laurie Essig: 'The married unit has always been a tool designed by and for the state—one that consolidated and created whiteness, wealth and heterosexuality'. Unfortunately, she was way off pitch on every count.

To begin with, marriage is not a creation of the state; it can be traced back at least 70,000 years, long before the state appeared. We are the only species to contract into formal relationships. Chimpanzees don't marry. Females are especially promiscuous and try to mate with as many senior males as possible. Because mothers only go back into heat when they have weaned their young, aggressive males will often kill the offspring to bring females back to sexual availability. For women in human relationships, marriage, not casual sex, has often been the best survival strategy, and in many societies still is. But here is where the similarity ends. Even in a loveless union, there is the consolation of having a child, and a marriage often endures because legitimacy is all important. The derogatory term 'son of a bitch' is such a powerful insult, not because it slanders one's mother, but because it calls into question one's legitimacy and therefore one's social position.

What also makes us different from chimps is the sexual division of labour. Early on, men hunted animals and women gathered plants, and the food was shared back at camp. Male chimps, by contrast, rarely share food with each other, although occasionally they do with females for sexual favours. Sharing gave rise to a family structure peculiar to human beings from which the practice of marriage first arose. With the invention of agriculture went the demarcation of land and people and the rise of family alliances and alignments. In post Stone Age societies, marriage became important for reinforcing political dominance hierarchies. A wife came to serve as a marker of a man's status. The clothing and jewellery she wore were usually a mark of her husband's status, not her own.

The cultural mechanisms that generate marriage have also constantly changed over the centuries—think of the courtly love poetry of the Middle Ages, the romantic novels of the eighteenth century, and the chick-lit that young girls read today. And some of you may recall from Orwell's dystopian vision of the future *1984*, the love's-young-dream rubbish that came off the printing presses of the Ministry of Truth. Marriage also has a distinctive cultural history (if you believe Marco Polo, the inhabitants of Xichang offered their wives to any visitor). In the West, women had to battle hard to win the 'right' to keep their own property. And as for the heterosexuality that Laurie Essig thinks bedevils the married state across cultures, same-sex marriages were known in Native American societies centuries ago; same-sex unions were also a feature of ancient Greece. Think of the Theban soldiers of the Sacred Band who were encouraged to enter into marriage bonds with each other so they would fight all the harder in battle to save the ones they loved most. These days, you can even enter into virtual marriages, too.

But, more than anything else, marriage serves a function, which is why it is to be found in every society and every age. It taps into the basic human need for sex and companionship. Human beings, said the philosopher Schopenhauer, only huddle together when the weather is cold. But that is far from true. We are social animals who need to forge close social and emotional bonds with others, as well as generate heirs. We also need passion in our brief lives though this is often dismissed by materialists. An especially vivid example of this is a paper written by the economist and Nobel Laureate Gary Becker in 1973 in which he hypothesised a mythical meeting in a forest between two people, male and female (rather tellingly M+F in his paper) who agree to exchange skills in cookery and car maintenance. Tellingly, in the few places in the paper in which he mentioned love, he put the word in quotes.

'War is a world, not an event', writes Svetlana Alexievich (Alexievich, 2017: 17). Indeed, it is. War has a life of its own, and it intersects with our lives in ways that we don't always understand, but if it is a world of its own, it is one which has two different but intersecting dimensions.

Historians encourage us to think of war largely in instrumental terms, i.e., largely in terms of politics. The instrumental dimension is that in which force is applied by the state or a political actor. Whether Greek city states, or Chinese Warring Kingdoms, or the Khanate of the Mongols, they have all had political ambitions, namely to augment their power and increase their wealth. As such, war is a rational instrument of state policy. As Clausewitz insists, war is or should be, 'the continuation of politics by other means'. It is a near-perfect formulation which is why it is quoted all the time, but no-one likes to be fixed in a formulated phrase, particularly when it is not of one's own coinage. And unfortunately, Clausewitz's dictum occludes more than it reveals. For without the human element—its existential dimension, war would be quite different.

'There were great numbers of young men who had never been in a war and were consequently far from unwilling to join in this one'. The quote comes from Thucydides' *History*, and you will find it inscribed on the walls of the Imperial War Museum in London. Many young men who go to war don't make it back; many more return home disillusioned, but for a lucky few, it is everything they hoped it would be and more. It is quite literally life-changing. As William Broyles, a US Vietnam veteran writes, 'if you come back whole, you bring back with you the knowledge that you have explored regions of your soul that in most men will always remain uncharted'. It is the only way, he adds, in which men can touch 'the mythic domain' (Mueller, 2010: 4). The phrase takes us back to our discussion of myths and their importance in our lives—it gives voice to an idea that some of us might prefer to evade, and others fear to express. But clearly there are people for whom the very act of going to war offers a chance to live more intensely. War is driven by such existential factors as gendered expectations—the need to prove oneself a man, by the age old need of the young to excel, by the social demands of class, all of which involve what it means to be human in a world saturated with public and private violence.

The mythic domain of war above all encompasses the individuality of experience. You and I might think that we should only go to war as a last resort, out of necessity, not desire, or a feverish search for glory. We may both believe that there is equal truth in the ordinary. But anyone who is conversant with military history will know that there are men who throw themselves into battle willingly enough. What the warrior prizes above all else is the recognition of his fellow men, and he is willing to hazard his life (as well of course, to take the lives of others) in order to secure it. He is willing to fight for honour, or a medal, or a flag, not because they have any intrinsic value in themselves, but because they are desired by others. Exclusive to the human species is desire—we desire not what we want but what others esteem. In some cases, we desire to outdo others—to rob them of what we wish to possess: their reputation.

That is why it serves little purpose to ask why so many men were willing to travel with Alexander all the way to the Indus and with Napoleon to Moscow. You and I may think it is a long way to go only to be killed, yet isn't there something humbling about the length of the journey? In Alexander's army, they were all volunteers; in Napoleon's army, many were conscripts, but there were also others who had followed him on campaign for years. What they wanted from war was the experience of involving themselves in something whose value was outside the self. It would be wrong to say they were trying to find some meaning in life; I think few warriors ever go to war for that. What they wanted instead, was the experience of being alive.

In *Heart of Darkness*, Marlow speaks of travelling to the 'culminating point' of his experience. The fact that for some war is a terminus, the place where the warrior ends up, is no help of course if you are trying to get somewhere else. But warriors have a desire to deny themselves nothing, and in so doing find themselves between two poles of existence. On the one hand, a determination to live life to the full, and on the other, a determination to take risks that most of us would not think of taking. And while most young men have joined up over the ages not really knowing what they are getting themselves into and have been robbed of their illusions very quickly, others in later life recall the personal acts of kindness and the friendships forged which are often far more intense than those they will ever know at home. War, above all, allows some men to discover their true selves—a man who thinks himself a coward can find himself a hero in the heat of battle; the inauthentic hero may discover that he is not as heroic as he once thought. That is one of the reasons some men embark upon a unique quest: to find glory in battle.

Memes: The Search for Glory

'Vix duellis nuper idoneus / Et militavi non sine Gloria' (Lately I have lived amidst battles credibly enough / and not without glory fought). This is an epigraph to Henry Reed's Lessons of the War to which he returns at the end in the final verses of his poem.

> Things may be the same again: and we must fight
> Not in the hope of winning but rather of keeping
> Something alive: So that we meet our end
> It may be said that we tackled whatever we could
> That battle-fit we lived and though defeated
> Not without glory fought (Hennessey, 2009).

The passage appears at the conclusion of Patrick Hennessey's book The Junior Officers' Reading Club. Every war involves long periods of boredom, but it is the battles that make it all worthwhile for some. The trouble is that these days we engage in fire-fights more than set-piece battles, while our enemies lack the romance of the Ashanti or the Zulus or even the Afghans of the past; they have been cut down to size. They are a sorry bunch of ethno-nationalists, military entrepreneurs who seize every moment to capitalise on the misery of others, Jihadists checking in their Kalashnikovs with their prayer mats and the internal exiles from life looking for anything that will divert them from the emptiness of their own lives. And we are rather conflicted about glory. Hennessey joined an army that he found was caught between a world that needs it and a society that looks for glory more often on a football pitch than on a battlefield (Hennessey, 2009). In the West, conditions have changed dramatically and for those for whom they have changed, the violent option, the hammer in the human behavioural 'tool kit' has become less practical, even less appealing.

In his Pulitzer Prize winning book, *The Right Stuff*, Tom Wolfe celebrated the lives of those young American men 'who sought glory in war' by becoming fighter pilots in the Korean War. Rapidly vanishing even then, however, were the days of aerial dogfights, so familiar to us from World War I and its most famous air ace, the German war hero Manfred von Richthofen, the 'Red Baron'. His nickname persists even today; it has been adopted by a pizza company, by a restaurant in Berlin Tegel airport, by a videogame and a Japanese anime series, and most famously of all, he's been transformed into Snoopy's arch nemesis by the cartoonist Charles Schultz. The Korean War (1950–3), as it happened, was the very last in which fighter pilots could compete with the early air aces. We find this conveyed rather poignantly in James Salter's novel, *The Hunters*. Salter was a West Pointer who became a fighter pilot and remained proud of his service to the end of his life. His pride is reflected in his autobiographical depiction of the hero of his novel, a young pilot who is driven by a 'compulsion to press close to death, to feel the purity that followed'. The airmen are described as 'knights in a game fit only for kings', though Salter tends to talk up the planes more than he does their pilots. 'Flashing like silverfish they broke through a low-blowing surf of clouds and into unmarked sky ... They were specks of metal moving through a prehistoric sky, contaminating an ocean of air with only their presence electrifying the heavens' (Salter, 1997: 69).

Some Korean War pilots later went on to work on the first manned space programme. What Wolfe called 'the right stuff' was courage—they were willing, even eager to take on the odds. It was not a quality, he added, that was much appreciated by the novelists of the time; it was the age, after all, of the anti-hero (McCrum, 2018: 268). And is it still appreciated by the movie makers of ours? Three decades separate the movie *Top Gun* (1987) from another *A Good Kill* (2015), and it shows. Where Tom Cruise duels with enemy pilots in an F-14, the drone pilots of the second movie operate 7,000 miles away, firing missiles at the behest of a CIA agent in the field. Where Cruise's character, Maverick, plays volleyball and rides horses in his spare time, Maj Thomas Egan gets drunk every night to forget the things he's witnessed not in the field but on a screen in his air-conditioned cabin.

And yet … young men and now women are still lured in by the search for something larger than themselves. Many would still like to write themselves into the history books or be honoured by their peers back home, and one way of doing that is to compete and even surpass the deeds of popular heroes. It is that very human aspiration that war exploits and which explains why it really does take on a life of its own. As René Girard wrote in his book *Deceit, Desire and the Novel*, we tend to attribute to our heroes a 'fullness of being' that we do not enjoy ourselves. That fullness of being can exist in the reader's imagination whether or not the novel is grounded in the realities of life. For the mimetic charge transcends the brutal reality of everyday life (Girard, 1965). It is also an example of a larger truth. Just as biologically we are the product of genes, so culturally we are the product of memes that may infect us, making us susceptible to the idea, for example, that it is glorious to die for one's country. That is why, suggested Barbara Ehrenreich, we should think of war as a self-replicating pattern of behaviour (Ehrenreich, 1997: 235). If she is right, then we might even think of it as contagious, and like any contagion, it can be fatal to the host. We may escape the imperatives of biology only to find ourselves entrapped by culture which has crueller imperatives of its own.

Unlike genes, which have no intelligent designer, memes can be designed in by politicians who are often abetted by poets. That is why the contemporary philosopher Slavoj Žižek talks of a 'military-poetic complex'. But are memes contagious in the same way as a virus—good for the meme, bad for the host? The philosopher William James thought that religion was a 'mystical germ'—it thrived because it created a sense of community among the believers (Dennett, 2006: 84). Richard Dawkins claims that, just as a virus parasitises a genetic mechanism of a host cell, when you plant a religious meme in a mind, such as the idea that you will be rewarded in heaven for martyrdom, it metaphorically parasitises a brain, turning it into a vehicle for its own propagation, though not, needless to say, the martyrs' (Dawkins, 1976: 207).

Martyrdom may indeed piggy-back on a much wider belief in the immortality of the soul, an appealing doctrine for all of us, even if it caters to wishful thinking. It is a powerful idea nonetheless. Seven centuries ago, it inspired young men in Europe to go on a crusade. We no longer hold them in fond memory today because we are encouraged to be so cynical about their motives. But many of them mortgaged their estates and in effect their families as well, entrusting them to the care of monasteries until such time as they returned, though many didn't (Riley-Smith, 1987: 256–7). The crusading spirit, which we were once taught to admire—we no longer do—may have been self-serving, but it owed its success to its peculiar ability to turn men's minds to serving the ends of the Christian faith. The crusading idea at least confronted knights with the idea that there was a larger purpose to warfare than the interminable quarrel over their own personal rights. And the authority of the Church at least anchored their warrior impulses to an ethical framework of sorts

(Keegan, 1993: 296). To be sure, the ideal had long degenerated before the crusading impulse flamed out.

If we jump forward to the twentieth century, we will find a vivid example of how pernicious memes can be. In his book *War of the World*, Niall Ferguson invokes the term 'virus of the mind' to suggest that in the twentieth century racism spread between peoples, not because it benefited them, but because it benefited racism (Ferguson, 2006: 111). But then again, not all memes are poisonous. Some ideas are good for us. They help keep a community united, and they encourage its members to bond together in times of danger. They often have an emotional power that seeds commitment to the group. Religion can indeed be a source of comfort; it can even steady nerves and allow people to find inner resources they never imagined they possessed.

But now, here is the real question, and it may have entered your mind already: do memes really exist? Memes, let us be clear, are hypothetical constructions. The idea was first floated by Dawkins back in 1976:

> A meme should be regarded as a unit of information residing in a brain. It has a definite structure realised in whatever medium the brain uses for storing information ... this is to distinguish it from phenotypic effects which are its consequences in the outside world (Dawkins, 1976: 192).

A meme, in other words, is merely a set of instructions, or to put it differently, the blueprint, not the product. It persists because it can be transmitted or copied, and its persistence is what makes it so dangerous. Dawkins, who by the way was one of Tinbergen's young researchers, produced an idea that has certainly caught on; today it is known far beyond the scientific conversation in which it was first coined.

Memes, let me reiterate, are inferred from observation of human behaviour; they can't be directly observed by putting them under a microscope or cultivating them in a petri-dish. They have their adherents like Susan Blackmore and Daniel Dennett, and their violent critics like the late Mary Midgley. Kevin Laland and Gillian Brown who once believed in them, but no longer do. But Dawkins' idea has become commonplace for a reason—it is catchy. If you like it, it is also parasitical: it tends to infect minds that come across it. Besides which, I would argue their actual existence is not that important. What makes the concept important, writes Dennett, is that it gets us to think about war's cross-cultural and cross-temporal appeal (Dennett, 2006: 350).

Explaining war away as mimetic may help us grasp how it exploits a very human predisposition for mimicry. And mimicry is central to our lives. We are in part, imitation machines. And in a digital age, ideas and images spread more quickly than ever; they often go viral. When an idea takes hold in millions of individual minds and is reinforced by repetition, it becomes a persistent thought, and a persistent thought can cross time and space. 'Achilles and Hector slain / fight, fight and fight again / in measureless memory', wrote the poet Edward Muir. They haven't stopped; they are fighting still.

Sportive Monsters

'Still is the bottom of the sea; who would guess that it harbours sportive monsters' (Nietzsche, 1998: 89). So wrote Nietzsche in his most poetic but also challenging work, *Thus Spoke Zarathustra* (in Part Two—*Of the Sublime Men*). Even today, he is still a controversial figure. For much of his life, he found himself out of harmony with his times; towards the end of it, confined in an asylum, he was out of harmony with himself. But he had a way of nailing down an argument in a vivid sentence or two, and the case he was making was that some human beings find sport in ruining the lives of others. Whether they see it as a sport or not, war attracts some very bad men, and it offers many others an opportunity to do some very bad things. It also breeds monsters. This is one of its most frightening realities. Some are already lost before they join the battle, others are claimed by the darkness it produces. It turns many otherwise blameless men into bad people. Every war confronts soldiers with the immediacy of moral choice, and not all of them behave as they have been trained to or for that matter would wish to. In the course of war, their psychic deterioration is often all too evident. Some men are so lost even to themselves that cruelty becomes natural to them, passing without notice in their minds.

We humans behave in very different ways. That is why, wrote the great English panjandrum G K Chesterton, it makes little sense to upbraid a lion for not being properly lion-like. In other words, we don't judge a lion by its general behaviour, but we do judge ourselves by our own actions. All lions, we claim, are brave, all donkeys are cowards, though a donkey, if asked, might well beg to differ. The same is not true of us largely because, as William James told us, we have far more cultural instincts than any other species and thus a greater range of behavioural traits. Some of us can be very inhumane which, regrettably, is often the mark of the species. At any time, even good people can be drawn into the nihilistic world that war often forges. Untethered to any moral code, when things go badly men will often kill with a good conscience. When a soldier is stripped of his socially acquired virtues and left in a moral vacuum, he is often in danger of returning to the primal state. Some men may even become so alienated from their own humanity that alienation is their way of being at home with themselves.

This is often true when they are encouraged by the knowledge that actions that in peacetime would lead to punishment are likely to be either sanctioned or simply overlooked. In the case of mercenaries and paramilitary units, which tend to thrive in conflict, there are few codes of honour to act as a restraint anyway. Soldiers are meant to be servants of the state, but war has always attracted its private contractors—men who because they wear a different uniform or no uniform at all are not deemed to make the state complicit in their own actions. They number among their ranks the Italian mercenaries who Machiavelli so much despised, as well as the *lansquenets*—seventeenth century mercenary German soldiers who were known for their unruly behaviour—and the members of the *Freikorps* who emerged from Germany's defeat in the First World War.

Probably the first novel to give these figures a voice was *The Adventures of Simplicius Simplicissimus*. It is a book with a long subtitle which was typical of the times: *The Description of the Life of a Strange Vagabond / Named Melchior Sternfels von Fuchshaim/ Where and How He Came Into This World/ What He Saw, Learned, Experienced and Endured in It;/ and Why He Left It Again of His Own Free Will/ Extremely Funny/ and Exceedingly Useful To Read*. It was not until the nineteenth century that the author was finally identified as Hans Jakob Christoffel von Grimmelshausen. The main theme of the story is quickly told. In the course of the Thirty Years War, the young Simplicius witnesses many senseless acts of wanton destruction. He describes as well the hideous tortures inflicted on his own family, and yet when later a mercenary himself, he finds himself entrapped in a life of wickedness by poverty and desperation. The mercenaries whom he joins at least offer him a family of sorts, though in the case of the leaders, grievance has become greed and opportunistic robbery for survival has long since become organised crime.

Grimmelshausen paints the picture of a world in which atrocities are both shocking and commonplace at the same time. Jacques Callot's pictures of the conflict that we've encountered already show peasant homesteads being pillaged and burned, women about to be raped and trees weighed down with the suspended bodies of civilians caught in the wrong place at the wrong time. *The Adventures of Simplicissimus* illustrates two recurring and popular motifs in the literature of the time—it shows the picture of a simple-minded man adapting himself to the absurdity and corruption of an age gone mad. And it depicts the grim humour of an age that, believing in nothing, could even laugh at its own anxieties. It was exactly at this time that Thomas Hobbes coined a wonderful phrase for the riot of private armies, warlords and criminal gangs who roamed around Europe, selling their services to the highest bidder. He called them 'worms in the intestines of the state' which were gradually sapping its life and diminishing its power (Hobbes, 1972: 375).

Two hundred and fifty years later we encounter the battle-hardened members of the German *Freikorps*. Its members came from a country that was so morally unhinged by defeat that many soldiers took refuge in the camaraderie of collective violence. One of them wrote in 1919: 'people told us that the war was over. That made us laugh. We ourselves *are* the war' (Ehrenreich, 1997: 151). Another of their number, Ernst von Salomon, wrote a highly revealing novel, *The Outlaws*. Salomon was an officer in the German Army before joining a *Freikorps* unit. He seems to have had some degree of self-awareness. The chapter titles of his novel are at least revealing: 1. The Dispersed; 2. The Conspirators; 3. The Criminal. These are the three stages through which his *Freikorps* members pass after the formal fighting between armies has stopped. And the reader is not spared a graphic description of their behaviour in the Baltic States where they relocated after the war.

> We burst into surprised crowds and stormed and shot and lashed out and hunted down. We drove the Latvians like hares across the fields and set fire to every house and pulverised every bridge to dust and

broke every telegraph pole. We threw the corpses into wells and threw hand grenades in after them. We killed everything that came into our hands, we burnt everything that would burn... There, where we had raged and where before had been houses, lay rubble, ashes and glowing beams like festering sores in a bare field... We lit a funeral pyre where more than dead material was burning; there our hopes were burnt, our longings; there burnt the bourgeois tablet, the laws and values of the civilised world... (Elias, 1996: 195).

Was such behaviour the result of personal choice, and individual psychology, or the product of circumstances? What is evident from reading Salomon's book is that he had no real insight into his own motives, although he was not only willing to admit to his darkest deeds but seems to have revelled in the anger that they were likely to evoke in others. But then, how often do we have an insight into our own? None of us unfortunately has a skeleton key that permits us to unlock the minds of other people. 'We don't know our own souls, let alone the souls of others', wrote Virginia Woolf. 'Human beings don't go hand in hand the whole stretch of the way. There's a virgin forest in each, a snowfield where even the print of birds' feet is unknown' (Carey, 2005: 23–4).

Only a novelist like Woolf herself can really know the interior lives of her own characters. Even a fictional character, however, even when vividly drawn by a great writer, may not know what makes him act badly. What makes people do what they do, and how much do they really understand their own impulses? Take for example Iago—one of Shakespeare's most famous villains. Iago is the ultimate 'sportive monster'—he toys with Othello and brings him to destruction. But what drives him on? The poet Coleridge talked of his 'motiveless malignancy'. For Iago 2, the man who betrays his commander repudiates everything that Iago 1 stood for: the ensign who would have died rather than allowed Othello's Colours to be captured in battle. We have known since Freud the extent to which we are prisoners of thoughts, fears and desires that we are not always consciously aware of. The point is that war offers us a stage on which our murderous impulses and desires can be played out, even if what is striking about Iago is that he becomes a monster off the battlefield, not on it (Bloom, 1999: 437). And in real life, malignancy is often motiveless too: war attracts people who have no motive to misbehave, political or otherwise, who join up for the opportunities it provides to engage in wickedness for its own sake.

Wickedness, however, doesn't make us any more interesting. Many of war's 'sportive monsters' today are rather pathetic creatures; they are often painfully banal. A recent report on the foreign fighters in Syria found that they tended to be 'thrill seekers' looking for adventure in a theatre where they thought they had impunity to act in any way they wished. Some of them were desperate to flee the oppressive emptiness of their lives back at home, though few who find themselves trapped in similar lives turn to terrorism to escape their predicament. Others had a hunger for experiences that could not be satisfied in the over policed societies of the Western world where risk taking is rarely unmediated (Darke, 2018: 12). What many were seeking was what a character in Chuck Palahniuk's novel *Fight Club* (1996) calls 'a near life experience'.

Given access to 500 hours of raw unfiltered footage of Jihadists filming each other often hours or days before mounting a suicide bombing, Thomas Small was able to see them in all their humanity. Wrestling with the traditional insecurities of all young men, they were idiotic, playful, plain stupid, and yes, murderous, willing to explode their way into our collective consciousness. In April 2004, while prepping his vehicle for a suicide attack, one of them posed in front of a camera. He took a fake number plate that he had made out of paper and held it to his face. Across the front, in Arabic script, is printed '72RWH' which, when turned around reads in English '72 virgins' (Small, 2018: 16). Such men do not always come into the world ready-made. Some become their characters by meeting with the challenges life throws at them, others as a result of chance (finding themselves in the wrong place at the wrong time). What is disturbing today is that they like posting videos of beheadings on social media which often go viral and transform them into the celebrities they aspire to become. Such behaviour calls to mind the claim by Norman Cousins: death is not the greatest loss of life: the greatest loss is what dies inside us while we are still alive (Black, 2018: 1).

Too often, in judging their actions we are guilty of what the social psychologist Philip Zimbardo calls the 'rush to the dispositional'. We try to find the roots of psychotic violence in individual psychology. But not all the evils of the world are born of dispositional tendencies; they often emerge from a specific context. We tend to ignore this because making sense of violence is usually a binary process: we tend to explain it away either by reference to the personal pathology of a soldier, or by reference to his society or culture and its unique biases and prejudices. But a soldier's true character is often revealed when he is placed in a unique context and forced to confront its unique challenges. When situational forces confront the individual with difficult choices, evil is driven not just by impulses unique to the person concerned, but also by situational forces such as peer pressure and group identity, and the failure of officers to exercise responsibility for the men under their command. Don't we all conform to peer pressure from time to time? To stick out can be dangerous. The Greeks knew that being ostracised, a word they coined, was a terrible fate; to be exiled from the city was a form of identity theft. The need to conform can be sufficiently strong to invalidate the moral rules of society that are meant to be internalised in the family and school, and when it comes to finding oneself under fire far from home, does anything else really matter than the opinion of one's peers?

Where Zimbardo goes further than many are willing to follow him is in his claim that we are entirely the victims of circumstances. He encourages us, when discussing evil, to take to heart Coleridge's profoundly dialectical intuition that extremes often meet. Don't forget that just as atrocities can be traced back to extreme situations, extreme acts of bravery can be traced back to the situations that evoked them too. The fact, he writes, that some of us are born brave allows us to draw a distinction between valour, which is innate, and bravery, which is situational too—an act born of the moment (Zimbardo, 2006: 275–7). That is why you can't court martial a soldier for not throwing himself on a grenade to save his friends. Goodness and evil cannot come to grips with each other without some common ground, and evil can take many forms, not all of them consciously malevolent. Ordinary people can be tricked by bad decisions or just bad luck: they can venture beyond the boundaries they know to be right only to find they cannot get back.

Given the brain's constitution and inputs, argues Zimbardo, its specific outputs—our behaviour—cannot but obey the laws of genetics. Functional magnetic resonance imaging (fMRI) brain scans can predict peoples' decisions up to 10 seconds before they are even conscious of having made them. If this is the case, then perhaps all acts, both heroic and aggressive, are the product of genetic inheritance and the environment in which we find ourselves. If that is true, then we are left with the rather disturbing thought that the traditional idea of moral responsibility, which presumes that people can choose to act well or badly, may be scientifically untenable. None of which detracts from the obvious that our lives are shaped for better and worse by our own actions and their inescapable consequences.

War and the Religious Appetites

We are a moral species. That is why it is so difficult to imagine war without religion. Take the famous story of David and

Goliath, which was captured in bronze by Donatello. We see a young boy with one foot poised on Goliath's severed head, holding his sling shot and pellets in his left hand and an outsized sword in his right. In real life (or so the Bible tells us), Goliath, standing seven-foot tall, encased in the latest Bronze Age armour, must have been a truly daunting figure. But then David had a few cards up his sleeve, which you won't find mentioned in the Bible. Goliath was probably suffering from gigantism, writes Malcolm Gladwell, one side-effect of which is a loss of peripheral vision. You can't always see what is going on around you, and David, we learn, danced around him like the youthful Muhammed Ali in his early encounters in the boxing ring. Possibly, poor old Goliath couldn't see what was happening much of the time. And David was armed with a sling, the deadliest weapon in the ancient world. Modern ballistics experts have found that a typical-size stone, hurled by a slinger from a distance of 30 metres with a velocity of 34 metres/second could either kill a man outright or knock him unconscious in a second. In other words, adds Gladwell, our heavily armed warrior had as much chance of prevailing against David as a Bronze Age warrior would have had against an opponent armed with a 0.45 automatic pistol (Gladwell, 2013: 12). True, but surely this also misses the point. If David had returned to the Israelite camp later in the day to be debriefed so that the army could engage in a typical exercise of 'lessons learned', he would have attributed his success almost certainly to the fact that his God was stronger than the God of the Philistines.

Sanctioned by priests through the ages, war has thrived. In the earliest years of tribal societies, the Gods were probably what one writer calls 'geopolitical lubricants' who forced both sides to honour the treaties they signed or suffer divine wrath for breaking them (Wright, 2009: 79). As the centuries rolled by, monotheistic deities stepped up to the plate. Victory for the Israelites depended not only on their martial skills but also on the seriousness with which they kept their covenant with their God (Ferguson, 1978). And in victory, the Chosen People knew what was expected of them. As Matt Ridley writes, Joshua was not being hypocritical when he killed 12,000 heathens in a day and gave thanks to the Lord afterwards by carving the Ten Commandments in stone, including the commandment 'Thou shalt not kill'. 'Like all group-selectionists, the Jewish God was considered to favour his own side' (Ridley, 1997: 192).

It is the function that religion serves that explains its power: religion meets various needs that are difficult to satisfy in its absence. The human mind is programmed for survival not truth, and if you see religion as a mechanism that gives some people a sense of meaning or purpose or direction in their lives then it is one of the factors that can make life more bearable. And the same is true of war, which has taken on much of the colouring and language of religion from the beginning. In fact, the two are inextricably interlinked. Both, after all, feed off the same passions, which is why we must look at religion at some length, and not dismiss it, as some atheists do, as merely an object of anthropological curiosity. Long gone are the days when it was possible to believe that it would disappear, fatally holed beneath the waterline by Enlightenment scepticism.

There are many scientific explanations for why we have religious beliefs and why they persist, why in short 'God won't go away' (Lewis-Williams, 2016: 290–1). One suggestion is that religion may be 'wired-in'. Neuro-scientists focus on the anterior convexity of the frontal lobe and inferior parietal lobe and their reciprocal interconnections. It is those interconnections that generate concepts of gods, powers and spirits. A sense of awe, ecstasy, or transcendence can also be attributed to altered states of consciousness that may lead people to think there is something cosmically larger than themselves and the life they observe every day. This may be the result of a spill over between the neural circuits of the brain which can be generated in turn by long periods of meditation and fasting. Paul Bloom attributes this to the dualistic nature of our minds which predisposes us to attribute consciousness to other things (such as the spirits of a place). We are psychologically predisposed to see a purpose in all things. We have a taste for teleology which turns into an appetite for religious explanation (Pagel, 2012: 140). This ability to ascribe agency to some other being—the understanding, for example, that lions are programmed to attack—is a survival mechanism. By knowing that a lion's purpose is to hunt, we can second guess its intentions and escape harm if we are lucky. We want events to have causes and, in discovering them, to establish a pattern that is sufficiently coherent to serve as a guide in the future.

Daniel Dennett refers as well to what he calls the 'intentional stance'. We may be inclined to see God in everything because of our sense of agency. We are causal beings who need to know why things happen as they do. Even chimps shake their fists at the sky in a thunderstorm. It is not an alpha male's challenge to another alpha male that can't be seen. Jane Goodall, who once observed this behaviour, put it down to 'an uncomprehending surge of emotion' (Wright, 2009: 482). And that is probably how our distant ancestors reacted as well. Later, with the development of consciousness, they chose to attribute storms to angry spirits. As Edward Taylor argued a century ago: 'spirits are simply personified causes' (Ibid: 470). From there it was only a step—though a big one—towards what philosophers call the argument from design. The fact that day followed night, and always had, and presumably always would, was deemed to be evidence of the reliability of the Creator. And the argument that God is the ultimate explanation of all things followed on naturally. He was the *ens necessarium*, the necessary being, without which there would be nothing at all. Even the most conservative of medieval theologians refused to believe he had created Himself, in other words that he had literally bootstrapped himself into existence (Holt, 2012: 108).

But then theology has never been as important as theologians like to think. If we confine our study just to theology, we won't grasp religion's great emotional power. If we focus only on the 'truth' of a given revelation, we will make the mistake of construing religion in purely metaphysical terms. Religion has an adaptive value that theology doesn't. Theological arguments have rarely converted anyone; religious experiences have.

In *The Varieties of Religious Experience*, a book based on the lectures that he delivered at the University of St Andrews in 1903, we find an eloquent defence by William James of experience against theology as the true backbone of most religious beliefs. It is the 'religious appetites', he argued, that explain why religion is an intrinsic and possibly ineliminable part of the human condition. It is the rituals and holy words and social practices that have done most of the psychological and emotional heavy-lifting. They have all helped to bind a congregation together by offering its members security, even consolation, against the evils of the world. Such a functional explanation of religion, not surprisingly, has rarely found favour amongst theologians or philosophers.

For James, religion not only encouraged devotion, it demanded it. It not only induced intellectual assent, it engendered emotional commitment. In that sense, it had far-reaching implications for human behaviour (James, 2003). Two especially striking examples are prayer and martyrdom. Prayer as an adjunctive repetitive behaviour (like nail biting or hair twisting which tend to calm us down) is a version of an otherwise helpful habit of asking other people for help. It also gives us the comforting illusion that if we pray long enough we can somehow control our fate (Asma, 2018: 178). When it came to martyrdom, the early Christians profoundly objected to Julian the Apostate's reluctance to persecute them because it had deprived them of the opportunity to martyr themselves. The church historian Sozomen, writing eighty years after Julian's death, insisted that the last pagan emperor had refrained from employing fire and sword against the beleaguered Christian community 'solely from envy of their *glory*' (Kelly, 2019: 24). It is an interesting conjecture, for martyrs were the celebrities of their day.

Glory, as we have seen, is also the lifeblood of war, and in its pursuit many warriors have discovered a vocation akin to a religious calling. Having a gun in one's hands, claimed Franklin Miller, was like a 'religious experience'. A former Green Beret, he received the Congressional Medal of Honor as well as seven other medals during his short career (Miller, 2003: 112). It is combat, wrote another American warrior Andrew Exum that is the adrenaline rush, the great leap of faith. It is combat which redeems war as a profession, for it gives the individual the chance to express his commitment to country and unit through the medium of sacrifice (Exum, 2005: 233). Another American soldier, Karl Marlantes, the author of the best-selling novel *Matterhorn* (2010), writing about his experiences as a former Marine in Vietnam, claims that any man who is engaged in killing or being killed struggles with a situation approaching the sacred in its terror and contact with the infinite. Many people might argue that there is nothing remotely spiritual about combat, but he would beg to disagree. Like a mystical or religious experience, it involves the constant awareness of one's own death, it requires total focus on the present moment, and it requires you to value other people's lives above your own: the band of brothers, a community that is not that different from a religious congregation. 'The big difference is that the mystic sees heaven and the warrior sees hell. Whether combat is the dark side of the same vision, or something only equivalent in intensity, I simply do not know' (Marlantes, 2011: 7–8).

Shawn Nelson, an American soldier fighting in Mogadishu in 1993, compared combat flow to an epiphany. 'Close to death he had never felt so alive; the only thing he could compare it to was the feeling that he found sometimes when he surfed, when he was inside the tube of a big wave and everything around him was energy and motion and he was being carried along by some terrific force' (Evans, 2017: 167). Such people are role models and their exploits live on. James liked saints because they were role models, and in their acts of charity genuinely created a social force. It followed that their sacrifice, in the language of Darwinism, had genuine adaptive value. 'One fire kindles another, and without the other, trust in human worth which they show, the rest of us would live in spiritual stagnancy' (James, 2003: 302). In wartime too, acts of self-sacrifice and heroism often inspire others to fight on when all appears to be lost. For those of us who will never be called upon to make a sacrifice for others, those who do are important—their lives have an emblematic, almost archetypal quality that makes their final act of self-sacrifice also our own. We read stories of heroic self-sacrifice for a reason, writes the cognitive psychologist Keith Oatley in his book *The Passionate Muse*. Reading really does make us different people; we tend to view life more positively. If we only watched the news on television every night, we would soon lose our faith in ourselves; reading an inspiring war novel makes it more likely that we can hang on to the idea of human goodness. Of course, we know in our hearts that the men who fight for us are often violent and never fully in control of their emotions; that they are often heroic, but usually as the last resort. Like most of us, they are weak, fallible human beings though they are also capable of moments of great strength of will. But we choose to think that our heroes do not have feet of clay in our need to believe in someone worth believing in.

Times change of course and we with them, and it is moot to ask whether, in a future in which warriors sit behind screens and robots do much of the fighting, courage will be much lauded. There is a striking passage in Orwell's account of working-class life in his most famous work of social commentary *The Road to Wigan Pier*. Orwell was not enthused by the contemporary vision of a world of machines which would save the workers from hard labour: 'machines to save thought, machines to save pain, hygiene, efficiency, organisation, more hygiene, more efficiency, more organisation, more machines' (Orwell, 1989: 180). His point was this: all mechanical progress aims not only at eliminating the need for labour but also at eliminating danger. It promises a world in which nothing can go wrong. He was critical of H G Wells' novel *Men Like Gods* for painting the picture of a world in which there was no need for godlike virtues, while peopling it at the same time with men who had them in abundance. Wasn't the whole direction of mechanical progress the elimination of physical effort? Why then insist on retaining the virtues we need to counter it? In a world from which danger has been eliminated, what need of physical courage? In a world in which there is no need for physical labour, what need of physical strength? 'Question not the need', rails Lear, when one of his ungrateful daughters seeks to reduce his retinue of servants. But Orwell did question the need, arguing that all the qualities we admire in human beings can only function in opposition to some challenge, difficulty or disaster. He came out firmly on the side of effort. He lampooned the 'softness' of his own society and what he called its 'degeneracy of vision'. Both the sentiment and the language in which it is expressed betray his times, but the general point he made is still well-taken. Does courage have any value in a totally mechanical world? Which is why he commended Bernard Shaw for imagining a Utopia in which a statue is erected to Falstaff, the first man who ever made a speech in favour of cowardice.

Will the same be true of war in the future? If it is indeed a 'human thing', and if we look at the qualities that we find most alluring: comradeship, trust in one another, a willingness to sacrifice oneself for a friend, what need of any of these in a world in which war is fought by robots? One day, we may find ourselves living in the world conjured up by Douglas Adams in his comic novel *Dirk Gently's Holistic Detective Agency*. In that world there are robots for every task you can think of. There is even a deluxe version called an Electric Monk which will believe in God for you.

A Warning to the Curious

War and technology are joined at the hip though it sometimes takes a vivid imagination to anticipate the consequences of our inventions. In *The World Set Free* (1914), H G Wells was the first writer to imagine an atomic war. Back in 1914, few if any scientists saw the possibility that atomic weapons might be built, and even those who did were blind to the future that would follow upon their use. Even Wells, I suspect, was not able to foresee where the story might eventually lead. Science fiction often fails us for that reason. As another science fiction writer, Frederik Pohl once remarked, there is no point anticipating the invention of the car if your imagination falls short of foreseeing the traffic jam.

As far as we know, in the almost 4 billion years of natural selection-driven evolution, only one species has developed this ability to think forward. It's a form of evolved curiosity that sets us apart from the rest of the animal kingdom. And it's been vital to war. Think of it this way. Viewed from one angle, war is an unmitigated evil that blights the lives of all of us and destroys the hopes of many. Viewed from another, you might come up with a striking counterpoint to this view. It powers scientific progress. Look again and you may catch a glimpse of one of the most powerful psychological mechanisms that distinguishes our species—the power of intellectual curiosity, which governments are all too eager to exploit. One of its greatest 'success' stories was the invention of the atomic bomb that was dropped on Japan in 1945. At Hiroshima, the future that Wells had envisaged finally caught up with us.

Many nightmarish visions were birthed by the bombing. One of the bleakest was Aldous Huxley's novel *Apes and Essence* (1948), which offered the reader a picture of a post-apocalyptic California that had reverted to barbarism. Mutated children are killed at birth, sex is seasonal and a 'Lord of the Flies' god, the Bomb-Bringer, is appeased with prayers and human sacrifice. Huxley lifted the title of the novel from Shakespeare's play *Measure for Measure* in which Isabella speaks of man's 'glassy essence like an angry ape' which 'plays such fantastic tricks before high heaven / as make the angels weep'. In Huxley's moral parable, the apes have taken over. Intelligent baboons fight twenty-first century war with scientific greats like Einstein as mascots on a leash. All of this by the way is very unfair to apes. Animals do not kill for honour or reputation or even for the pleasure of it. Most are not gratuitously cruel; unlike us, they harbour no racial or cultural prejudices. They don't kill their own kind because they have a circumcised penis, or an uncalloused palm, marking them out in the case of the former as Jews or in the case of the latter, members of the hated bourgeoisie. And if they did possess atomic bombs, they wouldn't set out to kill each other for ideological principles.

Apes are also quite unlike us in another way. We are distinguished by what the Elephant Boy in Kipling's tale calls 'satiable curiosity'. It is not, of course an attribute that is unique to us. New Caledonian crows are especially curious creatures. Through trial, error and observation, baby crows learn how to fashion sticks into barbed hooks with which to extract grubs from holes, but young humans are much more adept at noticing the novel, the accidental and the serendipitous, and once their curiosity is peaked, they are unlikely to stop. When we light upon a new discovery, a dopamine 'hit' is delivered to the reward pathways of our brains which makes it likely that we won't forget what we have discovered (Henderson, 2017: 196).

Personality also plays a much larger role for us than it does for any other animal. And personal traits in science vary enormously. Some scientists pursue a goal-minded approach, others are great experimentalists who stumble upon and explain away the unexpected. But the most indispensable characteristic is a passion for work and a near-obsessive interest in seeing it through to a conclusion. Scientists are driven by the need to succeed, so much so that many have no scruple about where their work might lead. An especially egregious example is Wernher von Braun who made the big mistake, after emigrating to the United States and working on the Apollo space programme, of allowing Hollywood to turn his life into a biopic. The 1960 movie *I Aim at the Stars* is rarely remembered today without the comedian Mort Sahl's suggested subtitle, 'But Sometimes I Hit London'. During the war, he had worked on the V1/V2 missile programmes which had led to the second blitz of the city in the summer of 1944. In a famous scene in the movie, von Braun tells his mother about the deal he has cut with Hitler to further his research. 'Long ago, they said witches made a pact with the Devil so they could fly on broomsticks', his mother remarks. Her son replies: 'my broomsticks fly without the Devil's help. But if they didn't, I guess I'd be willing to sign with him'. In real life he did indeed make his pact with the Devil. In recent years, evidence has emerged of his complicity in the death of 12,000 slave labourers in the factories that built his missiles. We now know that he was fully conversant with this fact at the time (Piszkiewicz, 1998: 50–4).

There is another psychological trait that allows war to exploit our human curiosity: social deviance. Scientists are often 'odd men out'. They are removed from society or remove themselves at an early age because they are considered to be different. But then, perhaps all creativity is deviant. As Nadine Gordimer wrote of her own profession as a writer, 'powers of observation heightened beyond the normal imply extraordinary dis-involvement'— the ability to stand outside society and its norms (Atwood, 2002: 29). Scientists, after all, are often much more enthralled by the elegance of a design or a mathematical formula than they are about the uses to which their inventions may be put. Is not the creative process itself often blind? Doesn't pride in technical achievement cancel out every other consideration?

There is little reason, alas, to wax optimistic about the future. The greatest threat to us has always been our own ingenuity. It is killing the planet thanks to global warming. It has been responsible for pushing up population growth since the mid-nineteenth century. It has also taken war into two new domains: space and cyberspace. We also live with a new threat that our ingenuity brings. In Frederik Pohl's novel, *The Cool War* (1981), the Great Powers of the day find themselves in conflict once again. Trying to sabotage the economy of its rival, one devises a new weapon, a deadly flu virus that targets thirty- to fifty-year-old adults, 'prime of life' individuals who run business and government in the industrialised countries (Pohl, 1981). Today you can shut down a whole industry by planting a cyber virus. In the future, workers may have no jobs to go back to.

But biological warfare is still a clear and present danger. In 2011, two scientific teams, one in Wisconsin and another in the Netherlands showed that it was surprisingly easy to make the influenza virus both more virulent and more transmissible. Three years later, the US government put an end to any further research for fear of where scientific curiosity might lead. The Covid-19 pandemic should concentrate our minds even more—in the early days, there were rumours aplenty that it had been concocted in a biological warfare laboratory in Wuhan. Scientists, as we have seen, have often been suspect because the questions they ask are often shaped by the needs of war, not science. It is possible that sometime soon a scientist, whether for profit or ideological conviction, may put herself in the service, not of a state but some terrorist group. Even now, someone you've never heard of may be working on a biological weapon of war even more terrifying than the atomic bomb.

ON THE EDGE OF TOMORROW

One of today's fashionable scientific ideas is that there are multiple universes out there. If so, perhaps there is an alternative planet Earth where the rules of evolution are different. What might this planet look like? Perhaps, one in which there are no Great Powers and so no Great Power conflicts. Perhaps, a world in which there are no civil wars between people of different ethnic identifies, religious beliefs or political allegiances. Perhaps, the inhabitants share only one identity and have never dissolved into tribes. Perhaps, no species has ever fought in the name of different gods because it has only ever worshipped one, or even none. There might even be a universe which has found that getting rid of war is just a matter of changing the channel.

Unfortunately, we face a problem. 'You're on Earth, there's no cure for this'. This is the reality we confront, and it was put pithily by Samuel Beckett in *End Game*. Beckett, to be sure, was an arch pessimist: he wrote plays that depicted life as a punishment for being born. He thought that life was meaningless, and tedious to boot, and that its tedium could only be relieved from time to time by excessive acts of violence. But he was surely right about one thing—this is our world and there is no escaping from it, which is why we must understand what makes us tick.

We are about to enter what is often called a post-human world. We are seemingly intent on engineering the next generation of humans by using gene-editing technologies like CRISPR, melding our minds with artificial intelligence and with hardware more resilient than our shambling bodies. We are intent on introducing brain–computer interfaces, though our thoughts are embodied in networks of millions of neurons, using a code that neuroscientists have still not cracked. We expect that AI will supercharge the ability of computers to process data and deduce patterns beyond human cognition. And all of these changes, so we expect, will impact upon war in ways that have been explored already by Hollywood and many science fiction authors. France's Defence Innovation Agency has set up a team of sci-fi writers to propose scenarios that might not occur to military planners while trying to anchor the scenarios they come up with to what is humanly possible. All of which of course, may call into question whether war will continue to remain 'the human thing', and how far, or for how much longer, Tinbergen's model can be invoked to explain it.

Most sci-fi writers in fact remain rooted in reality; very few conjure up a utopian world where war is no longer a feature of life. In Liu Cixin's novel *The Supernova Era*, everyone over the age of thirteen has been killed by radiation from a supernova. The world is run by children. Wars are still fought but this time for fun, the organising principle of their new life. The logic of war, the author suggests, is encoded in our DNA, now transmuted into a bloody form of entertainment. In other works, human beings are upgraded through neurological interventions. Published over forty years ago, Joe Haldeman's book *The Forever War* (1974) offers the reader a bleak vision of a post-human future in which soldiers learn everything they know not in a classroom but through 'feedback kinesthesis' (a form of cyber-netics) wired into a collective brain. They are implanted with pseudo-memories, in this case vivid pictures of an extra-galactic race who at this stage no-one has seen, carrying out atrocities against distant colonists. As it happens, the memories are not real but manufactured. But they are real enough in the soldiers' minds to help commanders to tap into their primal urges and so to cultivate their aggressive instincts. And Haldeman suggests they don't have to tap down very far. For the aim is not to bypass human rationality, but to get soldiers to think sub-rationally. 'Back in the twentieth century they had established to every-body's satisfaction that "I was just following orders" was an inad-equate excuse for inhuman conduct ... But what can you do when the orders come from deep down in the puppet master of the Unconscious' (Haldeman, 1999: 67). As it happens, we may not have to delve that far to implant false memories. We can already coax the mind to create richly detailed virtual worlds that we've never actually experienced but may think we have thanks to the use of the drug DMT (dimethyltryptamine).

In other fictional iterations of the future, we find intelligent machines interacting with their human operators. In Leo Frankowski's novel *A Boy and His Tank*, a group of soldiers on an alien planet come to bond with their smart tanks and their smart tanks to bond with them. One of the most telling lines in the book is the commander's: 'Kid, if your tank is loyal, you don't have to be'. What the novel captures, as we shall see is a future reality: we will be treating machines as collaborators not tools, members of the same team. Then there is the *Terminator* fran-chise in which the machines have taken over and written us out of the script. In SkyNet, which first appeared on the cinema screen in 1984, we have a hostile super intelligence that we will ourselves have created. It's our last invention. A famous article in *Wired* once asked a provocative question: does the future still need us? Some science fiction writers suggest that it won't be very long before we will have to ask the same question about war.

Let's try, however, to add some perspective to the past and the future. The past does not exist unless frozen in the fossil record, or in stone or in the few written histories that have survived. Perhaps, says Septimus in Tom Stoppard's play *Arcadia*, one day the missing plays of Sophocles will be pieced together from the papyrus rolls that we are constantly discovering from excavating the trash heaps of the ancient world. But the unrecorded future also doesn't exist. It is at most a possibility. This is why predictions date quickly. If you had gone to see Stanley Kubrick's masterpiece *2001: A Space Odyssey*, as I did when it first hit the screens in 1968, you might have hoped that you would be flying to the moon within thirty years courtesy of Pan Am. But the airline went out of business in 1991, and we haven't even set foot on the moon again since 1972. The value of science fiction at its best is that it captures a world on the brink, a world already here, conceived, but not yet born. The best sci-fi authors are able not only to inhabit the historical moment but also to transcend it at the same time by seizing upon the contemporary trends that they find most interesting and extrapolating them into the future. Science fiction differs from mainstream fiction in many respects, but one of the most important is that it observes tendencies of behaviour 'that exist but are barely recognised in contemporary life' (Amis, 2012: 82).

In fact, in none of the stories I have related has war been transformed beyond the point of ready recognition, which is why I'm going to argue that Tinbergen's model will still be useful for some time to come. Even Liu Cixin's world engages with a question increasingly urgent to our own. War has always entertained children—think of the toy soldiers I used to play with when I was a child. War begins in childhood with the stories that children learn and the games they play. Today, sitting behind computer screens, they can zap aliens or villains closer to home; they are already locked into a world of war which one day may become real enough. In the US, the military, always on the look-out for tomorrow's cyber warriors, now attend VR conventions to identify potential recruits, some as young as eleven. One day, predicts one author in a note of desperate resignation, we may choose to 'decorate' children for their hand-eye-coordination skills (Graham, 2011: 222).

But we may be about to embark on a quite different journey. Possibly, the best way to think of the soldier of the future is as an integrated mobile weapons system like a Bradley fighting vehicle or an Abrams tank, part human, part machine, 'an F-16 on legs' as one member of the US Army Future Force Warrior Program put it some years ago ('The March of Technology', *The Economist*, 10 June 2006). Soldiers are rapidly becoming the technology they use. And even though in our technology-fixated times our lives are not simply defined by machines—we still have emotional lives, as well as aspirations and beliefs, we live in technology's shadow. Every age leaves its imprint on humanity and ours will too, a point that was first made in another novel by H G Wells, one that you may well have read.

Man-Machine Hybrids

The War of the Worlds (1898) is still probably his most popular tale. It tells of the invasion of Earth by a race of Martians who are far more intelligent than humans, and even more ruthless. Their weapons are more deadly still—they roam around the English countryside where they have first landed in vast machines and use poison gas and death rays with complete impunity. Imagining the future, of course doesn't mean creating it, and so far, at least, Martians have not arrived. But Wells anticipated the use of poisoned gas on the battlefields of the Western front a few years later, and his death rays are probably not far behind. But what is most striking about the novel is that in a brilliant note towards the end of the book when the Martians are destroyed unexpectedly by human bacteria against which they have no immunity, Wells casts doubt about whether it's appropriate to draw any absolute distinction between a Martian and a human being. As the Artillery Man declares, with unbounded enthusiasm, after looking into one of the Martians' abandoned machines: 'Just imagine this: four or five of their fighting machines suddenly starting off—heat rays, right and left, and not a Martian in 'em but men who have learned the way how'. What the Artillery Man envisages is the coming of an era in which human beings will undergo an evolutionary change; they will become indistinguishable from the machines they use. If you like, they will be rather like an F16—with legs.

We are already heading in that direction. We are already undergoing something of an ontological shift in the way we regard the world. Computer-mediated communication is already changing the world we know, just as biotechnology is beginning to change our bodies. We now talk of 'programming' our careers and 'interfacing' with life. The merging of cognitive intelligence and computer processing is additionally far more advanced than we commonly recognise. It is used for treating a wide range of medical conditions, and we are investing heavily in neural interface technologies that allow us to use a computer by brainpower alone, such as voice recognition programs. This could in time be extended into the military to create the first generation of iSoldiers.

To understand what may be happening, let's go back to where we began with Leo Tolstoy. Tolstoy was neither a philosopher nor a historian; he was a novelist, and his strengths lay in his acute observation of how people tended to react in critical situations. From his own military experience, he concluded that battles are lost or won thanks to isolated incidents of bravery and cowardice by groups of men who frequently have little contact with each other. Remember though that he didn't claim that there wasn't a pattern behind victory or defeat in battle, only that we had not yet discovered it. He believed, in fact, that there was a law of 'social dynamics'. He genuinely believed that eventually science would discover what he called the 'human differential' and that it would be disclosed by methods akin to Newtonian calculus. He looked forward to the day when scientists would be able to crack the human code.

There is no law of 'social dynamics', or, if there is, we still haven't discovered it. But could we produce something very similar through data-mining? There is a technique in manufacturing called Six Sigma that is designed to eliminate errors in the manufacturing process. It uses statistical techniques to eliminate glitches, the famous 'ghost in the machine'. A company that has a 99.99% success rate will make only 3.4 errors per million opportunities to err. In the future, might not social life be similarly objectified and reduced to a correct set of variables? In 2015, Mark Zuckerberg told Stephen Hawking that he suspected there was a fundamental mathematical law underlying all human relationships that governs the balance of who and what you care about (Jurgenson, 2019: 109). If true, then the discovery of the 'human differential' may not lie too far in the future.

But let's keep in mind that data as such has no absolute epistemological value, and number-crunching is not the only methodology to use. A society obsessed with data-driven stocktaking would be a fundamentally impoverished place. Learning to code behaviour wouldn't allow us to fully understand the complex interaction between the use of violence, the political context that gives it shape and the technical limitations and ethical constraints (if any) that determine success or failure. Nonetheless, in later life Tinbergen suspected that none of these thoughts would make any difference. In the second edition of his book *The Study of Instinct* (1969), he complained that even in his own field of study, ethology, a disproportionately greater effort was being channelled into finding out what caused animals to behave as they did rather than to discover the effects of their behaviour. He suspected why. 'It's tempting to ponder this over-emphasis on studies of causation. I believe that it is partly due to the fact that as the development of physics and chemistry have shown, knowledge of the causes underlying natural events provides us with the power to manipulate these events and 'bully' them into subservience' (Midgley, 2006: 153). This was the period when scientists were beginning to hope that we could change human behaviour by changing human nature.

Some scientists even hoped that decoding human behaviour would enable us to get out of the war business altogether. Could we not screen out, for example, the supposed gene for aggressive behaviour? It was not, at the time, an entirely fanciful ambition. If there was a gene for aggression and if it had been war's port of entry into history, couldn't we modify it for our own purposes, our own intelligent designs? Wasn't the destiny of humanity encoded in the double helix? Neither of these questions was absurd. For there is indeed a biology of fate. There is, for example, an alcoholic gene though few who carry it become alcoholics. Genes may give us a predisposition to behave in certain ways, but circumstances kick in immediately when we are born. The family we are born into or our country of birth may indeed change the odds of good and bad behaviour. Those fortunate enough to be able to make a life choice can cheat fate even when the odds are stacked against them.

But we now know what Tinbergen suspected; there isn't a single gene that makes us aggressive. And anyway, even if such a gene did exist it would be a useless tool to adapt because of the inter-connection between culture and biology. We may well have cracked the human genome, discovering the 3 billion biochemical letters of DNA that store our genetic inheritance. But it has taken far longer than the optimists originally expected to disentangle the function of individual genes and how they work together. Genes are not independent units. What brings DNA to life is the cellular environment in which it is embedded. Genetic theorists with little biochemical understanding have been profoundly misled by some of the metaphors that Francis Crick, the man who co-discovered DNA, applied to describe its workings. One of the most quoted is the idea of 'self-replicating' molecules. Left in a test tube, however, they would not be able to make copies of themselves. As Tinbergen's model shows, our behaviour is determined as much by culture as it is by biology, or rather by the interaction of the two. So, even if we could identify a gene for aggression, we could only achieve so much in modifying it. And our efforts would not necessarily have much impact on the effects of our behaviour.

Still, the artificial enhancement of biological performance is a theme of many Hollywood movies such as the *Universal Soldier* franchise. In the first and best of the series, the UniSols are given enhanced self-healing abilities and superior strength. They are also highly aggressive and largely impervious to pain. The movie raises an important question about enhancement—what happens when we can select genes that we think will increase performance while not really understanding how particular gene combinations work. Whilst striving for enhanced abilities, physical or mental, might we also genetically diminish our capacity for compassion which is one of the themes of Roland Emmerich's film?

One day, however, thanks to the organic melding of human and machine, it may not be so easy to tell humans and thinking machines apart. One day, enhanced humans may be able to see better in the dark and hear the songs of a whale and run further and faster than any long-distance runner. At that point we may be on the cusp of a new age in which a completely new hominid may emerge. There have been seven that closely resembled us, some of whom overlapped with each other (we overlapped with *Homo erectus* and Neanderthals for thousands of years before they disappeared from the historical record). One of the disturbing features of evolution is that species overlap before one is eventually displaced by another.

Taming the Terminators?

There is nothing quite as arresting as a headline from *The Economist*. 'Taming the Terminator' was the striking title of an essay that appeared in early January 2019. It was referring to a Hollywood icon, surprisingly not an actor straight from central casting, but a machine that has been hovering in our overheated imagination ever since 1984 when the first Terminator movie hit the screen. In its briefing, *The Economist* claimed that the Campaign to stop Killer Robots—the attempt by a number of campaigning groups to stop countries from building fully autonomous, self-programming and self-targeting missiles had found a catchy slogan, which imaginatively combined two of the most fearful tropes of science fiction: a particularly powerful weapon capable of destroying us, allied to a non-human intelligence, greater than our own, which might find it difficult, or simply unnecessary to appreciate the value of human life, or the significance of its loss. How do we ourselves measure the weight of an individual life in war? The question is, would a robot really care? This anxiety is not entirely hyped-up. We know that sometime in the future, software will no longer be designed, but instead evolve by selection among minor variations. Possibly, our preferences—what we program them to do (like killing) will no longer be the predominant selection force. If, and when they become fully capable of thinking for themselves, will we find ourselves facing a final reckoning: 'Judgement Day' as it is called in the *Terminator* movies? (*The Economist*, 19 January 2019: 26).

If you have seen them, you will know that the problem begins when the US Defense Department switches on the SkyNet system and changes history for ever. There was a SkyNet moment of a kind in the market at 9:30 a.m. Eastern time on 21 August 2012 when Wall Street's biggest trading outfit, Knight Capital, switched on the new automated program for buying and selling shares. One of the functions of the automated trading system was to break up large orders into smaller ones which could then be executed individually. Unfortunately, the trading system didn't register that the smaller trades were being completed, so it kept tasking them again, creating an endless loop of trades. Before the programmers were able to identify and fix the problem, the software made more than 4 million deals, racking up US$7 billion in bad trades, and almost bankrupting the company. Most worrying of all, it all happened in 45 minutes. Of course, we should also remember that the system worked as it was designed to; an automatic circuit breaker that had been installed specifically for this purpose soon cut in. When trading restarted 5 seconds later, prices stabilised and most of the losses were recovered. Even so, trading machines put human traders out of business long ago, and as algorithms advance beyond investing and accounting, machines will be taking more and more strategic decisions themselves.

What we are discussing, of course, is the impact of artificial intelligence (AI). Can you recall when you first heard the term? I doubt it. It has been a theme of movies and books for years. Artificial intelligence may have made the headlines, but it has been flying our commercial jets since the 1970s, controlling elevators in rush hour traffic as well as playing matchmaker on dating sites for the lovelorn. What has made AI so visible today is the relentless advance of algorithm technology. The AlphaGo machine, which was developed to play the board game, clearly demonstrates that a machine is algorithmically capable of learning and developing creative strategies, as well as solving problems through experience. It was even able to generate rules for itself that its human programmers had not specified in advance.

It would seem that there is no amount of acquired knowledge that can't be crunched into code and made accessible to people who have no expertise at all. No wonder that in 2016 an IT company in Hong Kong put an algorithm on its main board (Harari, 2015: 232). We can see what is coming. Amazon was able to outfox people who had been in the business of shopkeeping for generations—the knowledge they once had is now little regarded. Who needs doctors when an app can measure your vital life signs and diagnose any illness from which you may be suffering? A company called Enlitic already operates an algorithm that can detect lung cancer nodules more accurately and quickly than a team of highly trained radiologists. Who needs professors when all knowledge will soon be online? Who needs to know how to drive a car when cars become driverless? Narrative Science, a Chicago based company expects that one day very soon computers will be researching, analysing, transcribing, drafting, editing, and sub-editing many of the articles we will read. Soon robots may be writing articles about their own future, as well as ours.

Let's try to get some perspective, however. For the moment, machines can do the jobs that we still can do, but they can do much better. Possibly, the most important of the jobs they will undertake in future are those we don't know we want done, but that is something we will only find out when we get there. Today, they can already fly a fighter plane and a B-52 bomber more reliably than a human pilot. And they would be excellent for patrolling streets and clearing minefields: in other words, doing all the regular routine jobs that soldiers are asked to undertake, but which put them in danger all the time. They are also good at doing jobs we cannot do, and only they can. We don't have the attention span to look at a screen for 24 hours. Machines are also better at managing other machines. They are not only simply better at monitoring risks, assembling information, analysing data (finding patterns, if they are there to be found) and reacting faster. Because they are not self-aware, they are not continually plagued by thinking about past mistakes or obsessing about an argument they have just had with another computer half an hour earlier. They are completely focused on the job they are doing. The real danger is that they will break down. The algorithms are going to be so complex that the machines will continue to malfunction, and someone will have to fix them. It is a dynamic called 'the paradox of automaton's last mile'. Militaries of the future need not give up the benefits of human judgement in order to get the benefits of automation. Automation can perform the essential tasks better than we can but probably we will still be needed as moral agents and failsafes. The US C-RAM system is a good example. Designed to protect US bases from rocket, artillery and mortar attacks, it has resulted in more precision and accuracy, but humans are still kept in the loop to verify that the target is in fact a rocket or mortar and that there are no friendly aircraft in the engagement zone (Wallace, 2015).

Nevertheless, it's important not to stray into the wilder fields of science fiction. AI is still basic. It cannot, so far do what all other animals can do without thinking: recognising others, interacting with the environment, instinctively knowing what's dangerous or not. The trouble is that though we know how to make machines think, we do not know how to make them thoughtful. That is why we both need each other.

One example of this is Alpha Zero which within twenty-one days went from being a sub-par player to becoming the best in history. It certainly defeated the Korean world champion, but it also broadened the scope of the strategies that human players can now use. Similarly, a program call Centaur, which has given chess players access to every game ever played, has doubled the number of chess grandmasters there are in the world. Machines are not replacing us; we are using them to become more intelligent and creative. Machines are not our competitors, as much as collaborators, even if in the popular mind the competition is getting fierce. As their intelligence grows, we will have to learn to treat them, not as tools, but collaborators. We will have to work with them, not just exploit them. The most comprehensive analysis of the factors influencing human-robot interaction—the multi-authored *A Meta-Analysis of Factors Affecting Trust in Human Robot Interaction* (2011) begins with a discussion of human–robot teamwork. Already, the extensive coding required to create the algorithms that guide autonomous systems requires many different programmers to work on the same program, with none of them knowing the whole package. For this reason, there's been a push towards programming that will allow a system to communicate its decision processes directly to its user and thus increase the interaction between human and non-human entities. And for that to work, they will have to build up feedback loops which will improve their social skills. Which is why, insists Lanier, it is wrong to think that AI will replace us in terms of rational thought or common sense. And though AI fantasists might claim that one day we will be able to automate wisdom, might we not at least agree that it may be a long time before AI systems are able to generate it (Lanier, 2017: 336)?

AI Awakenings

But what happens when machines begin to think for themselves? What might happen if we lose control? In August 2010, US Navy operators on the ground lost contact with a *Fire Scout* helicopter, an unmanned aerial vehicle that was programmed to return to base if ground communications failed. Instead of following its programmed flightpath, it steered for Washington DC. As it happened, the aircraft was not armed, and before manned aircraft could be scrambled to take it down the operators had regained control. It was a simple case of malfunction, and machines, as we know, malfunction all the time. The incident might have called to mind the movie *Stealth* (2005) in which an autonomous fighter jet, code named Extreme Deep Invader (EDI) disobeys orders and takes out a military target with dire results in terms of human casualties. The premise is that though it has not been programmed to act independently, its designers have given it an AI system that has developed its own rudimentary code of ethics which no-one notices until it is too late.

Before we get too anxious about our fate let's go back to Tinbergen's model.

Origins. The origin of artificial intelligence is to be found in our need to improve performance, and especially what makes us human: our evolving understanding of our own agency in history.

Cultural mechanisms. These play a role here too. In order to use AI more effectively, the US military is building a cloud-based virtual replication complex operating environment (i.e., a single synthetic environment), the military version of the software that powers online video games such as *Fortnite*, a survivor zombie game with 125 million players. The military–entertainment complex is now as important as the military–industrial one was in the Cold War.

Ontogeny. Ontogeny or our evolving history shows that AI systems are merely the latest stage in the evolution of war. In its first AI strategy document in February 2019, the Pentagon tells us that it is poised to change the character of warfare once again. An equally intriguing question is whether it will also change its nature ('Battle Algorithm', *The Economist*, September 7, 2019). But that won't happen until they can genuinely think for themselves.

Functions. AI systems will continue to tap into the psychological and physiological factors that determine our lives. We have seen how we share many attributes with other animals. Indeed, we are like them in many more respects than we have cared to imagine, but we are also very unlike them in one respect more than any other. We are an imaginative, aspirational and intentional species. This allows us to understand reality and to reshape it at the same time (Fernandez-Armesto, 2019b). No other animal species can do this, which is why it is difficult to imagine any machine, however intelligent, replacing us soon. A machine doesn't have ideas.

Despite the constant interplay of chance and necessity, we are a species that sets itself goals. Like other animals, our lives are goal-directed; our instincts can be thought of as pulled towards attractors that help our growth, survival and reproduction as members of a social group. But we have many different purposes, thanks to culture. Other animals have purposes, but they do not appear to be conscious of them. And while they may well have a capacity to adapt, adjust and regulate their behaviour, we have a much greater capacity to change the way we behave by formulating ideas of how we should thanks to three unique features of our species.

First, our intelligence is motivated. Thanks to natural selection, we are governed by a mix of emotions, instincts and drives that are programmed into us so that we can reproduce. Natural selection gives us goals: to survive, and to dominate and control others. We are forced to balance those goals with our need to survive—we try to choose actions that are life-sustaining. Motivated intelligence is intensely social. The early twentieth century philosopher Edmund Husserl argued that a human being is 'a source of intentionality'. We attribute intentionality to the people with whom we find ourselves cooperating or competing. 'Orders of Intentionality' is a term the philosopher Daniel Dennett introduced to help us think about how social intelligence works. As Dennett writes, if I believe you to know something, then I can cope with one order of intentionality. If I believe that you believe that I know something, then I can cope with two. If I believe that you believe that my business partner believes that I know something, then I can cope with three. We humans regularly encounter at least three orders of intentionality in everyday life; Dennett believes that if need be, we can cope with up to five. This is what social intelligence requires; an entity that is not motivated is not one that can be networked into social life on other than the most basic terms (Dennett, 2017: 130).

Machines may soon be able to read our thoughts, but understanding them is a very different challenge. One of the best examples of this difference can be found in a conversation in William Gibson's novel *Neuromancer* (1984):

Can you read my mind, Finn?
Minds aren't read. See, you've still got the paradigms print gave you and you are barely print—literate. I can access your memory, but that's not the same as your mind (Gibson, 1993: 37).

Gibson is applying, quite correctly, a computer-mediated metaphor to explain a change in human subjectivity. The old metaphors related to the Gutenberg universe of print really are fading fast, but they still hold in one respect, as Finn admits. For we still don't program our lives, we live them, with all the messy compromises and negotiated rites of passage involved; we still rely on emotional intelligence to negotiate life successfully.

Secondly, unlike us, machines are also non-teleological. They don't set themselves ends to which to aspire. Normative ethicists are fond of organising their field into three different categories:

duty, virtue and utility. But although it was only the last of these that the philosopher Elizabeth Anscombe derisively termed 'teleological' for its exclusive attention to the results of an action, the truth is that all three are invested in questions of 'ends'. For many philosophers, agency is ultimately consequential: we have a responsibility to anticipate, as far as we can, the outcome of our own actions before deciding whether to act or not.

This explains why we ask questions all the time, such as: 'what am I doing here'—'why are they shooting at me?' 'Why am I taking risks?' 'Am I willing to die and for what: religion, country, family, or if they are in danger my friends who are serving with me?' All of these involve a sense of purpose, identifying an end to which we can aspire. A man who has not questioned the value of his own existence, claimed W H Auden is still a child. For Auden, the ability to ask questions about life constituted the ultimate privilege of being human (Auden, 2002: 179). War is perhaps the most intense experience of all, for in the course of it we may come to know ourselves much better. Which is not to deny that it also attracts what Joseph Conrad called the 'hollow men', those who are left emotionally detached, as well as nature's psychopaths who just go along for the experience and have no capacity to empathise with friend or foe.

In a letter that he wrote to a friend about one of his most famous characters, Augie Marsh, the novelist Saul Bellow insisted that his hero was the embodiment of a peculiar human trait: the willingness to serve others. He is a man who insists: 'For God's sake, make use of me, only do not use me to no purpose'. Surely, he added, the greatest human desire is to be used, or at least to be useful (Bellow, 2016). *Augie March* made Bellow famous. It is a picaresque and often surreal novel which includes an episode in which the hero joins the merchant navy (as Bellow did) at the onset of the Second World War and has his ship torpedoed (which Bellow's wasn't). He then endures a long trip in a lifeboat with a crazed survivor determined to explain the meaning of life and death to him. So far, so human. Being 'used' or 'useful' is part of the package together with everything else in life. Today's young Jihadists are often only too willing to martyr themselves; the wish to be useful can often end in martyrdom. A machine, by contrast may well be programmed to self-destruct, but it is not a choice and therefore not a gift, as it is for a soldier who throws himself on a grenade to save his friends.

To put it more simply, if reductively, human 'being' externalises itself in activity which is why *Homo sapiens* is also *Homo Faber*. Identity is derived from the work we do which has value in the eyes of others, and which because of this also allows us to value ourselves much more. It's this fusion of the inner and outer worlds that gives war its appeal. Many soldiers require not only implicit confirmation of their identity through everyday contact with others but an explicit and emotionally charged confirmation that others bestow on them.

Thirdly, the social world we inhabit is the product of rationality, not logic. Reason, not logic plays a central role in our lives, though we must not fall into the trap of thinking, as did our ancestors, that it is the human essence. As a species we are beyond any single classification. And that is because we are not always rational, and whenever we are, we don't always act reasonably. We are quite capable of course of being logical when we want to be. We invented mathematics and science, and both put an emphasis on logical deductions. But for most human activities we've discovered that logic can be dangerous because it is often contrary to common sense. The physicist Niels Bohr put it very well when he told a student: 'Stop being so bloody logical and start thinking!' This is not quite as savage a rejoinder as Robert Oppenheimer's remark to one of his own PhD students at Princeton's Institute for Advanced Study: 'You are so young and *already* you have achieved so little' (try to get away with a remark like this today). If you wanted to be wholly logical, you would soon find yourself facing the same dilemma as the young Wittgenstein. Believing that we could infer the logical structure of reality from the logical structure of language, he eventually came to recognise the attempt couldn't account for the illogical things that mark our lives, such as religion and aesthetic experience. Resigned to the fate of not being able to speak about them logically, he advised we shouldn't speak about them at all.

Because machines are governed by logic, they are remarkably good at learning competitive tasks with binary outcomes, but they would struggle if asked to make judgement calls. And here is where the real danger may lie. The everyday decisions that commanders take in the field will one day be taken by algorithms. When autonomous systems eventually arrive, we will have to encode them with some set of moral guidelines so that they can take morally informed life and death decisions. We will have to program in a utility factor: do they take out a target if there is a significant risk of collateral damage? If we accept that collateral damage can't be avoided, how much can it be mitigated? But that is where the real problem lies. We humans have found by trial and error that there is a critical difference between what you have a right to do in law, for example, and what can sometimes conflict with it—what is the right thing to do. Being better at making decisions is not the same as making better decisions. That is why I suspect that arming a robot to independently choose when or not to fire would be a war crime waiting to happen.

In fact, machine intelligence doesn't have to be superior to our own to be dangerous; in the absence of embodied intelligence it may be quite dumb. The real danger, in fact, may lie in outsourcing more and more key decisions to machines that are not nearly as smart as we are in navigating through life. We have come up with moral laws and conventions that date back millennia, but moral life is not algorithmic. This is the source of one of our main fears about 'autonomous systems'—they are likely to plough through life with complete indifference to the nuances of the social world we have constructed for ourselves.

So far, AI has been very effective in gaming. AlphaZero learned to play a chess grandmaster in nine hours and AlphaGo in thirteen days. Algorithms are also excellent at playing war games with well-defined rules which allow a multiplicity of possible moves, but which also prohibit others. But they are not so effective at playing games where players cheat (i.e., break the rules). And we break the rules all the time, not only because we are perverse (we often act 'out of character') but because we are also creative. A story you are not often told is that after Kasparov lost to IBM Deep Blue, he devised a new kind of chess (Advanced Chess) in which a computer and human act together against a machine, and tend to win every time. The combination proves unbeatable, and the reason? Humans simply are more creative, and thus more effective when teaming up with machines.

Creativity is the act of turning new and imaginative ideas into reality; it is a way of making connections between seemingly unrelated ideas. Machines can indeed recombine different ideas; programs can learn from their environment and increase their 'fitness value' and recombine those programs in turn to increase the fitness value of a new program. A US navy robot was able to do this when learning how to navigate its way successfully through a minefield (Denning, 2019: 349). But many scientists believe that the intelligence that we have developed to navigate through the social world is inherently social. It is networked through language, through conversation with other people, and is generated through social connectiveness. We often overlook this because we are encouraged to think that our brains are computers and our minds their software, but our brains are structured to produce multiple cross-connections which give rise to consciousness and that is true of most animals, even the smallest like ants. Consciousness and thought arise through the networking of actions in the brain which translate into actions outside it—behaviour. If that is indeed the case, then it may well be that human intelligence is not actually computable.

All this could change, of course, if genuinely self-conscious systems were to emerge that might shape their own evolution by rewriting the codes with which we have programmed them into a language we couldn't even begin to understand. This possibility is one of the challenges that Cambridge's Centre of the Study of Existential Risk is now pondering. Darwinian evolution, which has lasted for 4 billion years, is about to be superseded by secular intelligent design, and tomorrow's designers may not be us. We have been around for 200,000 years. Twelve other hominid species made it that far. We may not have much longer. Remember what happened when the Neanderthals no longer offered any competition. We didn't go out of the business of competing. As one writer observes, we merely redrew the battle lines, competing as nations, religions, races and ideologies and acquiring ever more lethal weapons of mass destruction. It's possible that our first competitive encounter with a non-human competition may soon be a software tweak away (Poundstone, 2019: 99).

That is why the fear that an intelligence greater than our own might one day turn upon us is no longer science fiction. It has morphed into a bad horror movie. For there is no reason to be confident that a super intelligence would feel any attachment to us. Or that it would have any emotional resonance or sympathy for us, even though it may have an algorithmic understanding of our behaviour. And what if it comes to identify us as bottlenecks in its own development?

We have to ask such questions because we are working in the dark. What many scientists suspect is that advanced AI is likely to be fundamentally alien. Nick Bostrom has argued that a biological extra-terrestrial race would probably have more in common with us than machine intelligence of our devising. If aliens do exist, they would presumably have developed drives and instincts very similar to our own, if we assume, as we must, that they are governed as we are by the law of natural selection. They would probably try to avoid bodily injury, to reproduce and seek security. There's no reason to think, however, that machine intelligence would necessarily have any of these desires. Bostrom has argued that intelligence is orthogonal to an entity's goals, such that any level of intelligence could in principle be combined with any final goal (Bostrom, 2012). This would mean that a super intelligent AI could have any set of values from playing the perfect game of chess to wiping out the competition. And although there's no reason to think that it would be inherently hostile to us, that doesn't mean it would value human life either, especially if it were to decide that our atoms could be used for something it might consider more useful.

Mention of aliens, nevertheless, puts me in mind of another possible outcome, a less menacing one, which is worth considering as it gets to the heart of Thucydides' understanding of war as 'the human thing'. In his book *The Eerie Silence*, Paul Davies asks the question: where are the aliens? The question has haunted us ever since it was first asked by Enrico Fermi. Davies comes up with an interesting answer. It's more than likely that any biological lifeform would find it impossible to undertake deep space exploration because of the physical challenges. Forget asteroid belts and gamma rays and radiation. Were a carbon life form to land on another planet, it would immediately be exposed to bacterial infections that might kill it off as quickly as the native peoples of the New World were killed off by smallpox which the Spanish brought with them. Quite probably, if there are civilisations out there older than our own, they will have dispatched robots to explore space. And as their intelligence continued to evolve, they may well have reached the conclusion that space exploration is not for them; they might well have decided unilaterally to abandon their mission. If so, then they are probably to be found parked in the coldest recesses of deep space working on mathematical equations quite beyond us (Davies, 2010). Even now, they may be orbiting the cool, steady glow of an M-dwarf star running endless simulations of the world around them.

Why would a super-intelligence wish to make war on us, any more than it would wish to explore the universe? In the SkyNet scenario, the machines nuke us; but what if they were to take all the high-tech weapons out of our hands for safe keeping? If they ever do switch out of the system, our militaries would probably find themselves astoundingly ignorant of even the basics of survival—how to navigate without GPS, or to communicate with one another without a computer link. Our survival skills are atrophying all the time.

Envoi

> There I saw one I knew and call him, crying
> Stetson! You were with me in the ships at Mylae (T S Eliot, *The Wasteland*, 1922).

Many of you may not share my own scepticism, my belief that our behaviour won't change any time soon and that we are likely to be stuck with war for some time yet. Let me be the first to admit that this is a cheerless note on which to end.

T S Eliot put the case better than I can in his poem *The Wasteland* (1922). If a contemporary British general had glanced at the poem, he would probably have dismissed it as unreadable; if he had bothered to read it, he might have denounced it as decadent. Well, let's not go there. It remains one of the seminal poems of the war-torn twentieth century. The reference to Mylae is to an obscure naval battle in the first Punic War. A Roman victory, their first at sea, which was fought in 260

BCE. Eliot could have cited a battle from the First World War that had only recently concluded though there are some oblique references to it in the poem. One is when he writes of the crowds crossing London Bridge: 'I had not thought death had undone so many'. The words are Dante's and describe the Damned. Here they refer to the survivors of war returning to a world that has been undone by it. Then a door opens on another scene—a woman in a London pub who refuses to bring children into the world. Her husband Albert is coming back from the war, but both will find each other much changed. But the point Eliot was making in citing an obscure naval battle fought two centuries before Christ was that every war is the same: one gives rise to another, as one power falls and another rises in its place. It is an endless cycle in which we find ourselves trapped. And the same is true of non-state actors too, who find themselves locked into age-old conflicts, revenging their ancestors or repaying old scores, and reproducing the same baseline cruelties. Even today, the Sunni–Shia rivalry in the Middle East is really the outcome of an ancient and deadly family dispute.

Will we ever see the end of war? Perhaps, one day, but for now just recall the long story of war that is woven into the deepest textures of human life. A Macedonian king makes it all the way to the Indus; a Chinese general executes a gaggle of silly girls for refusing to comply with his commands; an Italian artist shows battle in a new light, thanks to the art of perspective; a group of *Freikorps* soldiers run riot through a Baltic village; two aboriginal tribes in Australia are observed in the 1920s fighting in a way that hasn't changed in 7,000 years; an American soldier in Vietnam tries to be an actor in his own movie; a movie franchise shows a future in which our inventions have turned on us with a vengeance. And a Russian author writes the greatest novel about war that has yet been written or is ever likely to be. Shades of the past, intimations of the future, all rolled into the present time, the time it has taken to read this book.

BIBLIOGRAPHY

Adams, Thomas K., 'Future Warfare and the Decline of Human Decision Making', *Parameters*, 31, 4 (2001).

Ahern, Daniel, *Nietzsche as Cultural Physician*, University Park, PA: Penn State University Press, 1995.

Alexievich, Svetlana, *Boys in Zinc*, Andrew Bromfield (trans.), London: Penguin, 2017.

Allen, Barry, *Knowledge and Civilisation*, Boulder, CO: Westview, 2004.

Amis, Kingsley, *New Maps of Hell*, London: Penguin, 2012.

Amis, Les, *Commemorating Epimetheus*, West Lafayette, IN: Purdue University Press, 2009.

Appleyard, Bryan, *Understanding the Present: Science and the Soul of Modern Man*, London: Picador, 1992.

Armstrong, Karen, *The Great Transformation*, London: Atlantic Books, 2006.

Asma, Stephen, *Why We Need Religion*, Oxford: Oxford University Press, 2018.

Atwood, Margaret, *Negotiating with the Dead: A Writer on Writing*, Cambridge: Cambridge University Press, 2002.

Auden, W.H., *Lectures on Shakespeare*, Kirsch, Arthur (ed), Princeton, NJ: Princeton University Press, 2002.

Axe, David, 'An Iraqi Shi'ite Militia Now Has Ground Combat Robots,' *War is Boring*, 23 March 2015, https://warisboring.com/an-iraqi-shi-ite-militia-now-has-ground-combat-robots

Babel, Isaac, *Collected Stories*, London: Penguin, 1994.

BIBLIOGRAPHY

Baricco, Alessandro, *An Iliad: A Study of War*, Edinburgh: Canongate Books, 2008.

Barker, Ernest, *The Nation-State and National Self-Determination*, London: Fontana, 1969.

Barkow, Jerome H, Cosmides, Leda, and Tooby John, *The Adapted Mind: Evolutionary Psychology and the Generation of Culture*, Oxford: Oxford University Press, 1995.

Barnett, S, 'Cooperation, Conflict, Crowding and Stress: An Essay on Method', *Interdisciplinary Science Review*, 4, 2, (1979), pp. 106–31.

Bartov, Omer, *Murder in our Midst: Industrial Killing and Representation*, Oxford: Oxford University Press, 1996.

Bass, Thomas, 'Information Pathology' in Brockman, John (ed), *This Idea is Brilliant*, London: Black Swan, 2017, pp. 408–10.

Bateson, Patrick and Laland, Kevin, Tinbergen's Four Questions: An Appreciation and an Update, *Trends in Ecology and Evolution*, 28, 12, (2013), pp. 712–18.

Bauman, Zygmunt and Lyon, David, *Liquid Surveillance, A Conversation*, Cambridge: Polity, 2012.

Baxandall, Michael, *Painting and Experience in Fifteenth-Century Italy*, Oxford: Oxford University Press, 1972.

Bell, Clive, *Civilisation*, London: Chatto & Windus, 1928.

Bellow, Saul, *This is Simply Too Much to Think About: Collected Non-Fiction*, New York: Penguin, 2016.

Berger, John, *Understanding a Photograph*, London: Penguin, 2013.

Bering, Jesse, *The God Instinct: The Psychology of Souls, Destiny and the Meaning of Life*, London: Nicholas Brealey, 2011.

Black, Jeremy, *War and Technology*, Bloomington: Indiana University Press, 2013.

Black, Sue, *All That Remains: A Life in Death*, London: Black Swan, 2018.

Blakely, Rhys, 'Society Not Nature Makes Girls Play Safer Than Boys' *The Times*, 19 March 2019.

Blomberg, Catharina, *The Heart of the Warrior: Origins and Religious Background of the Samurai System in Feudal Japan*, London: Routledge, 1994.

Bloom, Harold, *The Western Canon: The Books and Schools of the Ages*, London: Papermac, 1996.

BIBLIOGRAPHY

——, *Shakespeare: The Invention of the Human*, London: Fourth Estate, 1999.

——, *Genius*, London: Fourth Estate, 2002.

Blythe, Ronald, *Writing in War*, London: Penguin, 1982.

Boehm, Christopher, *Moral Origins: The Evolution of Virtue, Altruism and Shame*, New York: Basic Books, 2012.

Borgmann, Albert, *Holding On to Reality: The Nature of Information at the Turn of the Millennium*, Chicago: University of Chicago Press, 2000.

Bostrom, Nick, 'The Super-Intelligent Will: Motivation and Instrumental Rationality in Advanced Artificial Agents', *Minds and Machines*, 22, (2012) pp. 71–85.

Boswell, James, 'On War' in Gross, John (ed), *Oxford Book of Essays*, Oxford: Oxford University Press, 1991, pp. 98–103.

Bowden, Mark, *Black Hawk Down*, New York: Bantam, 1999.

Brockman, John, *What to Think About Machines That Think*, New York: Harper Collins, 2015.

Brocks, Paul, *The Darker the Night, the Brighter the Stars: A Neuropsychologist's Odyssey*, London: Allen Lane, 2018.

Brooks, Michael, *At the Edge of Uncertainty*, London: Profile, 2015.

Buchanan, Mark, *Small World: Uncovering Nature's Hidden Networks*, London: Phoenix, 2002.

Burgess, Anthony, *The Ink Trade: Selected Journalism, 1961–1993*, Manchester: Carcanet, 2018.

Burkert, Walter, *Homo Necans: The Anthropology of Ancient Greek Sacrificial Ritual and Myth*, London: 1983.

Byatt, Antonia S, *On Histories and Stories*, London: Vintage, 2000.

Calasso, Roberto, *The Unnamable Present*, London: Allan Lane, 2019.

Caputo, Philip, *A Rumour of War*, London: Pimlico, 1999.

Carey, John, *What Good are the Arts?*, London: Faber & Faber, 2005.

Carlin, John, 'Inside the Hunt for the World's Most Dangerous Terrorist' *Politico*, 21 Nov. 2018.

Cartledge, Paul, *The Greeks: A Portrait of Self and Others*, Oxford: Oxford University Press, 2002.

Chabon, Michael, *Bookends: Collected Intros and Outros*, New York: Harper, 2018.

Chamayou, Grégoire, *Drone Theory*, London: Penguin, 2015.

BIBLIOGRAPHY

Chan, Dean, 'Dead-in-Iraq': The Spatial Politics of Digital Game Art Activism and the In-Game Protest, in Payne, Matthew and Huntemann, Nina (eds), *Joystick Soldiers*, London: Routledge, 2010.

Chatwin, Bruce, *Anatomy of Restlessness: Uncollected Writings*, London: Jonathan Cape, 1996.

Chesterton, G K, *Orthodoxy*, London: Hodder and Stoughton, 1996.

Christian, David, *Origin Story: A Big History of Everything*, London: Penguin, 2018.

Cioran, E M, *The Temptation to Exist*, London: Quartet, 1984.

———, *Tears and Saints*, Chicago: University of Chicago Press, 1995.

Cook, Theodore, 'The Chinese Discovery of the New World', in Cowley, Robert (ed), *More What If?: Eminent Historians Imagine What Might Have Been*, London: Macmillan, 2001, pp. 85–104.

Cook, Michael, *A Brief History of the Human Race*, London: Granta, 2003.

Crane, Stephen, *The Red Badge of Courage*, Pizer, Donald (ed), New York: Norton & Co, 1994.

Cremin, Aedeen, 'The Lost City', *Mekong Review*, 13, October 2018.

Critchley, Simon, *Tragedy, the Greeks and Us*, London: Profile Books Ltd, 2019.

Critchlow, Hannah, *The Science of Fate: The New Science of Who We Are*, London: Hodder and Stoughton, 2019.

Cross, Tim (ed), *The Lost Voices of World War I*, London: Bloomsbury, 1988.

Danto, Arthur, *The Philosophical Disenfranchisement of Art*, New York: Columbia University Press, 1986.

Darke, Diana, 'How to be Militant', *Times Literary Supplement*, September 21, 2018.

Darwin, Charles, *The Expression of Emotions in Man and Animals*, London: John Murray, 1872.

Daseler, Graham, 'Perfectionist', *Times Literary Supplement*, 17 August 2018.

Davies, Paul, *The Eerie Silence: Renewing Our Search for Alien Intelligence*, New York, Houghton Mifflin, 2010.

Dawkins, Richard, *The Selfish Gene*, Oxford: Oxford University Press, 1976.

Dawson, Doyne, *The First Armies*, London: Cassell & Co, 2001.

BIBLIOGRAPHY

DeLillo, Don, *End Zone*, London: Penguin, 1986.

——, 'Human Moments in World War III', in *The Angel Esmeralda: Nine Stories*, London: Picador, 2011.

Dennett, Daniel, *Freedom Evolves*, London: Penguin, 2003.

——, *Breaking the Spell: Religion as a Natural Phenomenon*, London: Penguin, 2006.

——, *From Bacteria to Bach and Back: The Evolution of Minds*, New York: Norton and Company, 2017.

Denning, Peter and Lewis, Ted, 'Intelligence May Not Be Computable', *American Scientist*, 107, 6 (2019), p. 346.

De Waal, Frans, *Mama's Last Hug: Animal Emotions and What They Teach Us About Ourselves*, London: Granta, 2019.

Diamond, Jared, *The World Until Yesterday: What Can We Learn from Traditional Societies?*, London: Penguin, 2012.

Dickens, Charles, *The Pickwick Papers*, London: Penguin, 2003.

Dolman, Everett, *Can Science End War?* Cambridge: Polity, 2016.

Dunbar, Robert, *The Science of Love and Betrayal*, London: Faber & Faber, 2012.

——, 'How Conversations Around Campfires Came to Be' *Proceedings of the National Academy of Science*, 111, 39, (2014), pp. 14013–14.

Dunbar, Robert, and Wrangham, Richard, *Catching Fire: How Cooking Made Us Human*, New York: Basic Books, 2009.

Dutton, Dennis, *The Art Instinct: Beauty, Pleasure and Human Evolution*, London: Bloomsbury, 2009.

Dyer, Gwynne, *War: The Lethal Custom*, New York: Carroll and Graf Publishers, 2004.

Eagleton, Terry, *The Ideology of the Aesthetic*, Oxford: Blackwell, 1991.

——, *The Event of Literature*, New Haven: Yale University Press, 2002.

——, *Culture and the Death of God*, New Haven: Yale University Press, 2014.

Effross, Walter, 'Hi-Tech Heroes, Virtual Villains, Visions of Law and Lawyers in Cyberpunk', *Buffalo Law Review*, 45, 3, (1997), pp. 931–74.

Ehrenburg, Ilya, *The War, 1941–45*, London: MacGibbon & Lee, 1964.

Ehrenreich, Barbara, *Blood Rites: Origins and History of the Passions of War*, London: Virago, 1997.

Elias, Norbert, *The Germans: Power Struggles and the Development of*

BIBLIOGRAPHY

Habitus in the Nineteenth and Twentieth Centuries, Schroter, Michael (ed), Cambridge: Polity, 1996.

Ellis, John, *The Social History of the Machine Gun*, London: Pimlico, 1976.

Evans, Jules, *The Art of Losing Control: A Philosopher's Search for Ecstatic Experiences*, Edinburgh: Canongate, 2017.

Evans, Michael, American Irregular: 'Frontier Conflict and the Philosophy of War' in Cormac McCarthy's *Blood Meridian or The Evening Redness in the West, Smalls Wars and Insurgencies*, 22, 4, (2011), pp. 527–47.

Exum, Andrew, *This Man's Army: A Soldier's Story from the Frontline of the War on Terror*, New York: Gotham, 2005.

Fein, Helen, *Genocide: A Sociological Perspective*, London: Sage, 1993.

Fenves, Peter, *Chatter: Language and History in Kierkegaard*, Stanford: Stanford University Press, 1993.

Ferguson, Brian, 'Pinker's List: Exaggerating Prehistoric War Mortality, in Fry, Douglas (ed), *War, Peace and Human Nature*, Oxford: Oxford University Press, 2013, pp. 112–31.

Ferguson, John, *War and Peace and the World's Religions*, Oxford: Oxford University Press, 1978.

Ferguson, Niall, *War of the Worlds: History's Age of Hatred*, London: Allen Lane, 2006.

Fernandez-Armesto, Felipe, *So You Think You're Human: A Brief History of Humanity*, Oxford: Oxford University Press, 2004.

———, 'False Starts', *Literary Review*, 472, February 2019a.

———, *Out of Our Minds: What We Think and How We Came to Think It*, Berkeley: University of California Press, 2019b.

Fick, Nathaniel, *One Bullet Away: The Making of a Marine Officer*, New York: Houghton Mifflin, 2005.

Fitch, Tecumseh, 'An Instinct to Learn' in Brockman, John (ed), *This Will Make You Smarter: New Scientific Concepts to Improve Your Thinking*, London: Black Swan, 2012, pp. 154–6.

Flannery, Tim, *Here on Earth: A Twin Biography of The Planet and the Human Race*, London: Penguin, 2010.

———, *Europe: The First 100 Million Years*, London: Penguin, 2018a.

———, 'Raised by Wolves' *New York Review of Books*, 5 April 2018b, https://www.nybooks.com/articles/2018/04/05/raised-by-wolves/

BIBLIOGRAPHY

Ford, Dennis, *The Search for Meaning: A Short History*, Los Angeles: University of California Press, 2007.

France, John, *Perilous Glory: The Rise of Western Military Power*, New Haven: Yale University Press, 2011.

Frayn, Michael, *Constructions: Making Sense of Things*, London: Faber and Faber, 1974.

Freedman, Lawrence, 'Defining War' in Lindley-French, Julian and Boyer, Yves (eds), *The Oxford Handbook of War*, Oxford: Oxford University Press, 2012, pp. 17–29.

Freeman, Charles, *AD 381: Heretics, Pagans and the Christian State*, London: Pimlico, 2008.

French, Shannon, *The Code of the Warrior: Exploring Warrior Values Past and Present*, Boston, MA: Rowman & Littlefield, 2003.

Fried, Morton, *The Evolution of Political Society*, New York: McGraw Hill, 1967.

Fry, Douglas, (ed), *War, Peace and Human Nature*, Oxford: Oxford University Press, 2013.

Fussell, Paul, *The Bloody Game: An Anthology*, New York: Scribners, 1991.

Gabbert, Elisa, *The Unreality of Memory and Other Essays*, London: Atlantic Books, 2020.

Gat, Azar, 'Long Childhood, Family Networks and Cultural Exclusivity: Missing Links in the Debate Over Human Group Selection and Altruism, *Evolutionary Studies in Imaginative Culture*, 2, 1, (2018), pp. 49–58.

Geertz, Clifford, *The Interpretation of Cultures. Selected Essays*, New York: Basic Books, 1973.

——, *Available Light: Anthropological Reflections on Philosophical Topics*, Princeton, NJ: Princeton University Press, 2000.

Gellner, Ernest, *Nationalism*, New York: New York University Press, 1984.

Geuss, Raymond, *Changing the Subject: Philosophy from Socrates to Adorno*, Cambridge, MA: Harvard University Press, 2017.

Gibson, William, *Neuromancer*, London: Harper Collins, 1993.

——, *Distrust This Particular Flavour: Encounters With a Future That is Already Here*, London: Vintage, 2012.

Girard, Rene, *Deceit, Desire and the Novel*, Freccero, Yvonne, (trans), Baltimore: Johns Hopkins Press, 1965.

BIBLIOGRAPHY

Gladwell, Malcolm, *David and Goliath: Underdogs, Misfits and the Art of Battling Giants*, London: Allan Lane, 2013.

Gleick, James, *Time Travel: A History*, London: Fourth Estate, 2018.

Glover, Jon and Silkin, Jon (eds), *The Penguin Book of First World War Prose*, London: Viking, 1989.

Gooding, Francis 'All the News is Bad', *London Review of Books*, 41, 15, 1 August 2019.

Goodwin, Brian, *How the Leopard Changed Its Spots*, London: Orion Books, 1994.

Goody, Jack, *The Domestication of the Savage Mind*, Cambridge: Cambridge University Press, 1995.

Gottschall, Jonathan, *The Rape of Troy: The Evolution of Violence in the World of Homer*, Cambridge: Cambridge University Press, 2008.

———, *The Storytelling Animal: How Stories Make Us Human*, New York: Harcourt Mifflin, 2012.

Graham, Stephen, *Cities Under Siege: The New Military Urbanism*, London: Verso, 2011.

Gray, Jay Glenn, *The Warriors: Reflections on Men in Battle*, Lincoln: University of Nebraska, 1999.

Gray, John, *Seven Types of Atheism*, London: Allen Lane, 2018.

Greenblatt, *The Rise and Fall of Adam and Eve*, New York: Norton, 2017.

Greenfield, Susan, *Mind Change: How Digital Technologies are Leaving Their Mark on our Brains*, New York: Random House, 2014.

Griffin, Jasper, *Homer on Life and Death*, Oxford: Clarendon Press, 1983.

Habermas, Jurgen, *The Divided West*, Cambridge: Polity, 2006.

Haldane, J B, *On Being the Right Size and Other Essays*, Oxford: Oxford University Press, 1985.

Haldeman, Joe, *The Forever War*, London: Millennium, 1999.

Hale, John, *War and Society in Renaissance Europe*, London: Fontana, 1985.

Hall, Edith, 'Asia Unmanned: Images of Victory in Classical Athens,' in Rich, John and Shipley, Graham, *War and Society in the Greek World*, London: Routledge, 1993, p. 167.

Hamilton, Paul, *Historicism*, London: Routledge, 1996.

Hanson, Victor Davis, *The Western Way of War: Infantry Battles in Classical Greece*, Berkeley: University of California Press, 2000.

BIBLIOGRAPHY

———, *The Father of Us All—War in History—Ancient and Modern*, London: Bloomsbury, 2010.

———, 'Gunpowder and Geeks', *The Times Literary Supplement*, 19 July, 2013.

Harari, Yuval Noah, *Sapiens: A Brief History of Mankind*, London: Harper Collins, 2015.

Harris, Marvin, *Cannibals and Kings: The Origins of Culture*, London: Collins, 1978.

Hassan, Robert, 'Network Time' in Hassan, Robert and Purser, Ronald, *24:7: Time and Temporality in the Network Society*, Stanford: Stanford Business School, 2017.

Heaney, Seamus, 'Crediting Poetry' in *Nobel Lectures for the Literary Laureates, 1986–2006*, New York: New York Press, 2007, p. 166.

Heinrich, B, *Racing the Antelope: What Animals Can Teach Us About Running and Life*, New York: Cliff Street, 2001.

Hemingway, Sean, *Hemingway on War*, New York: Scribner, 2003.

Henderson, Casper, *A New Map of Wonders: A Journey in Search of Modern Marvels*, London: Granta, 2017.

Hennessey, Patrick, *The Junior Officer's Reading Club*, London: Allen Lane, 2009.

Herr, Michael, *Dispatches*, London: Picador, 1977.

Hersey, John, *Life Sketches, New York: Vintage*, 1991.

Hesse, Hermann, *If the War Goes On: Reflections on War and Politics*, London: Panther, 1985.

Hobbes, Thomas, *Leviathan*, Macpherson, C B (ed), London: Pelican, 1972.

Holmes, Richard, *Acts of War: The Behaviour of Men in Battle*, London: Cassell, 2004.

Holt, Jim, *Why Does the World Exist?* London: Profile, 2012.

Huysmans, Joris-Karl, *Against Nature*, London: Penguin, 2005.

Hynes, Samuel, *The Soldier's Tale: Bearing Witness to Modern War*, London: Pimlico, 1998.

Ignatieff, Michael, *Blood and Belonging*, Toronto: Viking, 1993.

Jacques, Martin, 'Civilisation State Versus Nation State' 15 January 2011, http://www.martinjacques.com/articles/civilization-state-versus-nation-state-2/

BIBLIOGRAPHY

James, William, *The Varieties of Religious Experience: A Study of Human Nature*, Gifford Lectures on Natural Religion, Gomes, Peter Jay (ed), New York: Signet, 2003.

Jeffrey, James, 'Iraq is Always with You', *The Guardian*, 18 March 2013, https://www.theguardian.com/world/2013/mar/18/iraq-is-always-with-you-veteran

Johnson, Dominic, *God is Watching You: How the Fear of God Makes Us Human*, Oxford: Oxford University Press, 2016.

Johnson, Steven, *Emergence: The Connected Lives of Ants, Brains, Cities, Software*, London: Penguin, 2001.

Jones, James, *The Thin Red Line*, New York: Dell, 1998.

Jünger, Ernst, *A German Office in Occupied Paris: War Journals 1991–1994*, Hanse, Thomas (trans), New York: Columbia University Press, 2019.

Junger, Sebastian, *War*, New York: Harper Collins, 2010.

Jurgenson, Nathan, *The Social Photo: On Photography and Social Media*, London: Verso, 2019.

Kahan, Dan, '"Tribe Before Truth": Why Scientific Knowledge Without Curiosity Can Be Polarizing', *Scientific American*, 18 December 2018.

Kant, Immanuel, *Observations on the Feeling of The Beautiful and the Sublime*, Goldthwait, John (trans), Berkeley, CA: University of California Press, 1991.

Karkazis, Katrina, and Jordan-Young, Rebecca, 'The Myth of Testosterone', *The New York Times*, 3 May 2019.

Keegan, John, *A History of Warfare*, London: Hutchinson, 1993.

Kelly, Christopher, 'A Shocking Story', *London Review of Books*, 41, 4, 21 February 2019.

Kinsbourne, Marcel, 'The Expanding In-Group,' in Brockman, John (ed), *This Will Make You Smarter*, New York: Doubleday, 2012.

Kissel, Mark and Kim, Nam, *Emergent Warfare in Our Evolutionary Past*, London: Routledge, 2018.

Knott, Marie Luise, *Unlearning with Hannah Arendt*, London: Granta, 2013.

Korsgaard, Christine, *Self-Constitution*, Oxford: Oxford University Press, 2009.

Krylova, Anna, *Soviet Women in Combat: A History of Violence on the Eastern Front*, Cambridge: Cambridge University Press, 2010.

BIBLIOGRAPHY

Kundera, Milan, *Immortality*, London: Faber and Faber, 1991.

La Boetie, Etienne, *Discourse on Voluntary Servitude*, Garner, William (ed), New York: Adagio, 2016.

Laland, Keith, 'How We Became a Different Kind of Animal', *Scientific American*, September 2018.

Lanier, Jaron, *Dawn of the New Everything: A Journey Through Virtual Reality*, London: Vintage, 2017.

Latour, Bruno, *Reassembling the Social*, Oxford: Clarendon Press, 2007.

Leblanc, Steven, *Constant Battles: Why We Fight*, New York: St Martins, 2003.

Le Guin, Ursula, Introduction, Burnett, Gilbert (trans), *Utopia* (Thomas More), London: Verso, 2017.

Lendon, J E, *Soldiers and Ghosts: A History of Battle in Classical Antiquity*, New Haven: Yale University Press, 2005.

Levi, Primo, *The Drowned and the Saved*, London: Michael Joseph, 1988.

Levitin, Mia, 'Around the Campfire', *Times Literary Supplement*, 28 June 2019.

Lewis, Simon and Maslin, Mark, *The Human Planet: How We Created the Anthropocene*, London: Pelican, 2018.

Lewis-Williams, David, *The Mind in the Cave: Consciousness and the Origins of Art*, London: Thames & Hudson, 2016.

Lewis-Williams, David and Pearce, David, *Inside the Neolithic Mind*, London: Thames & Hudson, 2018.

Lieven, Dominic, *Russia Against Napoleon*, London: Penguin, 2016.

Losurdo, Domenico, *Heidegger and the Ideology of War*, New York: Humanity Books, 2001.

Lukacs, John, *At the End of an Age*, New Haven: Yale University Press, 2002.

MacGregor, David, *Hegel and Marx After the Fall of Communism*, Cardiff: University of Wales Press, 1998.

MacGregor, Neal, *Living With the Gods*, London: Penguin, 2018.

MacIntyre, Ben, 'The Arms Race That Was All in The Mind', *The Times*, 6 April 2019.

Mailer, Norman, *The Naked and the Dead*, New York: Reinhart & Co, 1948.

Marche, Stephen, 'Back in the MLA', *Times Literary Supplement*, 7 June 2019.

Marlantes, Karl, *What's It Like to Go to War?* London: Corvus, 2011.

Maschner, Herbert and Reedy-Maschner K L, 'The Evolution of Warfare' in Bentley, Alex (ed), *The Edge of Reason*, London: Continuum, 2008, pp. 57–64.

Mayer, Adrienne, *The Amazons: Lives and Legends of Warrior Women in The Ancient World*, Princeton, NJ: Princeton University Press, 2014.

McCarthy, Cormac, *Blood Meridian*, London: Picador, 2010.

McCrum, Robert, *The 100 Best Non-fiction Books*, Cambridge: Galileo Publishers, 2018.

McEwan, Ian, 'Literature, Science and Human Nature' in Wells, Robin Headlam and McFadden, Johnjoe (eds), *Human Nature: Fact and Fiction*, London: Continuum, 2006, pp. 40–62.

McGrath, Alister, *Dawkins' God: Genes, Memes and The Meaning of Life*, Oxford: Blackwell, 2005.

McLynn, Frank, *Napoleon: A Biography*, London: Jonathan Cape, 1997.

Meinertzhagen, Richard, *Kenya Diary 1902–1906*, London: Elan Books, 1984.

Mendelsohn, Daniel, 'A Little Iliad', *New York Review of Books*, 5, 122, 24 June 2004.

——, *The Bad Boy of Athens: Classics from the Greeks to Game of Thrones*, London: William Collins, 2019.

Midgley, Mary, *Wickedness: A Philosophical Essay*, London: Ark, 1984.

——, *Science and Poetry*, London: Routledge, 2001.

——, *Evolution as Religion: Strange Hopes and Even Stranger Fears*, London: Routledge, 2002.

——, *Beast and Man: The Roots of Human Nature*, London: Routledge, 2006.

Miller, Franklin, *Reflections of a Warrior*, New York: Pocket Books, 2003.

Millett, P C 'Winning Ways in Warfare', in Campbell, Brian and Tritle, Lawrence A (eds), *Oxford Handbook of Warfare in the Classical World*, Oxford: Oxford University Press, 2013.

Montgomery, James (ed), *War Songs*, New York: New York University Press, 2018.

BIBLIOGRAPHY

Moody, Oliver, 'Why Dolphins and Whales Are Even Cleverer Than We Thought', *The Times*, 16 October 2017.

Morris, Ian, *War: What's It Good For? The Role of Conflict in Civilisation from the Pyramids to Robots*, New York: Profile, 2014.

Mount, Ferdinand, 'The Seducer', *London Review of Books*, 2 August 2018.

Mueller, John, *Remnants of War*, Ithaca: Cornell University Press, 2004.

Nagel, Thomas, 'Ways to help', *The Times Literary Supplement*, 20 November 2015.

Nicolson, Adam, *The Seabird's Cry*, London: William Collins, 2017.

Nietzsche, Friedrich, *Human, All Too Human*, Hollingdale R J (ed), Cambridge: Cambridge University Press, 1986.

———, *Ecce Homo*, Hollingdale R J (trans), London: Penguin, 1992.

———, *Untimely Meditations*, Hollingdale R J (trans), Cambridge: Cambridge University Press, 1995.

———, *Thus Spoke Zarathustra*, Hollingdale, R J (trans), Cambridge: Cambridge University Press, 1998.

Nikolaou, Paschalis, 'The Troy of Always: Translations of Conflict in Christopher Logue's "War Music"', in Salama-Carr, Myriam (ed), *Translating and Interpreting Conflict*, New York: Rodopi, 2007.

Nolan, Cathal, *The Allure of Battle: A History of How Wars Have Been Won and Lost*, Oxford: Oxford University Press, 2017.

Nussbaum, Martha, *The Monarchy of Fear*, New York: Simon & Schuster, 2018.

O'Brien, Tim, *The Things They Carried: How to Tell a True War Story*, New York: Scribners, 1990.

———, *If I Die in a Combat Zone*, London: Flamingo, 2003.

Orwell, George, 'Second Thoughts on James Burnham', *Collected Essays*, London: Secker & Warburg, 1975.

———, *The Road to Wigan Pier*, London: Penguin, 1989.

Ousby, Ian, *The Road to Verdun*, London: Jonathan Cape, 2002.

Pagel, Mark, *Wired for Culture: The Natural History of Human Cooperation*, London: Allen Lane, 2012.

Paret, Peter, *Imagined Battles: Reflections on War in European Art*, Chapel Hill: University of North Carolina Press, 1997.

Parker, Geoffrey, *The Thirty Years' War*, London: Routledge, 1997.

BIBLIOGRAPHY

Pavel, Thomas, *Fictional Worlds*, Cambridge, MA: Harvard University Press, 1986.

Payne, Matthew, *Playing War*, New York: New York University Press, 2016.

Petter, Olivia, 'Why Reading Jihadist Poetry Might Help Combat Extremism,' *The Independent*, 1 September 2017, https://www.independent.co.uk/life-style/jihadist-poetry-literature-read-help-combat-extremism-isis-terrorism-elisabeth-kendall-a7924041.html

Pick, Daniel, *The War Machine: The Rationalisation of Slaughter in the Modern Age*, New Haven, CT: Yale University Press, 1993.

Pinker, Steven, *The Blank Slate: The Modern Denial of Human Nature*, London: Allen Lane, 2002.

Piszkiewicz, Denis, *Wernher von Braun*, Conn: Praeger, 1998.

Plumb, J H, 'Churchill as Historian' in Taylor, A J P (ed), *Churchill: Four Faces and the Man*, London: Allen Lane, 1969, pp. 149–50.

Pohl, Frederik, *The Cool War*, New York: Del Ray Books, 1981.

Porter, Jane, 'The Neuroscience of Imagination', *Dialed*, 02 18, https://www.fastcompany.com/3026510/the-neuroscience-of-imagination

Poundstone, William, *How to Predict Everything*, London: One World, 2019.

Power, Henry, 'Epic Patchwork', *Times Literary Supplement*, 3 August 2018.

Radinger, Elli, *The Wisdom of Wolves: How Wolves Can Teach Us How to Be More Human*, London: Michael Joseph, 2019.

Rai, Tage Shakti and Fiske, Alan Page, *Virtuous Violence: Hurting and Killing to Create, Sustain, End and Honour Social Relationships*, Cambridge: Cambridge University Press, 2015.

Raulff, Ulrich, *Farewell to the Horse: The Final Century of our Relationship*, London: Allen Lane, 2017.

Remarque, Erich Maria, *All Quiet on the Western Front*, London: Vintage, 1996.

Rhodes, Steven, *Lifelines: Biology, Freedom and Determinism*, London: Penguin, 1997.

Ridley, Matthew, *The Origins of Virtue*, London: Penguin, 1997.

Rihll, Tracey, 'War, Slavery and Settlement in Early Greece' in Rich, John and Shipley, Graham (eds), *War and Society in the Greek World*, London: Routledge, 1993, pp 69–86.

Riley-Smith, Jonathan, *The Crusades: A Short History*, New Haven: Yale University Press, 1987.

Roberts, Adam, *Science Fiction*, London: Routledge, 2000.

Roco, Mihail and Bainbridge, William S, *Converging Technologies for Improving Human Performance: Nanotechnology, Biotechnology, Information Technology and Cognitive Science*, Washington, DC: National Science Foundation, 2003.

Rosen, Stephen, *War in Human Nature*, Princeton, NJ: Princeton University Press, 2005.

Rosenbaum, Ron, *Explaining Hitler: The Search for The Origins of His Evil*, London: Macmillan, 1998.

Rousseau, Jean-Jacques, *Discourse on the Origin of Inequality*, Oxford: Oxford University Press, 1994.

———, 'State of War: 1755' in Brown, Chris, Nardin, Terry, and Rengger, Nick (eds), *International Relations in Political Thought: Texts from the Ancient Greeks to the First World War*, Cambridge: Cambridge University Press, 2002, p. 416.

Runco, Mark, 'Creativity Has No Dark Side' in Cropley, David, Cropley, Arthur, Kaufman, James and Runco, Mark (eds), *The Dark Side of Creativity*, Cambridge: Cambridge University Press, 2010.

Rutherford, Adam, *The Book of Humans: A Brief History of Culture, Sex, War and the Evolution of Us*, London: Weidenfeld & Nicolson, 2019.

Ryan, Alan, *On Aristotle: Saving Politics from Philosophy*, New York: Liveright Classics, 2014.

Salter, James, *The Hunters*, London: Penguin, 1997.

Sandywell, Barry, *The Beginning of European Theorising: Reflexivity in the Archaic Age, Vol 2*, London: Routledge, 1996.

Sassoon, Siegfried, *Collected Poems*, New York: Viking, 1949.

Satia, Priya, *Empire of Guns: The Violent Making of the Industrial Revolution*, London: Duckworth, 2019.

Scheidel, Walter, *Escape from Rome: The Future of Empire and the Road to Prosperity*, Princeton, NJ: Princeton University Press, 2019.

Schopenhauer, Arthur, *The World as Will and Representation Vol 2*, New York: 1969.

BIBLIOGRAPHY

Scott, James, *The Art of Not Being Governed: An Anarchist History of Upland Southeast Asia*, New Haven: Yale University Press, 2009.

———, *Against the Grain: Deep History of the Earlier States*, Yale, NH: Yale University Press, 2017.

Sebald, Winfried, *Austerlitz*, London: Hamish Hamilton, 2001.

Sen, Amartya, *The Argumentative Indian*, London: Penguin, 2005.

Sennett, Richard, *The Craftsman*, London: Penguin, 2008.

Shane, Charlotte, 'Reader, I Parried Him', *Times Literary Supplement*, 1 March, 2019.

Sheldrake, Rupert, *The Science Delusion: Freeing the Spirit of Enquiry*, London: Hodder and Stoughton, 2012.

Shermer, Michael, *Skeptic*, New York: St Martin's Press, 2016.

Shulman, David, 'Off with Their Heads', *New York Review of Books*, 5 April 2018.

Silk, John, 'Animal Behaviour: The Evolutionary Roots of Lethal Conflict', *Nature*, 513, 7518, 2014.

Sinclair, Andrew (ed), *The War Decade: An Anthology of the 1940s*, London: Hamish Hamilton, 1989.

Sloan-Wilson, David, 'Why Richard Dawkins is Wrong About Religion' in Bentley, Alex (ed), *The Edge of Reason: Science and Religion in Modern Society*, London: Continuum, 2008, pp. 119–36.

Sloman, Steven and Fernbach, Philip, *The Knowledge Illusion: Why We Never Think Alone*, London: Macmillan, 2017.

Smail, Daniel Lord, *On Deep History and the Brain*, Berkeley: University of California Press, 2008.

Small, Thomas, 'Fully Human' *Times Literary Supplement*, 20 July 2018.

Smith, Kathleen, 'The End of Innocence', *Literary Review*, July 2019.

Smith, Monica, *Cities: The First 6,000 Years*, London: Simon & Schuster, 2019.

Snyder, Timothy, *The Road to Unfreedom: Russia, Europe, America*, London: Crown Publishing Group, 2018.

Sontag, Susan, *Regarding the Pain of Others*, London: Hamish Hamilton, 2003.

Spufford, Francis and Uglow, Jenny, *Cultural Babbage: Technology, Time and Invention*, London: Faber and Faber, 1996.

BIBLIOGRAPHY

Stephenson, Michael, *The Last Full Measure: How Soldiers Die in Battle*, London: Duckworth, 2013.

Stoppard, Tom, *Jumpers*, London: Faber and Faber, 1986.

Swofford, Anthony, *Jarhead: A Marine's Chronicle of the Gulf War*, London: Scribner, 2003.

Taylor, A J P, *Churchill: Four Faces and the Man*, Allen Lane: 1969.

Taylor, Timothy, 'Culture' in Brockman, John (ed), *This Will Change Everything: Ideas That Will Shape the Future*, New York: Harper Collins, 2010a, p. 162.

———, *The Artificial Ape: How Technology Changed the Course of Human Evolution*, London: Palgrave Macmillan, 2010b.

Thonemann, Peter, 'Light Armies', *The Times Literary Supplement*, 18 March 2011.

Tinbergen, Niko, *The Herring Gull's World*, New York: Basic Books, 1961.

Todorov, Tzvetan, *Facing the Extreme: Moral Life in the Concentration Camps*, London: Phoenix, 1996.

Toffler, Alvin and Toffler, Heidi, *War and Anti-War: Survival at the Dawn of the 21st Century*, London: Warner Books, 1983.

Tolstoy, Leo, *War and Peace*, London: Penguin, 1982.

Tomasello, Michael, *A Natural History of Human Morality*, Harvard University Press, 2016.

Tombs, Robert, *The English and Their History*, London: Penguin, 2014.

Tooby, John, 'Coalitional Instincts,' in Brockman, John (ed), *This Idea is Brilliant*, New York: Harper Perennial, 2018, pp. 496–99.

Tooley, Hunt, *The Western Front: Battleground and Home Front in the First World War*, London: Palgrave Macmillan, 2003.

Tritle, Lawrence, *From Melos to My Lai: War and Survival*, London: Routledge, 2000.

Truong, Thi Thuy Hang, 'Women's Leadership in Vietnam: Opportunities and Challenges', *Journal of Women in Culture and Society*, 34, 1, 2008.

Turner, Karen and Hao, P T, *Even the Women Must Fight: Memories of War from North Vietnam*, New York: John Wiley & Sons, 1998.

Updike, John, *Toward the End of Time*, New York: Random House, 1997.

Usborne, Simon, 'Why Women Win in the Long Run,' *The Financial Times*, 26 January 2019.

Van Creveld, Martin, *The Culture of War*, London: Ballantine, 2008.

Virilio, Paul, *Speed and Politics*, New York: Semiotexte, 1986.

Von Clausewitz, Carl, *On War*, in Heuser, Beatrice (ed), Oxford: World's Classics, 2007.

Wallace, Sam, 'The Proposed Ban on Offensive Autonomous Weapons is Unrealistic and Dangerous', *Kurzweil*, 5 August 2015, https://www.kurzweilai.net/the-proposed-ban-on-offensive-autonomous-weapons-is-unrealistic-and-dangerous

Warrick, Patricia, *The Cybernetic Imagination in Science Fiction*, Cambridge: MIT Press, 1982.

Watanabe, Takeo and Tamaki, Masoko, 'Night Watch in One Brain Hemisphere During Sleep', *Current Biology*, 26, 2016, pp. 1190–4.

Watson, Peter, *The Modern Mind: An Intellectual History of the 20th Century*, London: Harper Collins Perennial, 2002.

Wengrow, David, 'Civilisation before the State' in Almqvist, Kurt and Linklater, Alex (eds), *Civilisation: Perspectives from the Engelsberg Seminar 2013*, Stockholm: Axel and Margaret Ax: son Johnson Foundation, 2014.

Wilson, Edward, *Consilience: the Unity of Knowledge*, New York: Alfred Knopf, 1998.

———, *The Origins of Creativity*, London: Penguin, 2017.

———, *Genesis: The Deep Origin of Societies*, New York: Norton & Co, 2019.

Wilson, Michael, and Wrangham, Richard, 'Intergroup Relations in Chimps' *Annual Review of Anthropology* 32, 1, 2003, pp. 363–92.

Wolf, Maryanne, *Proust and the Squid: The Story and Science of The Reading Brain*, London: Icon, 2008.

Wolin, Richard (ed), *The Heidegger Controversy*, Cambridge: MIT Press, 1993.

Wong, Kate, 'The New Origins of Technology' *Scientific American*, 4, 2017.

Wrangham, Richard, *The Goodness Paradox: How Evolution Made Us More and Less Violent*, London: Profile, 2019.

Wrangham, Richard and Peterson, Dale, *Demonic Males: Apes and the Origin of Human Violence*, Boston: Houghton Mifflin, 1996.

Wright, Evan, *Generation Kill: Living Dangerously on the Road to Baghdad with the Ultra-Violent Marines of Bravo Company*, New York: Bantam, 2004.

Wright, Robert, *Nonzero: The Logic of Human Destiny*, London: Vintage, 2001.

———, *The Evolution of God*, London: Little & Brown, 2009.

Zaretsky, Robert, 'Roots, But No Frontiers', *Times Literary Supplement*, 17 August 2018.

Zimbardo, Philip, 'The Banality of Evil, The Banality of Heroism' in Brockman, John (ed), *What is Your Dangerous Idea?*, New York: Harper Collins, 2006, pp. 275–6.

INDEX

INDEX

INDEX

INDEX

INDEX

INDEX

INDEX

INDEX

INDEX

INDEX

INDEX

Murphy, Audie, 115
Mussolini, Benito, 101
mutualism, 101–2
My Early Life (Churchill), 96
mythology (Greek), 64, 76–80
myths, 82–7
   archetypes of, 82, 83–5

Nagasaki, bombing of, 158–9
Napoleon at Arcola, 107
*Napoleon Crossing the Bridge of
   Arcola*, 107
Napoleonic wars, 99, 146
Narrative Science (company), 204
Nataruk (Kenya), 132
national debt, 142
National Peace Council, 22
National Portrait Gallery
   (London), 95
nationalism, 99, 100–1
natural selection, 122, 188, 208
Neanderthals, 123, 130, 202
Near East, 131, 137
Nebuchadnezzar, 134
Nelson, Horatio, 142
Nelson, Shawn, 186
Netherlands, 191
Neuromancer (Gibson), 209
Nevada, 59
New Guinea, 32, 33, 126
New School for Social Research
   (New York), 85
New World, 131, 150, 151,
   152–3, 215
New Yorker, The (magazine), 85

Nietzsche, 19, 93, 104, 122, 141,
   145, 156, 173
9/11 attacks, 38, 88, 89, 117
nomadic invasions
   cycle of, 140
   great empires, 137–9
   in New World, 151–2
nomadic peoples, 131, 138
novels, 80–2
   science fiction, 194–6, 197–8
nuclear bombing, 157–60
nuclear weapons, 160
Nur Jahan (wife of Jahangir), 65

Oatley, Keith, 186
Odyssey, The (Homer), 61, 82
Ohio-class ballistic missile sub-
   marine, 160
Old Testament, 86
Old World, 150
Olivier, Laurence, 32
Olympian Odes (Pindar), 76
On Aggression (Lorenz), 10
On War (Clausewitz), 99
One Bullet Away (Fick), 86
One of Ours (Cather), 104
1066 and All That, 31
ontogeny, 11, 22–3, 158
   definition, 121
   human evolution, 121–3
Operation Achilles, 83
Opium War (1840–2), 154
Oppenheimer, Robert, 211
orangutans, 29–30
organised hunting, 39

INDEX

INDEX

INDEX

INDEX

wickedness, 178

Wilson, Edward O, 15, 45, 124

Wired (magazine), 195

Wisconsin, 191

Wittgenstein, 146

Wolf, Maryanne, 80

Wolfe, Tom, 169–70

wolves, 13

  communication, 39, 41

  organised hunting, 39

  social skills, 56–7

women

  abduction of, 60–1

  in armed forces, 20, 59–60, 68–70

  in Hollywood movies, 69

  hunting expeditions, 37

  as pirates, 65

  role in war, 62–6

Woolf, Virginia, 63, 103–4, 177

words Vs. images, 103

World of Warcraft (video game), 81, 117

World Set Free, The (Wells), 188

World Until Yesterday, The (Diamond), 129

World War I, 108, 175

World War II, 10, 32, 49, 68, 100, 210, 217

Wrangham, Richard, 47, 130

Wright, Evan, 116

Wuhan, 192

Yemen, 86

Young Woman's Christian Association, 22

youths

  joined armed forces, 20, 166–8, 171

  and Korean War, 169–70

  and video games, 116–17

Zimbardo, Philip, 179–80

Žižek, Slavoj, 171

Zuckerberg, Mark, 199

Zulu (film), 22

256